BIG
TEQUILA

EMANUELE MENSAH

BIG TEQUILA

A COMPREHENSIVE GUIDE TO
AGAVE SPIRITS

CIDER MILL PRESS

BOOK PUBLISHERS

To my daughter Zendaya

INTRODUCTION

Greetings, fellow spirits enthusiasts! As the soft clink of cocktail glasses and laughter echo through the air, I stand behind the bar, a bartender with ten years of experience. From the busy streets of London to the sun-kissed shores of Australia, I've mixed, muddled, and crafted countless cocktails, but it was in this whirlwind of flavors that I found my true passion—mezcal and tequila.

I felt an irresistible pull toward these traditional Mexican spirits. I immersed myself in their depths, as I studied their origins and the devotion behind their creation.

Then, my journey led me to an unforgettable adventure in Mexico—a pilgrimage to the land of tequila and mezcal. The distilleries tour was a kaleidoscope of sights, scents, and flavors that awakened my senses and left an indelible mark on my soul. Each encounter with the people working in the distilleries revealed a story of dedication, love, and a commitment to their craft.

As I stood in the agave fields, feeling the sun's warmth on my skin and witnessing the meticulous care given to each plant, a profound appreciation grew in me. The process of creating tequila and mezcal is more than just a process; it symbolizes the very essence of passion and devotion, a centuries-old art form passed down through generations.

The charm of these spirits lies not only in their history but in the symphony of flavors they orchestrate upon the palate. From the earthy smokiness of mezcal to the crisp, vibrant notes of tequila, each sip is an expedition through time and culture. Their stories are rich, steeped in traditions that have been kept alive for centuries.

With this book, my desire is to share the love and passion I've encountered on my journey with tequila and mezcal.

In the following pages, you'll find not only essential knowledge about tequila and mezcal but also a collection of handcrafted recipes. These concoctions are designed to take you on your own personal exploration of these spirits, to sip, savor, and fall in love with their charms in the comfort of your own home.

May this book be an invitation to rediscover tequila and mezcal, to embrace their heritage, and to celebrate the passion that breathes life into every drop. Together, let's raise our glasses to the artisans, to the lands that nurture the agave, and to the magical spirits that have won my heart—and I hope yours too. Cheers!

AGAVE

AN INTRODUCTION TO AGAVE

Let's start our journey talking about agave. Without it, we wouldn't have either tequila or mezcal. Agave is the secret to these beautiful spirits.

Although agave was first described in 1753 by Swedish botanist Carl Linnaeus in his book *Species Plantarum*, this plant has been part of human culture for a long time. Remains of agave used in human contexts date back ten thousand years.

It was considered a sacred plant by the pre-Columbian tribes of Mexico. It was nourishment and a water source. Agave fibers were also used to produce clothing, footwear, building materials, animal food, and paper.

Also called *maguey* (an imported term from the Antilles), agave was central to religious rituals and sacrifices. For example, it was used to produce pulque, an alcoholic milky-white beverage made from fermented agave juice (*aguamiel*). It was believed that pulque could purify the body and help the drinker communicate with gods. Captives drank it before a battle, and the priests and those who were sacrificed imbibed it during rituals. (See more about pulque on page 23.)

According to a theory, after distillation was introduced in Mexico by the Spanish, agave started to be used to make alcoholic drinks, mezcal, and tequila.

Nowadays, agave has many uses, not just for making spirits. For example, it is used as an anti-inflammatory ingredient in the form of a powder, infusion, or nectar. It is also edible and can be used as a paste or nectar while cooking.

But what is agave? It is a genus of succulent plants belonging to the family Asparagaceae. From the Greek word *agauē*, meaning "noble or illustrious," agave is native to southern parts of North America, Central America, the West Indies, and northern parts of South America. It grows in arid, semiarid, and temperate forests at about 9,000 feet (2,750 meters) above sea level.

There are more than two hundred species of agave found in a wide range of sizes and colors, from pale green to blue gray. Many are characterized by a rosette of thick, succulent, and strong fibrous leaves that bear teeth along the edges and, in most cases, a sharp terminal spine. They range from a few inches to 8 feet (2.5 meters) in length and up to 30 feet (9 meters) in height.

Pollinated by bats and insects, most species are monocarpic, meaning they flower once and then die. Just a few can bloom several times during their lives. Agaves grow slowly and bloom when they are about ten to twenty years old, and they can survive for up to thirty years.

TYPES OF AGAVE

As mentioned earlier, there are many different species of agave. Let's have a look at those most commonly used for tequila and mezcal.

Agave tequilana Weber Azul

Named after the French military doctor and botanist, Frédéric Albert Constantin Weber, who first described it, *Agave tequilana* Weber Azul (blue agave or tequila agave), is rich in fibers, with a slight blue layer on the leaves. Used for the production of tequila due to its high sugar content, blue agave grows up to 6 feet (1.8 meters) tall. The lance-shaped leaves end in a brown, sharp, terminal spine and margined teeth. Once flowered, the plant produces a stalk (*quiote*) with twenty to twenty-five branches and yellow flowers. After flowering, the rosette dies.

Agave angustifolia var. espadín

Between 80 and 90 percent of mezcal is made with espadín, a variety that belongs to _Agave angustifolia_, the same species to which _Agave tequilana_ Weber Azul belongs. With roasted agave notes, espadín is the most commonly used variety. It takes six to eight years to mature and can be cultivated easily. In addition, it is less fibrous than other agave species, so it is easier to process the fruit after roasting. Also, it contains a high inulin content, allowing for efficient alcohol production.

Agave potatorum var. tobalá

In Mexico, _Agave potatorum_ var. tobalá grows widely in Oaxaca. It grows at high elevations (between 4,000 and 7,000 feet) and is small in size. Tobalá takes between ten and fifteen years to mature. It relies on birds and bats to pollinate and spread its seeds. It has a low inulin content, making it hard to produce mezcal; therefore, tobalá mezcal, which has earthy and fruity notes, is quite expensive.

Agave karwinskii

There are wide varieties of *Agave karwinskii*. The most famous are madrecuishe, bicuishe, cuishe, tobaziche, barril, and cirial. These varieties are usually identified by a cylindric piña (the heart) with sharp needles at the tips. They can grow up to 12 feet (3.5 meters) in dry conditions. Karwinskii mezcal is often herbal with mineral notes.

Agave marmorata var. tepeztate

Tepeztate grows in many areas of Oaxaca, where the soil is rocky and arid. It is difficult to harvest because these areas are often inaccessible, so it needs to be carried out by hand. Tepeztate is pollinated by bats, moths, and hummingbirds. Low in sugar content, this variety offers a rich, earthy aroma with tropical fruit notes.

Agave americana var. oaxacensis arroqueño

Arroqueño grows wildly and needs twenty to twenty-five years to mature. It is the genetic mother of agave espadín and is now considered an endangered species due to the long time it requires to grow. That's why a few producers started sustainable projects to preserve and plant it. Arroqueño gives floral notes.

Agave durangensis var. cenizo

Cenizo is the most common agave used in the Mexican states of Durango and Zacatecas, and it can be found at high elevations (up to 8,500 feet/ 2,590 meters) where the conditions are cold and dry. Cenizo is quite fibrous and takes between nine and thirteen years to mature. The flavor profile of mezcal varies depending on the region where cenizo grows, but generally speaking, it gives fruity and earthy notes.

Agave cupreata

Agave cupreata grows at 4,000 to 6,000 feet (1,200 to 1,800 meters) in the Mexican states of Guerrero and Michoacán. It can take ten to fifteen years to reach maturity and gives earthy and tropical fruit notes. *Agave cupreata* is known as *maguey papalote* and is also called *Agave potatorum*, due to the resemblance in the structure.

Agave salmiana

Also known as the Green Giant (*Maguey Verde*) for its large size, *Agave salmiana* is originally from the highlands in Coahuila, Durango, and San Luis Potosí, but it is now cultivated in Central Mexico. It takes up to twenty-five years to mature.

AGAVE DISTILLATES

Traditionally all agave distillates are called *mezcal*, but due to legal restrictions, that can't happen anymore. That's why *agave distillate* describes a spirit coming from the cooking, crushing, fermenting, and distilling of agaves. The main agave distillates are mezcal, tequila, bacanora, and raicilla. Pulque is considered an agave product, but it's not distilled, while sotol, until not long ago, was considered an agave distillate, but the genus *Dasylirion* is no longer classified as agave; it is now classified as a member of the Nolinaceae family.

To begin, let's examine the differences among agave distillate products in more detail.

MEZCAL

Mezcal is a distilled spirit made from over thirty species of agave plants. It can only be made in the designated regions of Mexico, and it's regulated by the *Normas Oficiales Mexicanas* (NOM) and the *Consejo Mexicano Regulador de la Calidad del Mezcal* (CMR). Its smoky flavor comes from cooking the agave in underground pits. (See more information about mezcal on page 29.)

TEQUILA

All tequila is mezcal, but not all mezcal is tequila. That's because tequila, unlike mezcal, can be made only from *Agave tequilana* Weber Azul (commonly called blue agave or tequila agave), and it can only come from designated areas in Mexico. It is regulated by the NOM and the *Consejo Regulador del Tequila* (CRT). Tequila can be made of 100 percent blue agave or must contain at least 51 percent agave. Unlike mezcal, the agave is cooked overground. (See more about tequila on page 43.)

BACANORA

Named after the town of Bacanora in the Mexican state of Sonora, this agave distillate can only be produced from *Agave pacifica*, also called agave yaquiana (*A. angustifolia*), which only grows in the mountainous region of Sonora.

From 1915 to 1992, bacanora production was illegal. The governor of Sonora at the time was very religious and believed drinking and producing alcohol was immoral. Since 2000, Bacanora has had a Mexican DO (origin denomination) but not an international one, and since 2005, production methods have been regulated by the NOM and the *Consejo Sonorense Promotor de la Regulación del Bacanora*. To make bacanora, the agave hearts are cooked in underground ovens, crushed to extract the juices, fermented naturally in vats, and, finally, distilled.

RAICILLA

Produced in seven municipalities of Jalisco, specifically near and around the Pacific coast town of Puerto Vallarta, raicilla is made from the agave lechuguilla (*Agave inaequidens*) and agave pata de mula (*Agave maximiliana*). In 1997, the Mexican Council of Raicilla Promoters was established to protect production. Raicilla started to be imported into the US in 2014 and got the Denomination of Origin in 2019. To make raicilla, the hearts of the agave are cooked in aboveground ovens, fermented, and distilled in raicilla distilleries, which the *raicilleros* call *tabernas*. The alcohol content ranges between 35% and 45% by volume.

PULQUE

As mentioned before, pulque is not a distillate but a fermented alcohol product made from the agave's sap (called *aguamiel*, meaning "honey water"). It is the oldest agave drink, and in pre-Columbian times, it was considered sacred.

At the beginning of the twentieth century, pulque waned in popularity because it was seen as a drink of the lower class, while the Mexican upper classes preferred distilled spirits, believing them to be more modern and hygienic. Nowadays, pulque has regained popularity, thanks to young people who want to celebrate the past and protest against those who appreciate imported products. As a result, pulque now represents 10 percent of the alcohol consumed in Mexico. Modern pulque is made as it was in pre-Columbian times. The sap is collected from the agave hearts and then fermented in a barrel without cooking the agave. The liquid coming from the fermentation, which usually takes five to twenty days, has a milky color and a yeasty taste. The alcohol content of pulque is between 2% and 7% by volume. It is almost impossible to find pulque outside Mexico.

SOTOL

Produced only in the Mexican states of Chihuahua, Coahuila, and Durango, sotol is no longer considered an agave distillate, since *Dasylirion wheeleri* (commonly called desert spoon or sotol) has been reclassified as part of the Nolinaceae family. In 2002, sotol got its own Appellation of Origin, and it has been legally protected in Mexico since 2004 (but not internationally, meaning that outside Mexico, producers can label their product "sotol").

The agave hearts are cooked in aboveground ovens or boiled in earthen pits. Juices from the crushed plant are then fermented in open-air vats and distilled by column distillation or copper stills. Sotol can be found in Blanco, Reposado, or Añejo forms.

OTHER AGAVE DISTILLATES

Sikua was the mezcal produced in the state of Michoacán before it was included in the mezcal DO. Charanda, unlike the other distillates, is made from sugarcane, is produced in Uruapan, Michoacán, and has a designation of origin. Comiteco is made with an agave native to Comitán de Domínguez, Chiapas, and is produced by distilling fermented mead.

MEZCAL

AN INTRODUCTION TO MEZCAL

Called "elixir of the gods," the word *mezcal* comes from *metl* (agave) and *ixcalli* (cooked), two Nahuatl terms that combined mean cooked agave. As we have seen in the previous chapter, drinks made with agave already existed in the pre-Columbian time. There is an open debate about when mezcal and distillation were born. Some think the Filipinos brought the distillation technique, while others believe that distillation and a drink called *mezcalli* have been known for at least three thousand years. But many think distillery techniques were introduced when the Spanish arrived in Mexico. One theory explains that once the Spanish finished their supply of brandy, they started to distill pit-roasted fermented agave hearts to make *vino de mezcal,* the precursor to modern-day mezcal and tequila.

At that moment (the sixteenth century), alcohol consumption was only for a few, and vino de mezcal gained popularity to the point that, in 1636, it became necessary to obtain a license to produce agave distillates. But due to a reduction in Spanish wine and liqueur sales, in 1785 the Spanish king Carlos III banned the production of mezcal and pulque. The prohibition, though, didn't stop people from producing and drinking mezcal, so in 1795, King Carlos IV lifted the ban and began taxing mezcal.

At the beginning of the twentieth century, mezcal sales started to dip so far that the drink disappeared from the scene for a long time. It was only in the '90s that mezcal gained popularity again, thanks to Ron Cooper, founder of Del Maguey, who introduced the first line of fine mezcal in Mexico and New York. From that point, its success only grew.

FROM PRODUCTION TO DISTRIBUTION

Now that we know what agave is and how mezcal was born, we can proceed with how it is produced. First of all, let's specify what mezcal is.

Mezcal is a distilled alcoholic beverage obtained from the fermented juice of agaves. It can be distilled from over thirty species (we have seen the most common, beginning on page 16), and it must be produced in one of the following areas in Mexico: Durango, Guerrero, Guanajuato, Michoacán, Oaxaca, Puebla, San Luis Potosí, Tamaulipas, Zacatecas, and Sinaloa.

All the steps for making mezcal influence the final flavor of the product, including techniques passed down through generations. Another aspect that can affect the profile of the mezcal is the terroir, meaning the type of agave, the soil, the climate, and the water used to grow it. Every kind of agave has its own characteristics, giving various flavors to mezcal, from floral to earthy, fruity to mineral. And since agave grows in different regions, even the soil, water, and climate will affect the flavor profile. For example, a type of agave that grows in a subtropic area will differ from one grown in a desert.

Let's have a look now at the steps for making mezcal.

The first step is the **harvesting** of the agave. *Maestros mezcaleros* (mezcal experts) have many years of experience and have learned when agave needs to be harvested and when it needs to grow.

Once agave is ready to be harvested, the maestros mezcaleros cut the *quiote* (the stalk that grows out of the agave's heart) with sharp machetes (called *coa*) so all the sugar reverses into the *piña*, the heart of the agave, which will be used for making mezcal.

Once the piña has been harvested, then it's **cooking** time. Agave hearts are cooked underground in conical pits, which is the reason for mezcal's smoky flavor. This method is hundreds of years old. The pits come in different shapes and sizes, determining how many hearts can be cooked and how long it takes.

Once a fire is started at the bottom of the pit, stones are placed on and around it. After the fire reaches its peak, agave hearts are placed in the pit on the *bagazo*, a layer of moist agave fibers that will protect the hearts from the direct heat of the stones. Once they cover the hearts with another layer of bagazo, the mezcaleros seal the pit with a layer of earth. The agave hearts will now be cooked in the pit for a few days to allow the starch contained in the agave to be converted into sugar.

Next, it is time for the **milling** process. Once agave has been cooked, mezcaleros need to extract the juice and sugar from the hearts. Traditionally they are crushed through the *tahona*, a large stone wheel standing in a shallow basin, which is attached to a central axle and is pulled in a circle by a mule, a horse, or a donkey.

Another method consists of crushing the heart by hand with the help of a wooden mallet. In some cases, mechanical mills are used as well.

Then comes the **fermentation**. First, the pulp obtained from the tahona, called *mosto*, is mixed with water in tanks that are kept open to allow natural yeast to begin the fermentation and convert sugar into ethanol. When the sugar is converted, the brew obtained, called *tepache*, contains 8% alcohol.

There are some factors here that will play a role in the flavor profile of the mezcal. First, the tanks are left outside, so the weather, temperature, and geography will affect the fermentation time and the final result. Then the tank will contribute to the product profile, since it can be made of different materials such as wood, stone, steel, cement, plastic, or animal skins.

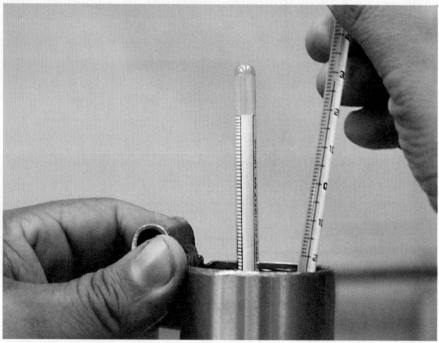

At this point, the *mosto* is transported to the stills for **distillation**. Mezcal must be distilled twice (but some are distilled three times) in copper or clay pot stills (which will contribute to variance in aroma). Another type of still used only in certain areas of Mexico, such as Michoacán, is the Filipino-style still, which is made of a wood-fire metal or clay pot, a hollow tree-trunk chamber, and a copper condenser where evaporation and condensation occur within the wooden chamber.

During the first distillation, the alcohol content fluctuates between 20% and 30%, but due to mezcal regulation, it needs to reach a content between 45% and 50%; hence the second distillation. The first alcohol coming from the stills, called *heads*, and the last, *tails*, contain impurities; that's why for the second distillation, only the *heart* is used, which is the pure alcohol between the heads and the tails.

After the distillation, mezcal must be certified, released, and bottled at the place of origin.

Mezcal can go through a third distillation called *pechuga* ("breast" in Spanish), and it happens when producers decide to add fruit or nuts to the still, or when they hang a chicken breast (or any other type of meat) above the kettle so the fumes absorb the meat flavor before condensing into alcohol.

Another type of distillation common in the area surrounding Ejutla, Jalisco, is the *refrescador*. This process allows makers to double distill in a single pass. The copper still is surrounded by a stainless-steel cylinder that is filled with water, which allows the upper part of the still to cool and to be used as a sort of condenser. Therefore, the alcohol vapor is sent back down into the boiler before being heated again.

The last step is **maturation**. Unaged mezcal is bottled straightaway and sold as is. Aged mezcal is placed in wooden barrels to mature for a minimum of two months.

CATEGORIES OF MEZCAL

In 1994, the Mexican government established the appellation of origin, *Denominación de origen* (Dominion of Origin), for mezcal and published the *Normas Oficiales Mexicanas* (NOM) that determine the production standards for the spirit. In 1997, the *Consejo Mexicano Regulador de la Calidad del Mezcal* (CMR) was formed to enforce those standards.

The NOM regulations establish that mezcal must be produced in one of the specified regions of Mexico (see page 30) and must be made with 100 percent agave (which must be stated on the label). The alcohol content must be between 35% and 55% by volume. An official permit is required to bottle mezcal, which must happen in the distillery. To export mezcal, the label should contain the CMR logo; the word *mezcal*; the type of agave used; the name, address, and official NOM number of the producer; the registered brand; the number of the batch; and the phrase "Made in Mexico" (or the Eagle's Head), to indicate that it was produced in Mexico.

The CMR sets out three different categories for mezcal that dictate the methods and equipment that can be used during the process. The categories are:

Mezcal: the most modern and industrial category that allows high-tech equipment, such as autoclaves for cooking the agave, stainless-steel tanks for the fermentation, and continuous column stills for the distillation.

Mezcal Artesanal: allows only a few modern tools. So the cooking happens only in pit ovens, but mechanical shredders are accepted for the milling, and copper stills can be used for distillation.

Mezcal Ancestral: the traditional way to produce mezcal, allowing only pit ovens, wooden or stone tanks, and clay pots.

Mezcal is then subdivided into four classes:

Blanco or Joven: unaged mezcal.

Maduro en vidro ("matured in glass"): stored in glass containers underground or in a room with minimum light, temperature, and humidity variations. It is aged for a maximum of twelve months.

Reposado: aged between two and twelve months.

Añejo: aged for at least one year.

Two additional classifications are:

Abocado con ("processed with"): mezcal that has been flavored or infused with ingredients that meet the NOM criteria, such as herbs and maguey worms, caramel, and fruits.

Destilado con ("distilled with"): a type of distillation (see page 35 for pechuga) that allows the use of ingredients such as regional fruits, meat, and herbs.

On the market, we can also find mezcal *ensamble* (or "ensemble"), which is made by combining two or more different types of agaves that are cooked, crushed, fermented, and distilled together in a single batch.

TEQUILA

CALAVERA TAPATIA.

A mí ninguno me muerde,
Pues soy calavera reata,
Que Jalisco nunca pierde
Y cuando pierde arrebata.

Y quien quiera paladear
Esta calavera fea,
Que no se atreva á mirar
Mi efigie, sin que me lea.

Han dicho que soy brincón
Muy hombre soy, á las pruebas,
Verán que en este panteón
Los.....dejo comiendo brevas.

O si versan de otro modo,
Nos vamos á la Tequila,
Que yo la verso de todo
Con calaveras de á pila.

Si por mi terreno fueran
A puños la versarían,
Y buen posole comieran,
Y muertos no se verían.

Porque por Guadalajara
No hay muertos que sean rajones,
Que allí se corta la cara
A los que tienen calzones.

Allí tengo mi morena
Refantaciosa y faceta,
Que ni la muerte la apena,
Tan reata como veleta.

Allí cualquier esqueleto
Está armado de tranchete;
Pero es tan bueno el sujeto
Que con ninguno se mete.

No envidia más que el amor
Y un buen sombrero jarano,
Un buen tequila, un habano,
Y un fierro de lo mejor.

Una baraja de Olea,
Y oro y plata por montón,
Y bebe y fuma y chulea
Hasta la muerte en acción.

A nadie provoca, es hombre
De raza la más bravía,
Mas quien le burle su nombre
Se va á la difuntería.

Y allí se queja á su suerte,
Pues el tapatío brincón,
Lo despacha con la muerte
A bailar un rigodón.

Mas yo no admito la duda
Y la calandria que cante,
Si se cree buena y forzuda
Muerte, que luego se plante.

Cargo mi cuchillo al lado.
Y no lo traigo de ocioso,
Que Dios coja confesado
Al que le guste el retozo.

Yo salgo de mi corral
Cantando á otro gallinero,
Y no hay quien me haga cabal
Porque el se muere ó me muero.

Que al cabo la muerte es flaca
Y no ha de poder conmigo,
Y ni el diablo me sonsaca,
Porque ya el diablo es mi amigo.

Hoy hago calaveradas,
Porque aunque se me llegó,
La muerte, patas rajadas,
Quiso entrarme y se rajó.

Yo no nací para prisco,
Ni mi valor acabó,
Calaveras de Jalisco
No cierren que falto yo.

El país tengo recorrido
Con mi cuchillo filoso,
Y nadie, pues, me ha tosido
Tan bien como yo le toso.

Porque aquel que la intención
Tuvo en toserme de veras,
Rodando está en el panteón
Con muertos y calaveras.

Aquí he matado poblanos,
Jarochos y Toluqueños,
Tepiqueños y Surianos
De Mérida y Oaxaqueños.

No resiste ni un pellejo
Mi cuchillo nuevecito;
He muerto de puro viejo
Pues fuí en mi vida maldito

Y á aquel que le guste el *duro*
El tequila y el posole,
Si muere, yo le aseguro
Que en la tumba bebe atole.

Pero que si no es rajado
Y trae cual yo sus dientes,
Aquí vivedescansado
Y....¡ay reata, no te revientes!

Que aquí no acaba los bríos
Ni la vida cuesta cara;
Que aquí están los tapatíos
Ygual que en Guadalajara.

Aquí soy hombre de veras
Cuando el sombrero me arrisco,
Y grité á las calaveras:
¡Muchachas, viva Jalisco!

Y que prevenga el cajón
Y sus ceras que prevenga,
Pues lo despacho al panteón
Le convenga ó no convenga.

Y á todo el mundo lo digo
Que yo ni muerto me dejo,
Y que el que sea mi enemigo
Pa mole su gallo viejo.

Es pues mi contestación
Ser de maneras sensillas,
Aunque esté ya en el panteón
Exhibiendo mis canillas.

Al que me mira lo azoto
O con mi fierro lo entuerto,
Que á mí no me espanta un roto
Con el petate del muerto.

Al catrín de vecindad
O trovador de velorio,
Lo mando á la eternidad
Sin rezarle un responsorio.

Con la muerte no me asusto
Porque á la muerte chongeó,
Pues que me retoza el gusto
Cuando en parranda me veo.

Imprenta de Antonio Vanegas Arroyo.—2a. Sta. Teresa No. 43. México.—1910

A BRIEF HISTORY OF TEQUILA

The history of tequila goes at the same pace as mezcal's history. While vino de mezcal started to be produced in the town of Tequila, it is believed that in the seventeenth century, Pedro Sanchez de Tagle established the first commercial mezcal distillery. He is considered by many to be the father of tequila (but this is just a theory). The distillery had to close when, in 1785, the Spanish government banned any mezcal production in favor of the importation of Spanish spirits.

But in 1795, King Carlos IV started to allow mezcal production. In that same year, the Cuervo family got the first license from the crown to produce mezcal wine and founded the first official Mexican distillery. It was also the first distiller to put tequila into bottles, rather than barrels, in the late nineteenth century. The distillery was established in Tequila, where blue agave plants were abundant.

To differentiate mezcal and pulque from the spirit produced in the city of Tequila, the latter was named tequila. But some stories say that Don Cenobio Sauza changed the name from vino de mezcal to tequila in 1873 to distinguish it from the mezcal produced in southern Mexico.

Regardless of the origin of the name, the definitive step that differentiated mezcal from tequila happened when, in the nineteenth century, a new method of production was introduced: tequila started to be produced with aboveground steam ovens instead of the underground processes used for mezcal. This new method allowed tequila to develop a milder flavor, and it became more suitable for a wider public.

In 1893, tequila started to be exported to the US and won an award at the Chicago World's Fair. In the twentieth century, the tequila industry kept growing, mainly because it became a symbol of national pride and the drink of freedom and progress during the Mexican Revolution (1910 to 1920). During Prohibition (1920 to 1933), it was smuggled across the border in great quantity. When the margarita was created in the 1930s, tequila became indispensable both in Mexico and US.

During World War II, tequila production kept growing, and agave fields expanded. The money coming in led many distilleries to modernize.

The 1968 Olympic Games in Mexico City gave tequila worldwide exposure, and in 1978 it received the *appellation d'origine contrôlée* (AOC—controlled designation of origin), which stipulated that tequila could only be produced in Mexico. In 1976, the *Normas Oficiales Mexicanas* (NOM) were established to regulate the process of making tequila.

In the 1980s, the real tequila boom exploded when a growing population of American tourists and baby-boomer visitors traveled to Mexico and discovered premium brands, which started to be sold in the US.

In 1994, the *Consejo Regulador del Tequila* (CRT) was founded to monitor tequila's production, bottling, and labeling to ensure compliance with legal requirements, and in 1997, Mexico signed an international agreement for all countries to recognize Mexico as the sole producer of tequila.

THE MAKING OF TEQUILA

Although tequila may not be aged for a long time, the process of making it takes years due to the slow growth of its raw materials. In fact, blue agave, which is the only agave used to make tequila, can take five to seven years to reach maturity. The maturation period can change depending on the area where blue agave grows. In some regions of Jalisco, the soil is volcanic, and agave is usually harvested after six to ten years, while in areas where the soil is ferruginous, or iron heavy, the agave contains more sugar, and the time until harvesting is longer, from eight to twelve years. As with mezcal production, the terroir is important and affects the final product. To make tequila, producers follow this process:

1. First, there is the **harvesting**. Once agave reaches its maturity, the *jimadors*, or agave farmers, cut the leaves with a flat-bladed knife, a process called *coa de limpiar*, until they extract the heart of the agave, the *piña*, which will then be transported to the distillery.

2. Then comes the **cooking**. This process definitively marks the difference between mezcal and tequila. Tequila producers use aboveground ovens, a method started in the 1850s that changed tequila's taste from the much smokier flavor of mezcal.

   Today, there are two cooking methods: brick ovens (*hornos de mampostería*) or steel containers (*autoclaves*). In both methods, the agave hearts are halved or quartered and then placed in the ovens to be steamed. With the autoclave, the process is quicker (it takes eight to fourteen hours), while the brick ovens take thirty-six to seventy-two hours. Both methods are designed to turn the natural starches of agave into fermentable sugars. A growing number of tequila producers are now using a more modern method, the diffuser, to obtain up to 20 percent more fermentable material than autoclaves.

The diffuser extracts the starches without the agave hearts first having to be cooked, using blasts of high-pressure water as agave hearts move onto a conveyor belt; the addition of acid hydrolysis releases fermentable sugars.

3. Once the agave hearts are cooked, it's time for **grinding** (which doesn't apply to the diffuser method). The juice needs to be extracted from the cell fibers through the *tahona* (see page 33, on mezcal) or the *molina*, a mechanical mill. If the distiller is making a mixto tequila, at this stage they will add other sugars, such as corn and cane sugar.

4. Now it's time for the **fermentation**. Unlike mezcal, which uses only wild yeast, yeast is added in the making of tequila (brewer's yeast, cultivated yeast, or natural airborne yeast) and will affect the final flavor of the product. The fermentation process occurs in stainless-steel containers (for hygienic reasons, the Tequila Regulatory Council [CRT] advised against wooden containers) and takes between twelve hours and several days. When yeast is added, the sugar contained in the liquid, called *mosto fresco* (fresh must), will be converted into a liquid called *mosto muerto* (dead must) with an alcohol content of 5% to 7% by volume.

5. At this point, it's time for the **distillation** that takes place in copper or stainless-steel pot stills or continuous distillation towers. Tequila is distilled twice (or sometimes three times, depending on the brand). The first distillation, called *destrozamiento*, takes a couple of hours and yields the *ordinario*, a liquid with an alcohol level of around 20% to 25%; the second distillation, *rectificación*, takes between three and four hours and produces an alcohol level around 55% to 75%.

During the *destrozamiento*, the liquid that comes out of the still has three parts: the head (the top), the heart (the middle), and the tail (the bottom). Only the heart will be used during

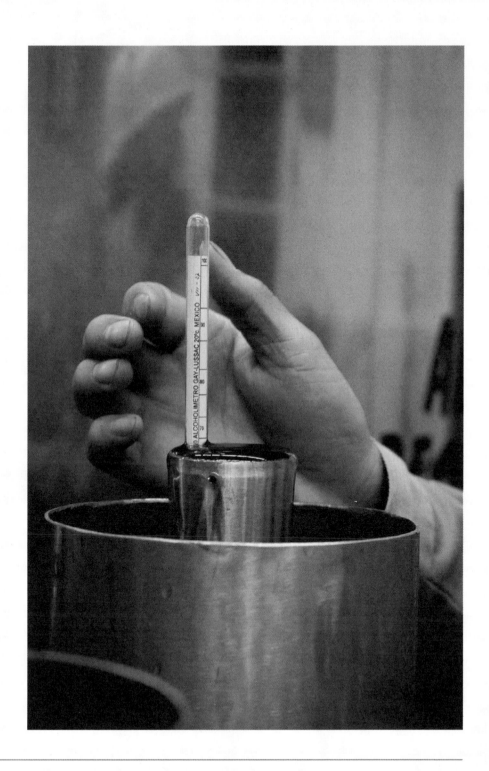

the *rectificación*; the rest will be thrown away because it contains most of the impurities. At the end of the second distillation, only the heart will be used for aging or bottling.

6. Finally, tequila can be **bottled** either straightaway or aged (see more on page 52).

CLASSIFICATION OF TEQUILA

Tequila is regulated by the NOM, which define the rules tequila must follow, and by the CRT, which checks that distilleries meet the NOM criteria.

The main criteria are the following: tequila must be made from the *Agave tequilana* Weber Azul and must be produced only in Jalisco, Guanajuato, Michoacán, Nayarit, and Tamaulipas; at least 51 percent of the alcohol content must originate from blue agave; and the alcohol content must be 35% to 55%.

The bottle's label is also regulated to ensure that important information can easily be found. It must include the registered brand, with its producer and distillery address; the NOM (the number that refers to the distillery where the tequila is produced); the word *tequila* and the category it belongs to; the net volume and the ABV; any additives present; the batch number; the description of origin (*Hecho en Mexico*); and information regarding health upon excessive consumption.

The NOM also distinguishes between 100 percent *Agave tequilana* Weber Azul tequila that is only bottled in Mexico and tequila made with at least 51% *Agave tequiliana* Weber Azul that may contain 49 percent sugar. The later, named *mixto* (although it's not a legal term), can be sold in bulk and bottled outside Mexico when the provisions set forth by NOM are met.

The NOM identifies five types of tequila:

- **Blanco or Plato** (but you may also find Silver, White, or Platinum, all referring to the same category): unaged tequila that has been bottled straightaway. It can be stored temporarily in steel tanks or large oak barrels for a maximum of sixty days.

- **Joven or Oro** (also called *Joven Abocado* or Gold): unaged tequila that has been adulterated with coloring and flavors, such as caramel, glycerin, or wood chips.

- **Reposado:** aged for at least two months. This tequila is richer and more complex than Blanco. The aging occurs in French oak or white oak barrels.

- **Añejo:** aged in sealed barrels of no more than 158 gallons (600 liters), usually around 52 gallons (200 liters), for at least one year in French oak or white oak barrels. Tequila often comes in contact with the wood, absorbing its taste and color.

- **Extra Añejo:** highly expensive tequila that has been aged for a minimum of three years in barrels that hold a maximum of 158 gallons (600 liters) but usually hold 52 gallons (200 liters). This category was introduced in 2006.

Another category, which so far hasn't been officially recognized, is *Cristalino*: any Reposado, Añejo, or Extra Añejo that has been filtered through activated charcoal to remove the color that comes from aging in oak barrels.

FROM THE MEZCAL AND TEQUILA BOOM TO SUSTAINABILITY PRACTICES

BEAM BRANDS
BOURBON WHISKEY
DSP-KY 230
D-160-P R0536
B14L06
TANK 220

THE BOOM FACTORS

Until the 1990s, tequila and mezcal were not taken seriously in the US. Tequila was seen as a cheap party drink, something to get drunk with; mezcal was advertised with a worm inside the bottle. A fortunate combination of factors helped shed tequila's (and later mezcal's) bad reputation.

First, those who spent time in Mexico knew that good-quality tequila and mezcal existed. US consumers recognized this fact when Mexican producers began exporting 100 percent agave tequilas, and not only mixto tequilas.

Patrón had a big influence on tequila's new reputation, branding itself as a luxury spirit and therefore attracting the mass market. They advertised Patrón as the world's greatest spirit, without even a hint at the word *tequila*, increasing sales—and soon tequila was everywhere.

In the 2000s, Carlos Camarena and Tomas Estes's concept of terroir in agave spirits set in motion another important step for tequila and mezcal: helping people understand the different types of agave and the factors that contribute to its growth, lending nuanced flavor to the final product.

Today, many producers apply Camarena and Estes's concept of terroir to their own productions.

"We use the term *terroir* to describe all localized characteristics of production—the earth, climate, biology, and production techniques of a region. These characteristics are the primary determinant of the profile of an artisanal mezcal. In any given area there will also be minor differences in soil and climate which impact the growth of individual plants, and so individual batches (partially accounting for batch variation)," said Ben Schroder, founder of Pensador Mezcal.

Today, the tequila and mezcal boom is unstoppable. GlobalData forecasts their sales in North America will grow by 31.2 percent in volume terms and by 38.6 percent in value between 2021 and 2026. This growth can be attributed to several factors:

- **Changes in consumer taste:** Consumers are increasingly looking for unique and high-quality products that can offer a distinct flavor profile.

  Jesse Estes from Tequila Ocho said, "I think the education that people like my father have been doing over the past several decades has finally reached a 'tipping point' of sorts. Bartenders, agave aficionados, and brand owners have all been extolling the virtues of drinking tequila, and it is now paying off. Enough people now understand and enjoy tequila, and are able to discern between different levels of quality."

- **Premiumization:** Tequila and mezcal have become premium spirits that can offer products made with traditional methods and high-quality ingredients that consumers are willing to buy. Master distiller Germán González Gorrochotegui from Tears of Llorona said, "Consumers in the United States are looking for better-quality tequilas. In my own experience, the first super-premium tequila, Chinaco, was exported by my father in 1983, so I believe he was the driving force behind this change."

- **Cocktail culture:** With the increasing popularity of cocktail culture, both tequila and mezcal have proven to be very versatile and can be used to make a wide range of cocktails.

A spokesperson from Camarena Tequila explained, "As more people have spent time at home over the past few years, they've been exploring new spirits and learning how to make and enjoy new cocktails. More trial has led to a greater appreciation and better understanding of tequila and its complexities. Additionally, the classic margarita has grown immensely in popularity, with CGA reporting it's the most sought-after cocktail in forty-three states."

- **Mexican culture:** Mexican culture has become increasingly popular, along with everything connected to it, such as food, music, art, and, of course, drinks. Mezcal and tequila are iconic Mexican spirits that keep attracting more and more people.

- **Celebrity-owned brands:** Many celebrities, such as George Clooney and Dwayne "The Rock" Johnson, have started their own tequila or mezcal brands, which have entered the mainstream, reaching millions of new consumers in the US.

Jesse Estes from Tequila Ocho said, "The sheer number of celebrity-owned or -endorsed tequila brands launched in the last few years is staggering, and this is, of course, drawing a lot of attention to the category."

PHIL BAYLY, FIRST GLOBAL MEZCAL AMBASSADOR

I had the pleasure to talk to Phil Bayly, the first Global Mezcal Ambassador, about his life and about agave.

His story is dictated by love for mezcal.

Many years ago, he was a photographer (and still is) in South Australia. At some point, he decided to visit Europe and bought a one-way ticket to London, where he ended up staying for six months. He then started to travel a lot, and during one of his trips, he went to Amsterdam, where he was supposed to stay just for a week. He ended up staying for nine years.

In Amsterdam, he started to work with a street artist on street views and for the Tropenmuseum. While he was working at the museum, Tomas Estes went to see an exhibition on a Mexican artist. After the exhibition, Tomas asked Phil if he could paint a palm tree in his Café Pacifico. Phil took the job and started to get more and more involved with Tomas and his Café Pacifico in Amsterdam, and then in London. As a matter of fact, he was involved in the opening of eighteen venues in six countries.

Because Tomas always talked about Mexico, Phil got curious and went on a trip there. He fell in love with Mexico so much that when he got back to Europe, Phil and Tomas started to host events about tequila tastings and margaritas in order to introduce the spirit to people. Phil got to know more and more about tequila, but there was always the mezcal element involved, so in 1985 he went to Oaxaca to learn more.

In 1991, he returned to Australia and opened his first bar in Sydney, named Café Pacifico. He ran it until 2013, when the landlord decided to demolish the building.

In 2003, Tomas Estes was named Global Tequila Ambassador by the National Chamber of the Tequila Industry (CNIT). In 2007, Phil and Tomas were on a French island for a three-day conference where big tequila producers and regulatory bodies were present. The CRT (*Consejo Regulador del Tequila*) met Phil and told him that they wanted him to be a tequila ambassador, but due to internal conflict, that didn't happen.

Later on, in 2014, Phil went back to Mexico and spent a long time researching and learning, because he wanted to do something involving tequila and mezcal. With time, he realized that people didn't know much about mezcal, and when they got to know it, they thought they could drink it like tequila, in shots. But mezcal is not a shot spirit, so Phil wanted to spread more information about mezcal and how to drink it, and make people understand the difference between tequila and mezcal. Thus Phil started a program called Agave Love in 2015 in Sydney. He invited twenty-five people from Mexico (key producers, CRT, CMR, CNIT) and created an event with ten venues. It took place in two days with forty-six talks and tastings. The venues were 200 meters from each other, so people could go from one to another. From there, he then went to Perth, Melbourne, and Brisbane.

Then, he brought the Agave Love program to other locations: Singapore, Hong Kong, Helsinki, Minsk, Saint Petersburg, Moscow, London, Seoul, Mumbai, Kuala Lumpur, and Japan.

In 2017, when he was in Hong Kong, he was named Global Mezcal Ambassador by the CRT (later on, he resigned from the position).

Nowadays, he is working on a book and on his own photos.

In regard to agave, I asked him his thoughts about what is happening with the production of the plant. He explained that there is an overproduction of agave, because people understood that it's more convenient to let the agaves seed and flower rather than actually buying the agave. So basically today it's better to be producers and distillers, because if the price of agave goes down, they can use their own agaves to make tequila; when the prices go up, they can just sell agaves and still make tequila.

Since the price of agave is currently high, people are thinking that they can make a fortune out of it. So they are planting agave everywhere; but in a couple of years, when they mature at the same time, the price, of course, will drop.

In the case of mezcal, they have a problem with timber: since producers use wood to cook the agave, the demand led to greater deforestation. So nowadays, producers should find an alternative solution. For example, some of them adopted solar power, which, with the help of mirrors, can cook the agave.

We also talked about the importance of terroir. The same type of agave that can grow in different areas will not taste the same, because the plants are influenced by the soil and the microclimate, creating different flavors. That makes mezcal the most "terroir" spirit on the planet.

Finally, I asked him what he thinks about aging mezcal and using it in cocktails. He does believe that there is no need for aging mezcal. That's because, compared to other spirits (such as gin, which needs botanicals to get flavors, or whiskey, which gets most of its flavors from the barrels), mezcal doesn't need to be aged to get more flavors. Since agave takes a long time to grow, it develops all the flavor that will go into mezcal. And in regard to cocktails, his choice is the Mezcal Negroni. So he approves of using mezcal in cocktails, but it really depends on the mezcal; the best choice is espadín, since it's affordable and strong enough.

THE IMPORTANCE OF SUSTAINABILITY

The boom in tequila and mezcal production has led to sustainability concerns associated with agave production.

Agave is a slow-growing plant that takes several years to mature before it can be harvested for tequila and mezcal production. The overall fear is that the limited supply could overinflate the prices or that there won't be enough growing agave to meet the demand.

To address these concerns, many tequila and mezcal producers have taken steps to promote sustainable agave farming practices. For example, some producers have implemented agave reforestation programs to ensure that there are enough mature plants for future harvests, or they are working to reduce waste.

Maestro Tequilero José Valdez from Partida explained, "We have invested in the correct disposal of the residuals of the tequila process, making compost with the cooked and squeezed agave fiber and the distilled fermented *mosto*. We minimize the use of water, using technology in the extraction and distillation process. We only used premium agaves that reach maturity, which means they cost more and take more time, but it is the natural way; we don't look for agaves that are fast cultivated with a lot of chemicals and fertilizer that generate big agaves in a short period of time but affect the soil."

Additionally, some producers have worked to support local communities by providing employment opportunities and investing in infrastructure and education. This has helped promote sustainable agave farming practices and ensure that the industry is economically viable for years to come. Ben Schroder from Pensador Mezcal added, "I think it's worth mentioning the adversity many of our producers have experienced. They live in one of the poorest agricultural areas in Mexico (and therefore the world), the land and the climate make farming very difficult, and roughly half of the young population is forced to migrate to urban areas in Mexico or the United States—dangerous journeys with uncertain rewards. By buying mezcal, you are giving these families a crucial lifeline and opportunity to stay in their homeland and support their communities."

EMILIO FERREIRA RUIZ, OWNER OF EL BUHO TEQUILA SHOP

When I was in Mexico in early 2023, I had the great opportunity to chat with Emilio, owner of El Buho shop, the biggest tequila shop you can find in Mexico.

Emilio was born in a small town near Guadalajara, in the highland of Jalisco. Since there were no opportunities, his parents decided to move to Guadalajara when he was two years old, so he, and later on his siblings, could have a good education.

Emilio started to work when he was young and did all sorts of jobs. After he graduated from college as a chemical engineer, he found a job in a big pharmaceutical company where he had to make medicines. He likes to say, "I used to make medicines for the body, but now I am selling medicines for the soul."

In 1979, he decided that he didn't want to work for someone else anymore and that he wanted to open a liquor store. So with his brother, he bought the oldest liquor store in Guadalajara, El Tecolote. At that time, the shop sold around ten to fifteen tequila brands, but today, under Emilio's brother's ownership, at least two thousand different brands are available.

In 2022, Emilio decided to open his own shop, this time exclusively selling tequila: El Buho. This came from different sources: first of all, from his memories. His father used to drink tequila at home with his family and friends, and he always had a great time drinking it. Plus, Emilio tried many kinds of spirits, just to realize that his was tequila.

El Buho is a must visit if you are a fan of tequila and you are in Jalisco. You will find so many brands that, unfortunately, are not exported outside Mexico. The shop is open every day, and if you happen to meet Emilio, you will be amazed by his knowledge of tequila.

And soon enough, if you are there, you will be able to taste his own tequila. I, for sure, can't wait to go back just to taste it!

Here is where you can find him: C. Juárez 164-B, Centro, 45500 San Pedro Tlaquepaque, Jalisco, Mexico. Elbuhotequila.com

DISTILLERY PROFILES

In this chapter, you will embark on a journey through the world of mezcal and tequila. The brands featured here have been carefully selected for various reasons, each holding a unique characteristic. Some are my personal favorites, while others have gained such fame that they simply cannot be overlooked. Additionally, I've included some lesser-known yet interesting small brands that I believe deserve greater recognition.

Within these pages, you'll find a long list of the mezcal and tequila brands. Visiting some of these distilleries has been a privilege, and I encourage you to do the same if you have the opportunity. The dedication and hard work behind these brands are remarkable, making each one exceptional.

Every tequila and mezcal in this book represents something special. They embody various aspects, such as community, sustainability, innovation, and quality. While some brands have a rich and long history, others have used the power of strategic marketing to gain acclaim for their products. Each sip of these spirits holds a story of its own, and together, they create flavors and experiences that will leave you amazed. Through this exploration, we'll gain a deeper understanding of the intricate world of mezcal and tequila and the stories that have shaped them.

AGUA MÁGICA

Agua Mágica was founded by an all-Mexican team, with Rafael Shin and Don Rogelio Juan Hernandez as cofounders. Don Rogelio Juan Hernandez is a fourth-generation mezcalero who returned to Mexico after having lived in the States for a long time. He had a dream of opening his own distillery, one that came true when he met Rafael Shin, a former food and beverage finance specialist within the Latin American market, who was looking for a partnership in the mezcal market.

Agua Mágica's *palenque* (or distillery) is located in the town of San Juan del Río, and the producer won bronze at the 2021 San Francisco World Spirits Competition.

Agua Mágica only uses espadín and tobalá agaves, harvested in San Juan del Río, where the soil is rich and a perfect climate, fresh river water, and a high-mountain altitude help the agaves retain less water and increase their sugar concentration, resulting in a complex and robust flavor.

Agave hearts are harvested and cleaned by hand, covered in banana leaves, and cooked in underground earth pits on red-hot rocks. The agave hearts are then crushed by a horse-pulled tahona wheel, fermented in open-air wood vats, and double distilled by maestro mezcalero Don Rogelio. At Agua Mágica, they produce only small batches of their product, Ensamble.

Agua Mágica supports the program Empowering Mezcaleros by donating 5 percent of their yearly profits to five family-run palenques and helping them obtain all the certifications to sell their mezcal.

AGUA MÁGICA ENSAMBLE

Agua Mágica Ensamble was made to prioritize quality; hence, Agua Mágica encourages drinkers to sip it neat. Made with a seven-year-old espadín and a fifteen-year-old tobalá, it won the triple gold medal for Spirits and the triple gold for Design at MicroLiquor Spirit Awards 2021. Ensamble is fermented for seven to eight days and double distilled in copper pot stills. On the nose, it presents aromas of cooked maguey, with slight notes of smoke, bananas, and almonds. On the palate, it offers mineralized herbal and fresh notes, with hints of cooked maguey, caramel, banana, almond, and mango. The finish is rich and smooth, and the ABV is 40%.

TEQUILA ARETTE

Arette was founded by master distillers Eduardo Orendain Sr. and Jaime Orendain in 1986 and takes its name from the Mexican horse called Arete, which won the first Olympic gold medals for Mexico at the 1948 London Olympics. The two brothers are fifth-generation tequila producers.

Their story starts with Don Eduardo Orendain, who opened a distillery in the early 1900s called El Llano and began to produce Orendain Tequila. In 1960, the Orendain family moved the production to a new, larger distillery, but Eduardo Sr. and Jaime Orendain rebuilt and returned to the original building in 1978 and founded Tequila Arette in 1986.

Arette is made from 100 percent estate blue Weber agave, from the Orendain fields surrounding Tequila. They produce small batches, starting by cooking the agave hearts in autoclaves for fifteen hours at 120°C. Then, the hearts are shredded with a mechanical mill and fermented in stainless-steel or concrete tanks for four to five days (depending on the expression) days with a cultivated yeast strain and wild yeast, without the use of any chemicals or accelerators. The distillation takes place in stainless-steel pot stills, and the aging process occurs in used bourbon oak barrels. Finally, the tequila is carbon filtered and then bottled.

Arette offers the following varieties, known as "expressions" in the world of mezcal and tequila:

- Artesanal: including Suave Blanco, Suave Reposado (aged for eleven months in American white oak barrels), Suave Añejo (matured for more than eighteen months in American white oak barrels), Gran Clase Extra Añejo (rested for at least thirty-six months in American white oak barrels), and Fuerte 101 (Blanco tequila without dilution).

- Clásica: including Blanco, Reposado (aged for six months in American white oak barrels), and Añejo (matured for fourteen to eighteen months in American white oak barrels).

- Gran Viejo: aged for six years in American white oak barrels.

- Agave de Oro Reposado: matured for six months in American white oak barrels.

ARETTE BLANCO

Arette Blanco is clear in color and one of the unaged expressions from Tequila Arette. On the nose, it presents aromas of cooked agave and herbal notes; on the palate, it offers flavors of vanilla, cinnamon, and pepper. The finish has hints of spices and agave notes. The ABV is 38%.

TEQUILA ARTENOM SELECCIÓN

ArteNOM was founded by Jacob Lustig in 2010 and works with several distilleries, showing the different characteristics agave can have when growing in different places, at different altitudes.

Jacob Lustig was born in California and spent much of his childhood in Oaxaca. In the 1990s, he moved to Oaxaca to complete his studies on the various methods of producing mezcal. Then, he renovated a distillery in Santa Catarina Minas and started to produce his own mezcal, Don Amado, in 1995.

At the same time, a large liquor distributor, Southern Wine and Spirits, hired him as an in-house agave spirits expert, and he spent the next eleven years working closely with more than forty distilleries. With time, he discovered that his favorite Blanco, Reposado, and Añejo tequilas were all from different distilleries, and he wanted to produce them. But, by law, tequilas were not allowed to be distilled in different distilleries under the same brand name. So, after a multiyear struggle, the Tequila Regulatory Council (CRT) granted him the authorization to produce them in 2010. He started to work with different distilleries with different altitudes, heritage, agave cultivations, and distillation techniques in the highland region.

Tequila ArteNOM Selección works with the following distilleries:

- NOM 1579: Felipe Camarena produces Blanco Clásico at the El Pandillo distillery in Jesús María at 6,788 feet (2,069 meters) above sea level.

- NOM 1123: Blanco Histórico is produced by the Rosales family at their Destilería Cascahuín in El Arenal, Jalisco. Master distiller Salvador Rosales Torres steam roasts the agave hearts and crushes them with a gear-spindle roller mill. The distillation takes place in pot stills and is barrel-conditioned for twenty-eight days in used mezcal barrels from Oaxaca.

- NOM 1414: This selection is produced in Destilería El Ranchito, owned by the Vivanco family since 1994 (though the family started to cultivate the agave in the early 1900s), in Arandas, Jalisco.

- NOM 1146: This selection is produced by master distiller Enrique Fonseca at La Tequileña in Tequila. The agave hearts are steam roasted, and the juice is extracted with a screw-press method. Fermentation occurs in stainless-steel vats with Mendoza wine yeast strains, and distillation takes place in copper pot stills. The tequila is aged in used Cabernet Franc wine barrels (from the Loire Valley in France) for a minimum of fourteen months and is then rested for a further fourteen months in toasted American white oak previously used for Canadian whiskey or Tennessee rye whiskey.

ARTENOM SELECCIÓN NOM 1414

Produced by the Vivanco family, the agave heart of the NOM 1414 is steam roasted, and the juice is extracted with a gear-spindle crusher. Fermentation occurs in stainless-steel vats with indigenous yeast strains, and distillation takes place in a copper pot still. The master distiller is Sergio Cruz. The tequila is aged for four months in third-fill American white oak barrels previously used for bourbon whiskey.

Very pale straw in color, the NOM 1414 presents aromas of vegetal chaparral and roasted sweet potato; on the palate, it offers flavors of vanilla cookie and allspice. The ABV is 40%, and may vary up to 41.2%.

ARTENOM SELECCIÓN NOM 1579

Produced by Felipe Camarena, the agave hearts of the NOM 1579 are slowly cooked in brick ovens and crushed by a roller crusher. The distillation occurs in small copper pot stills, and the tequila is aerated before bottling. Half rainwater and half filtered water (from the on-property well) are added for proof adjustment.

Clear in color, NOM 1579 presents aromas of spring rain, mint, and roasted agave on the nose; on the palate, it offers flavors of white pepper and spearmint candies, with a wine-like texture. The ABV is 40%, and may vary up to 40.7%.

3 BADGE BEVERAGE CORPORATION

3 Badge Beverage is a private, family-owned company run by August Sebastiani II, a fourth-generation vintner, operating out of an old firehouse in Sonoma, California—the same firehouse where August's grandfather and father were volunteer firefighters. The name comes from the old fire service badges belonging to the family.

3 Badge Beverage Corporation's story begins with Samuele Sebastiani, who blended his own wine and sold it in the early years of the 1900s, expanding his winery business with the acquisition of land and facilities from the Franciscan fathers. In 1944, August, Samuele's son, introduced new varietals and proprietary blends to their portfolio, becoming renowned throughout the California wine industry.

In 1980, the company was taken over by Don Sebastiani, August's son, who helped increase production and sales with innovation.

In 2005, Don's son, August Sebastiani II, founded a wine company, The Other Guys, with the goal of becoming a premium négociant. In 2014, August managed to buy the vacant firehouse from the Sonoma City Council, and in 2016 changed the name from The Other Guys to 3 Badge Beverage Corporation, which, after pioneering the wine industry, turned to looking for premium spirits from the finest distilleries. Two of them are Bozal Mezcal and Pasote Tequila.

BOZAL MEZCAL

Bozal translates to "wild" or "untamed." That's because 3 Badge Beverage Corporation wanted to reconnect to the wild species of Mexican agave grown in the uncultivated lands of Oaxaca, Guerrero, and Durango. They also wanted to refer to the untamed traditions used to distill small batches in those locations.

Bozal Mezcal is a 100 percent artisanal product. The wild agaves used by Bozal take between seven and nineteen years to mature, and when they are ready, they are harvested by hand. The hearts are cooked in conical, grounded pit ovens, then crushed by a stone tahona wheel. The open-air fermentation occurs in either wood tanks or clay pots without the addition of artificial yeast, and finally, it undergoes a double distillation. Then the mezcal is bottled into rustic ceramic bottles reminiscent of the traditional terra-cotta *copitas* used for drinking mezcal. Bozal's expressions are:

- Ensamble: made with espadín, barril, and Mexicano agaves.

- Single Maguey: focused on one variety of agave, made with the artisanal method in a copper pot still. The line includes the following mezcal:

  - Cenizo: 100 percent *Agave durangensis*, harvested from the hillsides of Durango at 8,500 feet (2,590 meters).

  - Cuishe: 100 percent *Agave karwinskii*, made in Zoquitlán Rio Seco, Oaxaca.

  - Sacatoro: 100 percent *Agave angustifolia*, harvested in Escuchapa, Guerrero.

  - Tepeztate: 100 percent *Agave marmorata*, made in Santa Ana del Río, Oaxaca.

  - Tobasiche: 100 percent *Agave karwinskii*, produced in Río de Ejutla, Oaxaca.

  - Madrecuishe: 100 percent *Agave karwinskii*, harvested in Miahuatlan, Oaxaca

- Sacrificio: produced in small batches, suspending locally sourced protein, fruit, and grains at the final stage of the distillation. The line includes:

  - Borrego: made with agave espadín and barril in Río de Ejutla.

- Guías de Calabaza: made with *Agave angustifolia* in Río de Ejutla.

- Jamón Ibérico: made with espadín, Mexicano, and tobasiche in Río de Ejutla.

- Pechuga: made with 100 percent *Agave karwinskii* in Río de Ejutla, Oaxaca.

- Reserva: limited release mezcal made with the ancestral method in a clay pot still. The line includes:

  - Barril: 100 percent *Agave karwinskii*, made in Santa Catarina Minas, Oaxaca.

  - Castilla: made with 100 percent *Agave angustifolia* in Durango.

  - Cempasúchil: 100 percent espadín, produced in Etla, Oaxaca.

  - Chino Verde: made with the extremely rare agave Chino Verde in Sola de Vega, Oaxaca.

  - Coyote: 100 percent *Agave americana*, made in Sola de Vega.

  - Jabalí: 100 percent *Agave convallis*, produced in Sola de Vega.

  - Tobalá: made with 100 percent *Agave potatorum* in Sola de Vega.

- A special limited edition from Bozal was the Advent Calendar, launched in fall 2022.

For every agave harvested, Bozal plants two in a mountainside wild nursery. After one or two years, they will be transported back into the wild.

3 Badge Beverage Corporation provides small villages financial support for education and women's health care in order to aid their community effort.

BOZAL ENSAMBLE

Bozal Ensamble is made with 100 percent agave espadín, barril, and Mexicano, growing in Miahuatlán y Etla, Oaxaca. It follows the artesanal method by cooking the agave hearts in earthen pit ovens, then crushing them with a horse-drawn stone tahona. It's then fermented with airborne yeast and double distilled in a copper pot still. Clear in color, it offers citrus and floral notes on the nose, followed by smoky and herbaceous flavors on the palate. The finish is warm and viscous. The ABV is 47%.

Q & A WITH AUGUST SEBASTIANI II, OWNER OF 3 BADGE BEVERAGE CORPORATION

Tell me a bit about the company.

We are rather proud of being a private, family-owned company operating out of an old firehouse in Sonoma. It's the very same firehouse that saw my father and grandfather as volunteer firefighters. And, while our family history was pioneering the wine industry, having the opportunity to tackle the spirits sector has been quite an exciting adventure. In true négociant form, we scour the globe to source premium spirits from the finest distilleries. One of those premium spirits includes Bozal Mezcal, which is sourced from various states in Mexico.

Do you have any special releases or limited editions?

With so many exceptional mezcaleros, there is much opportunity to highlight their expertise with new releases. We were proud to have developed a limited-edition Advent Calendar this last fall. The calendar included twenty-four 200 ml Bozal expressions in their traditional ceramic bottles, which pushed our total unique releases to date to twenty-nine. It included two proprietary copitas and tealights to be lit on the final day, in reverence to mezcaleros and the traditions passed down from one generation to the next.

What do you think about using mezcal in cocktails?

We encourage bartenders and at-home mixologists to be creative and experiment with mezcal in a variety of cocktails. Fresh citrus and home-made syrups can add a refreshing layer to an already complex spirit. My personal favorite as of late is a mezcal Negroni with two parts Bozal Ensamble mezcal, one part vermouth, and one part Campari.

What do you think were the main factors in the mezcal boom?

Terroir is so prominent, with where the mezcal is harvested, the type of maguey, and the unique production techniques. This allows for a variety of expressions to be released and room for continued growth. Also notable is the opportunity for food pairings. We have seen mezcal offer a much more educational approach with opportunities to keep innovating in the market. All of which makes mezcal quite similar to wine, in many regards.

About the terroir, how can it influence the production of mezcal?

As mentioned, it is hard not to see the parallels between mezcal and wine. The terroir has quite a bit of influence on mezcal, including where and how the agave plant grows, its climate, the minerality in the soil, and many other factors that are all very impactful. And quite similar to that of grapes and wine. A variety of production techniques also can have a unique effect on rare mezcal offerings, whether it be the use of clay-pot fermentation and distillation, or having the creative outlet to use protein, fruits, and spices in the final distillation. This can very much affect the flavors of one batch to another.

What is a tradition associated with mezcal production?

Sacrificial mezcal—often referred to as pechuga—is an age-old tradition in Mexico that we are proud to share with our Sacrificio tier. Typically taking place at year's end, sacrificial mezcals are produced in small batches for fiestas or locals, often using a protein in the final distillation. Additional locally sourced ingredients that are used in the final distillation can be nuts, spices, and fruit. The natural smoke characteristics are softened noticeably with this production technique, making for a unique and rare mezcal experience.

PASOTE TEQUILA

Pasote Tequila, its name is a tribute to the Aztec warriors, was founded by 3 Badge Beverage Corporation and originally produced at El Pandillo distillery, owned by Felipe J. Camarena (Don Felipe Camarena's grandson) in Jesús María, Los Altos, Jalisco. Today, Pasote is produced at Tequila El Tepozan distillery in San Julián, Jalisco.

Pasote is produced with estate-grown blue agave. The agave hearts are cooked in brick stone and then shredded with a tahona or a roller mill. The fermentation occurs in an open-air, stainless-steel tank with a proprietary blend of cultivated local yeasts. The distillation takes place in stainless-steel pot stills, using volcanic-rock-filtered water from an in-house well. At Pasote, makers don't use any chemicals, glycerin, or added flavors. Once distilled, the tequila rests in American white oak barrels.

Pasote offers the following expressions:

- Blanco: bottled straight after the distillation.

- Reposado: aged in American oak barrels for a minimum of four months.

- Añejo: matured in American oak for a minimum of twelve months.

- Extra Añejo: rested in American oak for forty-eight months.

In 2021, Pasote revamped the packaging of their products to highlight the message that they produce tequila with 100 percent estate-grown blue agave, using sustainable production methods, pure rainwater, and no added chemicals.

PASOTE BLANCO

Made with estate-grown ripe blue Weber agave, Pasote Blanco offers fresh herb and citrus fruit aromas on the nose; on the palate, it presents an intense flavor of agave balanced with pineapple notes. The finish is long, with agave hints that linger in the mouth. The ABV is 40%.

BANHEZ MEZCAL

Banhez is a cooperative in the village of San Miguel Ejutla (central valley of Oaxaca) owned by the Unión Productores de Agropecuarios del Distrito de Ejutla de Crespo (UPADEC). Francisco Javier Perez Cruz, raised in Oaxaca, thought if he could find a way for the hardworking families to work and stay together, they could create something successful. That's how Banhez was born.

Francisco learned from his mother, who had started an agave nursery with neighboring women, how to grow strong agave plants. He works alongside his brother Bertoldo as well. Back in Ejutla with his family, Francisco was appointed treasurer of the village in 1996 and mayor in 1999. In 2004, he was elected president of the National Mezcal Council, and later he received federal funding to establish nurseries and reopen distilleries around Ejutla.

Today, Banhez, alongside its farmers and producers, forms the *Unión Productores de Agropecuarios del Distrito de Ejutla de Crespo* (UPADEC), run by Francisco's son, Luis. In 2017, Banhez won double gold and best mezcal at the San Francisco World Spirits Competition.

At Banhez, mezcals are made with several varietals of agave, and many of them are wild. The agave hearts are cooked for three days in underground wood-fired pits, then ground by a tahona. The fermentation occurs in wooden tanks, and double distillation takes place in the traditional Ejutlan still, refrescadora. Finally, mezcal is bottled by hand in Ejutla.

Banhez expressions are the following:

- Ensamble: made with 90 percent agave espadín and 10 percent agave barril.

- Cuishe: made by Luis and Donaciano Pacheco in La Noria.

- Tepeztate: produced by Apolonio Patricio Lopez in San Agustín Amatengo.

- Pechuga: made with 100 percent espadín by Juan Osorio in San Vicente Coatlán, and distilled with indigenous seasonal fruits and raw turkey breast.

- Arroqueño: made by Apolonio Patricio Lopez in San Agustín Amatengo.

- Jabalí: produced by José Espinosa in San Andrés Zabache.

- Tobalá: made by Gonzalo Hernandez Bigotes and Luis Pacheco in La Compañía.

- Mexicano: produced by Apolonio Patricio Lopez in San Agustín Amatengo.

Banhez is committed to sustainability by using artisanal techniques: earthen wood-fire ovens, a tahona pulled by horses, and a natural fermentation. The family that plants the agave makes sure that the fields are grown organically and naturally.

BANHEZ ENSAMBLE

Banhez Ensamble is made with a blend of two different distillations of different agaves: cultivated espadín and barril. That's to put less pressure on the maestros mazcaleros to produce only one type of agave and to promote diversity, fighting the increasing use of espadín.

Banhez Ensamble is blended at their San Miguel bottling plant and brought down to proof with water.

Crystal clear in color, Banhez Ensamble offers floral and fruity flavors, such as pineapple and banana. It can be sipped or used in cocktails, and the ABV is 42%.

Q & A WITH ALEX JANDERNOA, DIRECTOR OF EDUCATION AT BANHEZ

Could you tell us about Banhez?

Banhez Mezcal is 100 percent owned and operated by the UPADEC Cooperative in Ejutla, Oaxaca. This type of ownership is something that is not very common in the top-selling mezcal brands globally. The brand and co-op were both started by Francisco Javier Perez Cruz, and his vision of what it could be back in the early days is coming to fruition. We have older families that helped start the co-op who are seeing a far greater income for their work than they had for decades. Along with that, we have the younger generation that want to stay in Ejutla, and they are investing in mezcal and agave and plan to be co-op members for generations.

How do you choose which type of agave to use?

For our flagship, Banhez Ensamble, we wanted to include both espadín and barril agave. This blend is a common one found throughout Ejutla, as these agaves have been grown alongside their other crops (corn, squash, beans, chiles) and in their grazing land for generations. This not only ties into our history but is important to economic and environmental sustainability. barrils are a different species which take longer and are therefore worth more money. By including this in our flagship product, it gives incentives financially that agave should be grown and produced. This also gives incentives for the use of rotational crops and helps in not creating giant monocultures of espadín. Multicrop systems and rotational farming are incredibly helpful in environmental sustainability, but for that to take place there needs to be economic sustainability tied into it.

Every member of the co-op who grows agave traditionally grows more than espadín and barril. We see a huge variety of agave coming from the communities in Ejutla. So alongside the flagship, we offer seven other labels of Banhez sold internationally. Each label represents an agave found in Ejutla, and each bottling rotates through our different co-op members who produce small to medium-sized "lots" of mezcal from these agaves. This provides more income for members who can produce these, but doesn't center it on one family or member so that it becomes a burden or the quality goes down. It also allows newer members to gain a better stake in the co-op.

The co-op works together to set growing practices and harvest practices that everyone must abide by. These tend to go beyond the traditional mandates set up by the regulatory committee. For each cultivated agave you harvest (espadín and barril), we as a co-op must replant five in its place. For each semiwild or wild agave you harvest, we must replant two.

How can the terroir influence the production of mezcal?

This is why I have been with Banhez for over five years. Terroir has a huge effect on mezcal. More so than almost any other spirit in the world, in my opinion.

Agaves used in distillate production can take anywhere from four to thirty years to reach maturity. They grow in a multitude of spaces and very rarely (except for in the past five years) live their life alone. They are surrounded by a multitude of plants and animals that interact with the agaves every day. One species can also grow within huge topography or only exist within a tiny microclimate. Agave can also reproduce across species. These types of genetic and morphological differences are all transferred to the end product: mezcal.

This is only one factor of terroir, with a multitude of unique and distinct regional production methods that can also affect terroir.

Is there anything that makes your production different from others?

Our mezcal is made specifically in Ejutla, Oaxaca. Our co-op families all use the traditional Ejutlan still called a refrescadora. While others around Oaxaca use this still, it is believed to have originated in Ejutla, and its use has been passed on from generation to generation.

For this reason, we affectionately call our mezcal and mezcal produced from these stills Mezcal Ejuteco or Ejutlan Mezcal.

The still's design is focused on efficiency and uses what we call the Happy Hour Distillation (two distillations for one pass). The still consists of a large pot which surrounds the head of the still and copper plates inside. The pot is continuously filled with cold water. This unique design causes a mezcal lighter in smoke, full of bright verdant flavors, and higher in ABV.

Are you involved in any initiatives to reduce the environmental impact of mezcal production?

As a larger brand we have quite a few initiatives, but baked into the co-op DNA is the idea of sustainable planting. Utilizing muticrop systems and setting prices at planting rather than at harvest have allowed us to avoid creating giant monocultures of agave and retain ownership of the land with the members. With this in place, we currently replant five agaves for every cultivated species and two semiwild agaves for genetics that are typically found in the wild. This is key to all our other initiatives.

One of our newer initiatives is using *bagazo* (agave waste) to make bricks for buildings in Ejutla.

We also have a reforestation program, where each family in the co-op (seventy-five as of 2023) plants one hundred trees in their community.

Alongside this we have placed bathouses throughout Ejutla and the United States to help promote the health of nocturnal pollinators in communities we work and sell in. Bats are the main pollinators for agave and need our help to survive if we want to keep drinking these spirits.

What do you think were the main factors that contributed to the mezcal boom?

There is a tendency to fetishize maestros mezcaleros as moonshiners and rural cowboy types. While there is some truth to this, for me this mindset doesn't allow room for all the modernity we find in mezcal. The folks who craft this spirit are scientists, botanists, engineers, all wrapped into one. Many of them are pushing the boundaries of spirits on a worldwide scale; however, because they are based in Mexico versus Copenhagen, NYC, or

London, we as the consumers don't give them the same type of respect. Someone who tends to look like me has to be the person who "discovers" it. I do believe this is changing, because the voices who talk about mezcal are starting to diversify as well. My hope is that we begin to talk about these producers, big and small, with the same reverence we have for modern cuisine.

Is there any change you would like to see in the industry?

More 100 percent Mexican-owned agave spirit brands. Ownership of your business and brand is how the makers and growers maintain their power.

How do you see mezcal growing in the next few years?

Europe is just scratching the surface on what's available. I also think we have just started to see the Asian market discover mezcal and find that it has some similarities to their local beverages.

Agave has always had great importance in Mexican culture, along-side tequila and mezcal. So how are they seen nowadays?

I think it has only grown. In Ejutla we've seen a huge boom in younger folks staying or returning to pursue a career in agave. Listening to the eighteen- to twenty-five-year-olds (who are technically my bosses), they are not only looking to its history but finding new ways it is tied into their current culture. The amount of agave memes I see is almost ridiculous.

Do you have any special releases or limited editions you can tell us about?

There are so many special projects that the members love to experiment with. We have some special things coming up this year that I think folks will find fun, fruity, and really fun to play with in cocktails.

Is there a traditional way to drink mezcal?

Two ounces at room temperature with a cold beer and a salty snack. There's nothing better, and if you are feeling fancy, opt for a nice sparkling dry rosé, which will play on the fun ferments in mezcal, and the bubbles still give you refreshment.

What do you think about using mezcal in cocktails?

We love it! Our Ensamble is a blend of all our members working together. This means that we can manage the environmental impact better as a unit as well as encourage more biodiverse plantings in the future. While keeping the money that comes with being a cocktail-based product in the community of Ejutla.

What are your thoughts about aging mezcal?

Personally, not a fan. The tannins of the barrel overtake the ferment notes that make mezcal special for me. That being said, if it appeals to people, they should drink it! Mezcal is not a static spirit; it's a spectrum!

BRUXO

Bruxo was created by a group of friends with different beverage professional experiences.

The brand ambassador, Anne-Sophie Vacher, explained the story to me: "Bruxo mezcal is an artisanal mezcal; the brand was created in 2008 by four friends from Mexico City. They went to Oaxaca to buy mezcal for the wedding of one of them and to celebrate the bachelor party. They fell in love with the spirit and did what they call a 'mezcal flight,' a moment of communion with Mexico after enjoying its nectar. They decided to create their brand after this trip. They came back to Oaxaca to visit sixty different palenques (distilleries in the state of Oaxaca) and created relationships with five families, as they were struck by their mezcal family recipes. We are still working with these families and six others. The idea is to preserve the distinctive character of each area of Oaxaca and the tradition of each family, and to honor the maestros without whom we would not be able to enjoy these special mezcals."

Bruxo mezcals are produced by different mezcaleros. As Anne-Sophie said, "The maestros choose their agaves according to their high maturity and sugar content. They are very careful concerning the agave production, in order to have the minimum impact on the environment and to always have the best agaves they can for the production of our mezcals."

In regard to their expressions, Anne-Sophie said, "Apart from Bruxo X, which was a later addition to the range, the whole range of Bruxo 1 to 5 are family recipes. We worked with five families in the beginning, and now they are eleven. As well as other companies, Bruxo has been working on sustainability."

Here are Bruxo's expressions and their characteristics:

- Bruxo No. 1: a variety to be produced by Lucio Morales Lopez (he passed away in 2021, and his son Juan took over), second generation of mezcaleros, and his son Juan in San Dionisio Ocotepec. It's made with agave espadín, cooked in a conical oven over pine and oak woods, and crushed with a horse-drawn tahona. The distillation takes place in copper stills. Every two years, they plant agaves and then replant them in San Dionisio Ocotepec.

- Bruxo No. 2: produced by Pablo Vázquez and Herminio Coronado in Agua del Espino, Oaxaca. It's made with 50 to 80 percent agave espadín and 20 to 50 percent agave barril, cooked in a conical oven, and crushed with a horse-drawn tahona. The distillation takes place in copper stills. The peculiarity of the Bruxo No. 2 is that it is a currado o abocado that is infused with cooked espadín agaves for two to three days, which gives it a round flavor with an interesting smokiness.

- Bruxo No. 3: produced by Felix Santiago in San Martín Lachilá. It's made with agave barril, cooked in conical ovens. The distillation takes place in copper stills. Felix started to produce mezcal in the 1950s, and, with time, he involved his family in the work. The peculiarity of the Bruxo No. 3 is the more dry, floral hints and the saltiness in the finish. Barril tends to get the salinity from the very mineral soil of San Martín Lachilá.

- Bruxo No. 4: produced by Cesareo, Pipino, and Epistacio Rodriguez in Las Salinas, Oaxaca. This Ensamble is made with 60 percent agave cuishe, 30 percent agave barril, and 10 percent agave espadín. The agave hearts are cooked in a conical oven and crushed with a horse-drawn tahona over mesquite wood. The distillation takes place in copper stills. Bruxo No. 4 has interesting herbal notes.

- Bruxo No. 5: produced by Candido Reyes in San Agustín Amatengo, Oaxaca. It's made with wild tobalá agave, cooked in a conical oven over pinewood, and ground with a horse-drawn tahona. The distillation takes place in copper stills.

Bruxo releases special and limited editions, but only for the Mexican market. In regard to that, Anne-Sophie said, "I was offered a bottle of one of the special editions, and after I opened it, I was told that it was the last one. So I share it with the people who will really appreciate this spirit!"

Bruxo is very environmentally conscious and participates in various projects with a view to protect the environment. Anne-Sophie said, "We want to produce, educate and develop the brand hand in hand with the families."

BRUXO X

Bruxo X is produced by Juan Morales, a third-generation mezcalero in San Dionisio Ocotepec, Oaxaca. It's made with agave espadín (matured from six to seven years) and barril (matured from ten to twelve years) and cooked in a conical oven over pine and oak woods. The agave hearts are ground with a horse-drawn tahona. The double distillation takes place in copper stills. Every two years, the Morales family plants its own espadín on the property.

Bruxo X is bright in color and on the nose offers aromas of citrus, flowers, and peanuts; on the palate, it presents flavors of citrus peel, chamomile, light mineral, and honey notes. The ABV is 40%.

Q & A WITH ANNE-SOPHIE VACHER, BRAND AMBASSADOR AT BRUXO

What do you think the best way to drink mezcal is?

I would say neat, but also it can be accompanied by slices of orange and *sal de gusano*, or worm salt.

What about drinking mezcal in cocktails?

I love to sip mezcal on its own, but I also think that mezcal cocktails can be a good introduction to the peculiar identity of this niche spirit. I really like a good mezcal cocktail; it gives the cocktail an interesting twist, and you can use mezcal in so many classics, like a mezcal Negroni.

And what are your thoughts about aging mezcal?

I think it depends on the result you want, if you age it in glass, and for how long. It will be lower in alcohol, due to loss through evaporation or "the angel's share," and will develop other flavors. If you age it in a wooden barrel, it will have a smoother taste, as the barrel will accentuate the vanillin compound naturally present in the agave.

Some brands who began selling mezcal many years ago decided to age it so it would be more familiar to the Mexican consumer, as it reminded them of tequila.

Do you think there are any misconceptions about mezcal?

I would say the classic misconception of having a worm in a bottle, thinking it is made of cactus or aloe vera, or the idea that shooting it is a good idea.

What are the Mexican traditions linked to mezcal?

Mezcal used to be produced for events, especially some specific preparations like *pechuga* when the mezcal is distilled a third time with meat inside the still. (It is traditionally distilled with chicken breast, but it can also be with spices, fruits, or other kinds of meat.) This mezcal was made in small batches for specific moments: births/baptisms, weddings, funerals.

In Oaxaca, during the nights of mourning, the families used to drink coffee with mezcal in it, as referenced by Lila Downs's song "La Cumbia del Mole."

How has the perception of the agave spirits changed?

Agave spirits are now a strong part of the local economy and way of life. They have also paved the way for ancient spirits from Mexico that are coming to light now, some made from agave as well as others, like sotol, raicilla, comiteco, and pox.

How can the terroir influence the production of mezcal? And does it affect the flavor of a singular batch?

Terroir influences many aspects: in my opinion, the idea of terroir includes the kind of plant you use to make mezcal, where it grows, the tradition of the geographical area where the mezcal is made, the family tradition of the maestro, his own mezcal recipe, the way he chooses the agaves, the time of cooking, the milling, the fermentation time, where the fermentation occurs or what is present around the fermentation tanks (if there are drying peppers close to the fermentation tanks, for example, or if there are other plants like rose bushes, the indigenous yeasts will impact the flavors), the altitude, the water he adds during fermentation (Is it from the well? If not, where does it come from? What is the pH?), what kind of fermentation vats he uses, the distillation (the kind of still, his cuts), then if there is a tradition of infusing the mezcal with anything (fruits, spices, etc.), if it is reduced with water or tails, and so forth.

In the past few years, we have witnessed a mezcal boom. What do you think were the main factors that led to it?

In my opinion, the boom is due to various reasons: bartenders are driving demand, and they are the first consumers and advocates of mezcal;

more people have traveled to Mexico and discovered mezcal there; and it accompanied the development of authentic Mexican cuisine outside of Mexico, replacing the Tex-Mex restaurants which have been around for a while.

How do you see mezcal growing in the next few years?

I see it growing, hopefully responsibly. Mezcal is developing, but we are still a niche spirit; more people are becoming aficionados and discovering different agaves, flavors, and traditions, and mezcal coming from other states than Oaxaca. It will be interesting to see if more states enter the NOM too.

Is there any change you would like to see in the industry?

Definitely: more people focusing on what is behind the label. The maestros *agaveros*, the maestros mezcaleros, and the strong tradition. Fortunately, in the industry, more and more people have been educating themselves.

Anything you would like to add?

We hope that the passion and the legacy of maestros agaveros and *jimadores* (very demanding and intense work) making such special spirits will be carried on by the generations to come.

MEZCAL AMARÁS

Amarás (or Amores, as it's known in the UK market) was founded by Santiago Suarez, and it is produced in San Juan del Río.

"The name Amarás is the future tense of *love* in Spanish, and our philosophy is that we're constantly striving to make things better for the world. That applies to the people that we work with, the people that are involved in all the planting of the agave or the distillation of the mezcal, and everybody that we can help in the supply chain. Our goal is to make the best liquid we can through a model that we call 'Seed to Sip,'" Santiago said.

Suarez was born in Mexico City and worked for an NGO before founding Amarás. He learned about the different agaves and mezcal production by going to mezcalerías and distilleries. He was seeing a lot of opportunities in mezcal, from elevating it to making it as a sustainable business. After meeting so many maestros mezcaleros, he found the right one to work with. "His palenque was very clean, he had a lot of different tools, and he was highly recommended by someone we really trusted at the beginning who was from Oaxaca. He had great liquid—the liquid was amazing; it was very smooth, and he was a great producer that understood a lot about mezcal," he said.

Mezcal Amarás was recognized in 2021 as the Best White Spirit in the World by the San Francisco World Spirits Competition.

Amarás collaborates with more than eighteen maestros mezcaleros and also produces mezcal at its distillery in Oaxaca. These mezcaleros use artisanal and ancestral methods, and Amarás respects their process, production time, and volume capacity; therefore, they buy from them only what they are willing to sell.

"I'm very excited about harvesting our own agaves. We harvest our own tepeztate this year, two years ago our first tobalá, and next year we're going to start harvesting a lot of different Americana species," said Suarez. "I'm very happy about that. Our philosophy excites me more, because what we're doing today and what's going to happen in five years' time is going to be quite impressive. The programs that we have totally create this horizontal growth. We will empower people not just by training and giving them loans, but also by creating a lot of income for them."

At Amarás, the fermentation is 100 percent natural: only wild yeast is used, and no chemicals are present in the process. The distillation takes place in clay pots for the ancestral method and in copper stills for the artisanal mezcal.

Amarás offers the following expressions:

- Mezcal Amarás: this line includes Espadín; Espadín Reposado, which rests for a minimum of three months in French and American oak; and Amarás Cupreata, made from thirteen-year-old wild agave plants from Guerrero.

- Mezcal Verde: crafted from eight-year-old agave espadín.

- Amarás Logia: launched in 2021, this is a collection of limited-edition mezcals, featuring specific mezcaleros and their distilleries. Amarás has five Limited Edition Logia: Cenizo (Nombre de Dios, Durango), which is cooked over mesquite and sweet acacia, and ax ground; Sacatoro, (San Lorenzo Albarradas, Oaxaca), made from *Agave angustifolia* and fermented in open-air rectangular vats; Tepeztate (Xochipala, Guerrero), which is aged in glass containers for more than thirteen months; Sierra Negra (Mitla, Oaxaca), made from *Agave americana* and cooked in stone-pit ovens with oak wood; and Tobalá (Tlacolula de Matamoros, Oaxaca), which is distilled in clay pots.

In terms of sustainability, Amarás is involved in several initiatives. Santiago said, "From day one, sustainability was embedded in the values of the business. It wasn't just a trend. It was one of the most important purposes of the business idea. I'm someone who's against 100 percent profit making, and I believe the world needs to find a middle ground where nonprofits and profit-making companies unite, so that initiatives can help the environment, the people, and the culture while creating profit for the investors."

Amarás follows a "Seed to Sip" philosophy that focuses on:

- **Community:** Recognized with the Equidad MX certificate (global workplace equality program promoting and designed to increase LGBTQ+ in the workplace across Mexico), they work with over twenty master distillers, preserving the tradition of mezcal; promote tutoring and training programs; and worked with more than forty artists to create their labels.

- **Terroir:** They produce a natural fertilizer (bokashi), plant seven agaves for every agave harvested on previously deforested land through organic methods, and have their own nurseries and a reforestation plan for local trees.

- **Love for the earth:** They work with the World Wildlife Fund on forest preservation and water care, were the first to produce carbon-neutral mezcal, and developed an "animal welfare of working Equidae in the mezcal value chain" program with the Universidad Autónoma Benito Juárez de Oaxaca to improve animal welfare.

Santiago said, "For me, the mezcal category is something that has to be taken care of, has to be done correctly, and has to be honored for the people that have created this category over the last four hundred years; we are working with master mezcaleros and agaveros from the third, fourth, fifth generation. So I'm excited about protecting it. I'm excited about making it work, and I'm excited about showing how you can create a business that is super eco-friendly and super sustainable, and has a huge impact in terms of fair-trade practices to show people that in Mexico, we can also create these beautiful companies that have an amazing impact for everybody that surrounds them. That's why I will always tell you *Siempre Amarás*, which means *you will always love* the future tense of love, where the name comes from, and by every day doing things better, I'm very excited to see the results in five years' time."

MEZCAL AMARÁS ESPADÍN

Sustainably made with 100 percent espadín agave, Mezcal Amarás Espadín is produced in the mountains of Tlacolula de Matamoros, Oaxaca. The agave hearts are cooked in a conical stone oven, then milled. The fermentation happens in pinewood vats, and the double distillation takes place in small copper pot stills.

Mezcal Amarás Espadín received a gold medal at the San Francisco World Spirits Competition in 2015 and earned the Chairman's Trophy at the Ultimate Beverage Challenge in 2015.

Crystal clear, it has aromas of bergamot and a touch of cherry blossom. On the palate, it offers smooth and sweet flavors with a smoky touch. The finish has cinnamon hints. The ABV is 41%.

MEZCAL AMARÂS VERDE

Mezcal Verde is made with espadín agave in Tlacolula de Matamoros, Oaxaca. The agave hearts are cooked in a conical stone oven with three different types of wood: ocote (*Pinus montezumae*), pirul (pepper tree), and encino (holm oak). It is fermented in pinewood vats and double distilled in a 500-liter copper still.

Mezcal Verde features a variety of label designs. It presents sweet jasmine notes on the nose, smoky notes of cooked agave and a touch of spice on the palate, and sweet caramel notes on the finish. The ABV is 43%.

CASA CORTÉS

Casa Cortés was founded by Rolando Cortés, son of Don José Cortés and a fifth-generation member of the Cortés family, and his son Asis in 2007. Rolando is the CEO of Casa Cortés.

He grew up in Santiago Matatlán and moved to San Francisco during his twenties. In the 2000s, he opened the Agave de Cortés brand, followed by El Jolgorio (2010) and Nuestra Soledad (2013), all under Casa Cortés.

The Cortés family, whose distilling activity dates back to 1840, produces mezcal in Santiago Matatlán, situated thirty miles southeast of Oaxaca City and one of the most geographically and biologically diverse areas in Mexico. They are one of the few mezcal companies that are still 100 percent Oaxacan owned, working with different mezcaleros around Oaxaca. Each Casa Cortés mezcalero preserves the tradition of mezcal by using traditional methods of production, passed down through the generations. All of them believe in the preservation of the culture, honoring the agave, and committing to sustainability.

In fact, Casa Cortés started to plant espadín agave a long time ago, before mezcal gained popularity, and today they carefully control production volumes and are investing in reforestation. They are also working to improve the local economy: they work with seventeen different families in sixteen different regions for the production of their mezcals. They deal with the production of mezcal, bottling, logistics, administrative management, and branding and marketing.

AGAVE DE CORTÉS

Maestro mezcalero Francisco Cortés Hernandez is in charge of Agave de Cortés. He lives in Santiago Matatlán, and for most of his life he worked with his father, Don José, in the palenque, until he inherited it.

Agave de Cortés produces mezcal with espadín cultivated in the mountainous Valles Centrales region, outside of Santiago Matatlán, and with the artesanal method. The agave hearts are hand harvested, cooked in an earthen pit oven, and crushed by a mule-drawn tahona. Then they are fermented in open-air wood tanks, using wild yeast, and double distilled in copper pot stills.

Agave de Cortés expressions are:

- Joven: the unaged expression.

- Reposado: rests for at least six months in second-fill bourbon barrels (charred American oak). The oak aging brings out a smoky richness with sweet notes such as caramel and cocoa.

- Añejo: rests for three years in French oak barrels. The barrel aging brings out caramel, vanilla, and lightly floral notes.

AGAVE DE CORTÉS JOVEN

Agave de Cortés Joven is made with 100 percent espadín, making it great for both cocktails and sipping on its own. As artisanal mezcal, it is made only with nonmechanized methods. On the nose, it presents vegetal ripeness, tropical fruit, and floral notes. On the palate, there are layers of flavor, from lemongrass to damp earth and mineral notes. The ABV is 45%.

EL JOLGORIO

Born in 2010, when the Cortés family reunited several distillers from around Oaxaca, El Jolgorio is nowadays represented by sixteen different families, working in ten different regions of Oaxaca.

El Jolgorio translates to "the revelry," and jolgorios are small festivals that celebrate births, deaths, weddings, and saints' days in remote mountain villages throughout Oaxaca.

In 2017, at El Jolgorio, they realized that certain varieties of agave would be limited, and therefore available only once per year. So they decided to package the batch coming from those agaves as rare editions in black bottles. Plus, as multigenerational mezcal producers, they are very attentive to the amount of wild agave that can be harvested in order to preserve and sustain them.

At El Jolgorio, agaves are generally sourced from different mezcaleros and in different regions, in order to reduce the pressure on one community and to spread financial benefits among families all over Oaxaca. After being harvested, the agave hearts are cooked in earthen ovens, ground, and then open-air fermented in wooden vats and double distilled in copper pot stills. On each bottle, El Jolgorio displays the species of agave, the year and age of harvest, the village of production, the name of the maestro mezcalero, the batch number, and the number of bottles produced.

Besides the special editions, the main El Jolgorio expressions are:

- Espadín, which must be rested in glass (*madurado en vidrio*) for a minimum of three years before bottling.

- Barril, Cuishe, Madrecuishe, and Tobasiche, each of these expressions has a vegetal and earthy flavor profile.

- Tobalá, with fresh and aromatic notes and rich, heavy fruits on the nose.

- Tepeztate, which delivers bright, green, and floral mezcal.

- Pechuga, made with 100 percent espadín, and with the addition locally harvested fruits, such as pineapple, lime, orange, plantain, apple, and pear, and the raw breast of a *guajolote* (regional creole turkey rooster) during the second distillation.

El Jolgorio also has a line of ancestral offerings that includes:

- Arroqueño, produced in Sola de Vega, Oaxaca.

- Coyote, a limited edition distilled from 100 percent agave coyote. It is produced by maestra mezcalera Doña Justina Ruiz Perez, Casa Cortés's first female master distiller, in Sola de Vega, Oaxaca.

EL JOLGORIO MADRECUISHE

Produced in Santiago Matatlán by maestro mezcalero Gregorio Martínez Jarquín, this mezcal is made with agave madrecuishe. Crystalline in color, El Jolgorio Madrecuishe presents earthy aromas on the nose. It offers mineral and eucalyptus flavors on the palate and a subtle salty note on the finish. The ABV is 48%, and each batch can vary a lot.

NUESTRA SOLEDAD

Nuestra Soledad is made with 100 percent agave espadín, cultivated in the remote mountain areas around the Valles Centrales region of Oaxaca.

Nuestra Soledad is a single-village mezcal that showcases the differences between the villages of Santiago Matatlán, La Compañía Ejutla, San Luis del Río, San Baltazar Guélavila, Santa María Zoquitlán, and San José Lachiguirí, Miahuatlán.

Each palenque (distillery) uses 100 percent espadín agave and centuries-old indigenous Zapotec methods. The agave is sustainably cultivated and then roasted in an earthen pit oven, fueled by oak and eucalyptus, and often lined with volcanic or river rocks to absorb and maintain the heat. The agave hearts are ground by using the traditional tahona method, passed down from father to son over many generations, and fermented in large open-air wooden tanks where local-source water is added. The natural fermentation lasts between six and ten days. Finally, the distillation occurs in copper stills, twice.

Nuestra Soledad is produced solely with cultivated espadín agaves from different communities, and at least two agaves are replanted for each one harvested.

Nuestra Soledad expressions are:

- Santiago Matatlán: produced by mezcalero Gregorio Martínez Jarquín in Santiago Matatlán, a rural town in the Valles Centrales region.

- San Luis del Río: named after a small village in the district of Tlacolula de Matamoros, the mezcal is produced by Ivan and Francisco Méndez, who carry on the legacy of their father, mezcalero Don Rafael Méndez Cruz.

- Lachiguí: named after the highest-elevation distillery in Nuestra Soledad, where Pedro Vasquez is the master distiller.

- San Baltazar: named after a small town in the district of Tlacolula de Matamoros; the master distiller is Gregorio Martínez García.

- La Compañía Ejutla: produced by Pablo Vásquez García.

- Santa María Zoquitlán: named for a village in the southeast of Santiago matatlán. The Maestro mezcalero is José Parada Valera.

NUESTRA SOLEDAD LA COMPAÑÍA EJUTLA

Nuestra Soledad La Compañía Ejutla is produced in La Compañía, a small village in the district of Ejutla. It is made with 100 percent agave espadín, cooked in a conical earthen oven, and milled by a tahona. It's then fermented in wooden tanks and double distilled using the traditional distillation method in Ejutla, the refrescador—a single extended distillation in a modified pot still with a cooling chamber.

Nuestra Soledad La Compañía Ejutla presents flower and mint aromas on the nose and savory and mineral flavors on the palate, and the finish is long and delicate. The ABV is 47%.

TEQUILA CALLE 23

Calle 23 was founded by French-born biochemist and engineer Sophie Decobecq in 2009. She is not only the owner but also the master distiller.

While studying for a dual PhD in biochemistry and engineering in France, she met the president of the Polytechnics Institute of Mexico City and decided to study fermentation in Mexico. She spent seven months in Mexico City, visiting distilleries in Guadalajara and Tequila and throughout the Mexican countryside, falling in love with Mexico, its culture, and tequila. Later, she took her first job as a consultant for an agave distillery in South Africa, but in 2003 she returned to Mexico, where she established an export company, IMEX International, and founded Calle 23.

Calle 23 won double gold at the 2009 San Francisco World Spirits Competition (Añejo), a gold medal for the Reposado, and a bronze medal for the Blanco expression.

Originally, Calle 23 was produced at Agaveros y Tequileros Unidos de Los Altos in Zapotlanejo, Jalisco, but later on, Sophie moved the production and her company IMEX International to Tequila Quiote in San Francisco de Asis in the Los Altos highlands. Today, Calle 23 is produced at Hacienda Capellania in San Jose de Gracia, Jalisco.

Calle 23 carefully selects their blue agave from Los Altos de Jalisco, between Tepatitlán and Arandas. The agave hearts are cooked in a stainless-steel autoclave for sixteen hours, then ground with a roller mill. Sophie uses two different wild yeasts, isolated from raw agaves in the fields and cultivated at the distillery's laboratory. One yeast strain is used for the Blanco and also placed into casks to age the Añejo expression; the other is used for the Reposado expression. The fermentation occurs in 25,500-liter stainless-steel tanks for seventy-two hours, and the distillation takes place in 5,000-liter stainless-steel pot stills, with copper serpentine coils inside the still. Finally, the tequila is labeled and sealed by hand.

Calle 23 offers the following expressions: Blanco; Reposado, which rests in bourbon oak casks for eight months, and Añejo, which matures for sixteen months.

CALLE 23 BLANCO

An unaged expression, Calle 23 Blanco is made with 100 percent blue agave, and it can be sipped or used in cocktails. Crystal clear in color, it gives aromas of cooked agave, hints of citrus, and herbaceous notes. On the palate, it is soft and gentle with a full agave flavor and fruit notes. With a lingering finish, it has an ABV of 40%.

CALLE 23 AÑEJO

Calle 23 Añejo is aged for sixteen months in bourbon oak casks. With a medium-dark amber color, it's a full-bodied tequila that offers aromas of oak, vanilla, and coffee on the nose, together with hints of herbs and spices. On the palate it presents flavors of wood, coffee, and tobacco. The ABV is 40%.

Calle 23 Blanco

Calle 23 Añejo

TEQUILA CASCAHUÍN

Tequila Cascahuín was founded by Salvador Rosales Briseño in 1904 in El Arenal, Jalisco. He opened the current distillery there in 1955. Today, the distillery is run by the fourth-generation Rosales family.

At the Cascahuín distillery, they use both modern and traditional methods to make tequila. The agave hearts are cooked in steam ovens or mezcal-style underground conical pit ovens, then milled either by a mechanical shredder or a tahona, or by hand with axes and mallets. The fermentation occurs in stainless-steel vats, in cement pits, or in wooden *tiñas* (vats) with airborne yeasts and warm water. The distillation takes place in a steel column still, copper pot still, or wooden Filipino still. For the aging process, they use several types of barrels, such as new or used, French oak or American oak, wine casks or cognac casks.

Cascahuín offers the following main expressions:

- Blanco: the unaged expression.

- Reposado: aged in American oak barrels (previously used for aging tequila for more than twenty years) from six to eight months.

- Añejo: matured in used American oak barrels for fourteen to sixteen months.

- Extra Añejo: aged in American oak barrels for forty-eight months and then an additional four years in sixty-year-old *pipones* (large wooden containers).

- Cascahuín 48%: a special edition to honor the founder, Salvador Rosales Briseño; not diluted or filtered.

- Extra Añejo finished French oak: a limited edition where Extra Añejo tequila is finished in French oak barrels for six months.

CASCAHUÍN TAHONA BLANCO

This is a Blanco expression that differs from the others in the Cascahuín core, because the juice is extracted from the agave hearts with the traditional tahona (they also offer a Reposado version).

Crystalline and transparent in color, Cascahuín Blanco Tahona presents aromas of mint, cooked agave, and citrus on the nose; on the palate, it offers sweet and herbal hints. The ABV is 42%.

CASCAHUÍN AÑEJO

This aged expression is matured for fourteen to sixteen months. With a natural amber color, Cascahuín Añejo offers aromas of raisin, almond, peach, and golden peanut on the nose; on the palate, it presents notes of wood and sweet cooked agave. The finish is silky, and the ABV is 40%.

CASA MAESTRI/
DESTILADORA DEL VALLE DE TEQUILA

Destiladora del Valle de Tequila, also known as Casa Maestri, was founded in 2008 by Michael and Celia V. Maestri, after they moved from Houston, Texas, to Tequila, Jalisco. At Destiladora del Valle de Tequila, 50 percent of the agave hearts are cooked in traditional brick ovens, and the other 50 percent are cooked in stainless-steel autoclaves. They are then crushed with a mill. The fermentation occurs in 7, 900-gallon (30,000-liter) tanks with natural yeast for forty-eight to sixty hours. The distillation takes place in alembic pot stills.

One of Mexico's most awarded distilleries (winning ninety-two medals since 2010 at the San Francisco World Spirits Competition), Destiladora del Valle de Tequila produces more than 128 brands. It is also the eleventh-largest tequila exporter.

Some of the brands it produces are:

- Casa Maestri: founded by Celia Maestri, it is the flagship brand of Destiladora del Valle de Tequila. The bottles represent the charrería culture (a celebration and competitive demonstration of the equestrian activities in the haciendas during colonial Mexico) and the mariarchi, and are made by ceramic artist Oscar Reynoso Becerra from Guadalajara. It has a Kosher Certificate, and it is made with traditional methods.

- Caballo Azul: comes in ceramic horse sculpture bottles in Añejo, Extra Añejo, and Extra Añejo Cristalino.

- Tuyo: designed to express the various aromas of the highlands and lowlands of Tequila, this brand ages in ten-year-old bourbon barrels.

- Chaquira Reserva de El Jaguar: this line is inspired by the Huicholes, indigenous people living in the mountainous area of northern Jalisco and North Central Mexico.

- Doña Celia: created in honor of Celia Barragán de Villanueva, Celia Maestri's mother, this tequila comes in hand-painted ceramic bottles.

- Identity: this brand includes the production of tequila, mezcal, and vodka (which is bottled at the Casa Maestri distillery). It was born to celebrate the LGBTQ+ community. For every bottle sold, Identity gives $1 to LGBTQ+ charities.

- Flask Spirits: this brand produces tequila Blanco, bourbon (aged for two years in oak barrels), rum (aged for four years), vodka (distilled five times), and 100 percent Canadian whisky. They all come in reusable 100 percent stainless-steel, glass-free flasks.

- Agavales: the first tequila produced by the Maestri family, it comes as Blanco, Gold, Plata, Reposado, and Añejo.

- Agave Boom: made with 100 percent blue agave, the bottles come with iconic pop-art features, designed for millennials.

- El Padrino de Mi Tierra: made by Celia Maestri in honor of her grandfather Pedro Barragán ("El Padrino"), who was well-known in Santa Inés in Michoacán for his work caring for the poor communities.

- Agavemio: Blanco tequila made with natural flavors, blood orange, chile and cucumber, and mango and pineapple.

- Miagave: this brand can be found in Blanco, Reposado, and Añejo, crafted by master distiller Agustín Sanchez.

- Don Romeo: Blanco, Reposado, and Añejo, made with 100 percent blue agave.

Casa Maestri Reserva de MFM Reposado

- El Tirador: inspired by the Mexican soldiers who fought in the Mexican Revolution in 1910, this tequila comes in hand-made ceramic bottles made by the artisans in Tonalá, Jalisco.

- General Díaz: in honor of General Porfirio Díaz, who was the president of Mexico for thirty-one years, this line offers Blanco, Reposado, and Añejo.

- India Bella: this brand offers a mezcal line made with 100 percent espadín and aged for fourteen years in oak barrels.

At Destiladora del Valle de Tequila, 50 percent of the agave hearts are cooked in traditional brick ovens, and the other 50 percent are cooked in stainless-steel autoclaves, and then they are crushed with a mill. The fermentation occurs in 7,900-gallon (30,000-liter) tanks with natural yeast for forty-eight to sixty hours. The distillation takes place in alembic pot stills.

CASA MAESTRI RESERVA DE MFM BLANCO

Bottled straight after distillation, Reserva de MFM Blanco presents aromas of fruits and citrus on the nose. On the palate, it offers flavors of black pepper and tropical fruits. The medium-length finish has a hint of spices. The ABV is 40%.

TEQUILA CORRALEJO

Tequila Corralejo is produced at Hacienda de Corralejo in Pénjamo, Guanajuato, one of the small communities authorized to produce tequila outside Jalisco. The hacienda was built in the eighteenth century as an agave farm and distillery at the birthplace of Miguel Hidalgo, leader of Mexico's fight for independence.

In 1994, Don Leonardo Rodríguez Moreno bought the hacienda, restoring it to a tequila distillery, as it was in the 1700s, in 1996.

Tequila Corralejo is made with estate-grown 100 percent blue Weber agave, hand harvested from their fields in the state of Guanajuato. The agave hearts are cooked in stone clay ovens for thirty-six hours and crushed with a roller mill. The fermentation occurs in stainless-steel tanks for thirty-six hours with a specially formulated yeast strain, "LCORRA1," cultivated from the very first press of the agave and developed with the Universidad de Guanajuato. The distillation goes through the Charentais method. The first distillation takes place in a continuous still, or column still. The second distillation takes place in an alembic copper pot still, imported from Tomelloso, Spain. Finally, the tequila is bottled in-house.

Besides the special editions, Tequila Corralejo's main expressions are:

- Silver: distilled from 100 percent blue agave and bottled straightaway after distillation.

- Reposado: aged for four months.

- Añejo: aged for twelve months in American, French Limousin, and Mexican oak barrels.

- Extra Añejo: aged for three years.

- 1821 Extra Añejo: 100 percent blue agave tequila aged for thirty-six months in second-fill charred American oak casks, previously used for bourbon.

- Reposado Triple Destilado: a triple-distilled Resposado tequila, aged for four months in French, American, and encino oak barrels.

- 99,000 Horas: aged for eighteen months in small, American oak barrels.

CORRALEJO REPOSADO

Corralejo Reposado is produced with 100 percent handpicked blue Weber agave in the state of Guanajuato, double distilled, and then aged for four months in American, French Limousin, and Mexican oak wood.

It has won several awards, such as the double gold medal at the San Francisco World Spirits Competition in 2007, 2009, and 2019, and the gold medal at the New York International Spirits Competition in 2022.

Light straw in color, Corralejo Reposado presents sweet vanilla, honey, and spice aromas; it offers lemon and lime, peppercorn, and oak flavors on the palate; and the finish is smooth and warm. The ABV is 40%.

CORRALEJO EXTRA AÑEJO

Winner of the gold medal at the New York International Spirits Competition in 2022 and the gold medal at the San Francisco World Spirits Competition in 2022, Corralejo Extra Añejo is made with 100 percent handpicked blue Weber agave, harvested in Guanajuato; double distilled; and then aged for three years in American, French Limousin, and Mexican oak.

Deep gold in color, it offers sweet and spice aromas on the nose; it presents smoke, citrus, and caramel flavors on the palate; and the finish is long and full-bodied. The ABV is 40%.

Q & A WITH RAFFAELE BERARDI, CEO OF FRATERNITY SPIRITS MEXICO

Can you tell us a little bit about Corralejo and its products?

Corralejo has been producing tequila for over twenty-five years, and we take great pride in our traditional methods and attention to detail. Our signature product is our Reposado tequila, made from 100 percent blue agave and double distilled for a smooth and balanced taste. We also offer aged tequilas for those who prefer a richer flavor profile.

Do you have any special releases or limited editions you can tell us about?

We do have some limited-edition releases from time to time, which typically showcase unique flavor profiles or aging techniques. One example of this was the Extra Añejo twenty-five-year anniversary.

Is there anything that makes your production different from others?

Our production process is rooted in tradition and craftsmanship, and we take great care to ensure that each bottle of tequila is of the highest quality. We also use 100 percent blue agave and follow all regulations and guidelines for producing tequila. In addition to this, we have a very special technique utilizing Charentais for our production.

How can the terroir influence the production of tequila?

Terroir can have a significant impact on the production of tequila, as the soil, climate, and other environmental factors can influence the flavor and quality of the agave plants. Each batch of tequila is unique, and the terroir can play a role in creating subtle variations in taste and aroma.

Can you tell us about any sustainable initiatives you are involved in?

We are committed to reducing our environmental impact by minimizing waste and water usage, and exploring new technologies and methods for sustainable tequila production. We also support efforts to protect the biodiversity of agave and other plant species in Mexico.

We are focused on the production and promotion of the blue agave, as it is the one we use for our tequila production. We have been supporting local communities in Guanajuato and other regions for the conservation of agave.

What do you think are the factors that contributed to the tequila boom?

The tequila boom has been fueled by a growing interest in craft cocktails and artisanal spirits, as well as a greater appreciation for the unique flavors and cultural significance of tequila.

Tell us more about the cultural significance of tequila.

Tequila has a long and rich cultural heritage in Mexico, and its production is steeped in tradition and ceremony. It is made from the blue agave plant, which has deep roots in the culture and mythology of the Mexican people.

What about agave and mezcal? How are they seen nowadays?

Agave, tequila, and mezcal are still highly valued in Mexican culture and continue to play an important role in traditional celebrations and rituals; in addition to this, Mexicans identify the agave as a judge of economic support for the country and as a job creator.

How do you see tequila growing in the next few years?

We anticipate continued growth and interest in tequila, particularly among younger consumers who are looking for new and unique taste experiences.

Is there any change you would like to see in the industry?

We would like to see more focus on sustainable and responsible production practices in the tequila industry, including reducing water usage and waste without changing the traditional way of creating the spirit.

What do you think about using tequila in cocktails?

We believe that tequila can be a versatile and exciting ingredient in cocktails, especially when paired with fresh citrus and other complementary flavors.

And what is, in your opinion, the proper way to drink tequila?

The proper way to drink tequila is to savor it slowly, either neat or on the rocks, with a side of salt and lime. Premium tequilas do not have to be drunk with lime and salt; by itself is the best way.

FAMILIA CAMARENA TEQUILA

Familia Camarena Tequila was founded by the Camarena family in 2010 and is produced at Casa Tequilera Herencia de Los Altos, Arandas.

Familia Camarena Tequila has won several awards, such as the gold medal for the Reposado and the silver medal for the Silver at the San Francisco World Spirits Competition in 2017.

Familia Camarena Tequila produces tequila with 100 percent blue agave harvested in the highest elevation of the Los Altos highlands, a process overseen by Mauricio Camarena, the sixth generation of the Camarena family.

The agave hearts are slow cooked in a traditional volcanic oven, then shredded by a mill. The fermentation occurs in fermentation vats with special yeast. The distillation takes place in small-batch pot stills. Finally, the tequila is bottled and labeled by hand.

Familia Camarena Tequila offers the following expressions:

CAMARENA SILVER

The unaged expression is a winner of several awards from competitions such as the San Diego Spirits Fair in 2017 and the New York World Wine & Spirits Competition in 2017. Perfect in cocktails, Camarena Silver tequila presents notes of fresh green herbs and citrus on the nose. On the palate, it offers the flavor of sweet vanilla, and the finish is soft and warming, with hints of savory brown spices and black pepper. The ABV is 40%.

CAMARENA REPOSADO

Camarena Reposado tequila is aged for two months in a combination of new and used bourbon American oak barrels. It's a winner of several awards in competitions such as the World Beverage Spirits Competition in 2017 and the Los Angeles International Spirits Competition in 2017.

On the nose, it offers notes of sweet toasted agave and soft spice. On the palate, it's soft and smooth, and the finish offers hints of vanilla and caramel. The ABV is 40%.

CAMARENA AÑEJO

Camarena Añejo tequila is matured for one year in American oak bourbon barrels. It can be enjoyed neat, and on the nose it offers aromas of toasted oak, nutmeg, baked apple, and citrus. On the palate, it presents flavors of cooked sweet potato, toasted oak, and vanilla. The finish is smooth and warm. The ABV is 40%.

Q & A WITH THE CAMARENA FAMILY

What do you think are the most important things to know about your company and your products?

Camarena Tequila's award-winning portfolio includes Añejo, Reposado, and Silver. All of the Camarena tequilas are harvested by hand from 100 percent blue Weber agave in Jalisco's Arandas Highlands, one of Mexico's most prestigious tequila districts, and distilled at the family's distillery through methods that blend traditional ovens, modern techniques, and proprietary ingredients. Camarena's portfolio is one of the smoothest and best-tasting tequilas on the market.

Bestowed with a gold medal in the 2022 Concours d'Spirits Awards and double gold, Best Tequila Winner of the 2022 John Barleycorn Awards, Camarena Silver Tequila is the company's flagship bottle and is made with fresh roasted agave, a hint of green herbs, and citrus overtones that are rounded out with a touch of sweet vanilla. It's soft and smooth with a warming finish, thanks to savory brown spices and black pepper. It's available in stores across the US.

How did you choose the type of agave?

Camarena has always stayed true to its founding family's heritage that traces back to Arandas, Mexico, an epicenter of artisanal highland tequila production. To create an award-winning tequila, the brand values the importance of using only the best ingredients, including the best agave that can provide the best fermentable sugars for the distilling of the tequila.

What do you think about using tequila in cocktails?

Using Camarena, a 100 percent blue Weber agave tequila, when making cocktails for family and friends, you give them a quality and smooth base that pairs well with various ingredients that complement the rich flavor profiles.

Camarena Silver Tequila's hint of green herbs and citrus flavors is delicious in cocktails like palomas, spicy margaritas, and bloody marias (made with tequila instead of the traditional vodka in the bloody mary).

What is the proper way to drink tequila?

Camarena uses modern blending techniques to consistently produce one of the smoothest and best-tasting tequilas around. Each Camarena variety has its own unique flavor profile, and to fully enjoy the complexity and liquid of each one, you must engage multiple senses, including look, smell, and taste.

To start, pour the tequila into a snifter, champagne flute, or any glass you may have around. Then, observe the color and identify any tones—you may find these in aged tequila, such as Camarena Reposado and Añejo.

After this, move on to sniffing the liquid. Turn the glass toward you and take small whiffs to identify citrus, herb, or flavor scents. The three areas you should make sure you cover are the top, middle, and bottom of the tilted glass rim.

And finally, time to taste! Inhale before you take a sip, and make sure you get just enough; swallow, and exhale through your mouth to fire up your taste buds and get a full mouth of flavor.

In the past few years, we have witnessed a tequila boom. What do you think were the main factors that contributed to that?

As more people have spent time at home over the past few years, they've been exploring new spirits and learning how to make and enjoy new cocktails. More trial has led to a greater appreciation and better understanding of tequila and its complexities. Additionally, the classic margarita has grown immensely in popularity, with CGA reporting it's the most sought-after cocktail in forty-three states. There has also been a recent boom in celebrity tequila brand launches that have helped bring attention to the beloved spirit category.

CORTE VETUSTO

Corte Vetusto was founded by David Shepherd in 2017. Born in Singapore, Shepherd grew up in Mexico City and moved to the US later on. He worked in brand management and new product development, but after tasting mezcal in a famous restaurant in Mexico City, he started to consider the potential for the spirit. So after a lot of research, he met Juan Carlos Gonzalez Diaz, a fourth-generation maestro mezcalero, and together they worked to create Corte Vetusto, a name that translates as "ancient cut," referring both to the cutting of the agave and the spirit during production, while also reflecting the fact that mezcal is the oldest spirit in the Americas.

Juan Carlos Gonzalez Diaz learned the making of mezcal from his father and grandfather. He also used to join his father on the journey to the villages to buy and sell mezcal, observing and learning from various maestros mezcaleros. Today, he is the maestro mezcalero for Corte Vetusto, with the help of Don Santiago, whose skills with a *coa* (a flat-bladed knife) are renowned throughout Oaxaca.

Corte Vetusto produces premium, single-estate, unaged, and artisanal mezcal, distilled in small batches in Mitla.

The agave hearts are slow roasted for three to six days in a traditional pit oven lined with volcanic rocks; the woods, such as mesquite, are placed in the center of the oven and covered by river stones. Before the oven is loaded, a ritual is performed: the raw agave hearts are beaten with a branch of piru or pepper tree to clear away any bad energy, and the workers ask the gods for their blessing on the batch. The agave hearts are then crushed by a tahona pulled by a horse called Payaso (Clown). The fermentation takes place in open-air wooden vats, with wild yeasts from the palenque's surroundings, for one to two weeks. Only the water coming from the mountains behind Mitla is added. The distillation takes place in wood-fired copper or clay pot stills. After a period of resting, the mezcal, distilled to proof, is ready to be bottled.

Corte Vetusto offers the following main expressions (all of them are winners of several awards):

- Espadín: made with agave espadín and distilled in copper pot stills.

- Tobalá: made with 100 percent agave tobalá.

- Ensamble II: a limited release that changes by batch, made with equal parts of espadín, tobalá, and madrecuishe. It's first distilled in a copper pot still, and second in an ancestral clay pot still.

CORTE VETUSTO TOBALÁ

Winner of the gold at the International Wine & Spirits Competition in 2020 and of the double gold at the International Spirits Challenge in 2020, Corte Vetusto Tobalá is made with 100 percent wild agave tobalá. The agave hearts are cooked in a conical earthen oven and milled by a volcanic stone tahona. After a natural fermentation, it's first distilled in a copper pot still, and then distilled in an ancestral clay pot still.

Clear in color, Corte Vetusto Tobalá presents earthy and dried herb aromas on the nose; it offers floral and apple flavors on the palate; and the finish is bright and fresh, with earthy notes. The ABV is 43.8%.

CONVITE MEZCAL

Convite was founded in 2013 by Oaxacan-born economist Jorge Vera with brothers Daniel and Cosmé Hernández Martínez, sixth-generation distillers, in the Zapotec mountains of San Baltazar Guélavila, Tlacolula de Matamoros, located in the Sierra Madre del Sur.

Convite takes the name of an Oaxacan gathering of friends and neighbors to celebrate every kind of event, from births and marriages to parades and festivals.

Convite has kosher certification and natural process certification.

The brand won the Best Mezcal Blends in the AGAVIT 2020 competition, and was awarded three gold medals in the Spirits Selection at the Concours Mondial de Bruxelles (in 2018 for the Wild Agave Blend, and in 2019 for its Coyote and Espadín Madrecuishe mezcals).

Convite mezcal is produced in small batches with wild agave harvested by hand. The agave hearts are cooked in a traditional conical stone oven using oak firewood, and then they are crushed with a tahona. The fermentation occurs with wild yeast and spring water from the Zapotec mountains of Sierra Madre del Sur. The double distillation takes place in copper pot stills. Convite's bottles are designed to recall the ancestral way of storing mezcal: in black clay pitchers that would serve to mature and preserve the characteristics of the product.

Convite offers the following main expressions:

- Ensamble Silvestre: made with tepextate, tobalá, madrecuishe, coyote, and tobasiche.

- Coyote: a fruity and floral mezcal.

- Tobalá: a floral and velvety expression.

Convite Ensamble Silvestre

- Tepextate: a spicy and earthy mezcal.

- Jabalí: a spiced and herbal expression.

- Espadín Madrecuishe: a mineral and citrusy mezcal.

Convite is active in many aspects of the Oaxacan community, supporting environmental sustainability and fair trade. They keep all their activities in Oaxaca, from production to packaging, and from administration to promotion. They employ farmers, cutters, and many others to create jobs and reduce emigration to the US.

They keep traditions alive, promoting festivities, music, local cuisine, and natural attractions.

In partnership with Lush Life Productions, they launched The Bartender Residency, a program for bartenders that helps them practice and learn the different techniques for making cocktails, offering training and education from the master distillers, the brothers Hernádez Martínez.

Finally, they are part of a reforestation plan: they plant wild agave in their San Baltazar Guélavila nursery, preserving the diversity of agaves in Oaxaca. They apply agroecological practices, including chemical-free polycultures and limited water consumption. They also transform agave waste into fertilizer for the fields.

CONVITE ENSAMBLE SILVESTRE

Convite Ensamble Silvestre is the combination of five wild agaves: tepextate, tobalá, madrecuishe, coyote, and tobasiche. Winner of several awards, such as the gold medal in the Spirits Selection at Concours Mondial de Bruxelles in 2022, Convite Ensamble Silvestre is double supervised by master distillers Cosmé and Daniel Hernández Martínez and offers flower and sweet flavors, with an intense note of lavender. The ABV is 46%.

CASA DON RAMÓN

Casa Don Ramón was founded in 1996 in Jalisco, and acquired in 2018 by Dialce, a subsidiary of the iiDEA Group.

In 2020, Casa Don Ramón launched a Tequila Don Ramón Limited Edition Collection, represented by global ambassador Pierce Brosnan. In the same year, Casa Don Ramón launched on the market its first mezcal Joven.

Casa Don Ramón harvests blue agave from the highlands of Jalisco, while using *Agave salmiana* for its Mezcal Joven, harvested from Zacatecas.

Once harvested, the agave hearts are slowly cooked in autoclave ovens, fermented in stainless-steel vats, and distilled in column stills. The maestro tequilero is Jesus Reza, who oversees the process of making tequila.

Besides the limited editions, Casa Don Ramón offers the following main expressions:

- Platinum:

    - Plata: the unaged expressions.

    - Cristalino Reposado: double distilled and matured in American and French oak barrels for four months, before undergoing a filtration process to remove the color.

    - Cristalino Añejo: double distilled and aged in American oak barrels for twelve months, before being filtered to remove the color. Both the Cristalino Añejo and Cristalino Reposado maintain a straw tint, because Casa Don Ramón's filtration method doesn't completely remove the color achieved during the aging process.

- Punta Diamante:

  - Silver: double distilled in steel pot stills.

  - Reposado: matured in white oak barrels.

  - Añejo: aged in American oak barrels for twelve months.

  - Lavender: silver tequila distilled with lavender infusion.

  - Tamarindo: silver tequila infused with natural tamarind.

- Casa Don Ramón Mezcal Joven: made from 100 percent *Agave salmiana* from Zacatecas, and double distilled in a pot still.

CASA DON RAMÓN PUNTA DIAMANTE REPOSADO

Casa Don Ramón Punta Diamante Reposado is made with 100 percent blue agave from the highlands of Jalisco and aged for a minimum of two months in white oak in order to get a deep and complex character.

Punta Diamante Reposado is golden in color and presents floral, herbal, vanilla, and chocolate aromas on the nose; it offers citrus, cooked agave, and herbs on the palate; and it has an herbal and citrus finish. The ABV is 40%.

CASA DON RAMÓN MEZCAL JOVEN 100% ESPADÍN

Casa Don Ramón also produces Mezcal Joven 100% Espadín. Mezcal Joven is double distilled in pot stills.

Clear in color, Joven 100% Espadín presents smoke, citrus, and floral aromas on the nose and herbal and vegetal flavors with hints of green peppercorns on the palate, with a long and lingering finish. The ABV is 40%.

Casa Don Ramón Punta Diamante Reposado

Casa Don Ramón Mezcal Joven

Q & A WITH CASA DON RAMÓN

What are the most important things to know about Casa Don Ramón?

Our jimadores carefully select the blue agave, using traditional methods perfected over generations. We take care of each step of the process and of the agave.

How did you choose the type of agave?

We wait an average of eight years to reach the point of maturation.

Is there anything that makes your production different from others?

We take advantage of the agave, extracting the liquid, raw. We set the fermentation stage with classical music to stimulate the aroma and the bouquet. We inject ozone instead of air to soften our products; that makes the tequila alkaline for a more enjoyable experience. We use naturally cleaner water from the depths of Lake Chapala, and our products have zero additives. Our bottles are aesthetically impeccable, and our packaging and labeling are 100 percent handmade, made by women who reflect their delicacy and talent in each piece.

Are you involved in any sustainable projects?

As far as *Agave salmiana*, a wild species whose harvest cannot be controlled, we make sure to always plant two more for each one harvested, to help preserve the species and not make a huge impact on the ecosystem. We only use six kilograms of agave (many major brands require up to twelve kilograms of agave in tequila and eighteen kilograms of agave in mezcal per distillation).

Is there any change you would like to see in the industry?

Industrialization has helped cover the rising demand in the last few years, and with that came the importance of focusing on sustainability and environmental responsibility. The process of making tequila can be resource intensive, requiring large amounts of water, energy, and land. That's why we are exploring ways to reduce the environmental impact, such as using renewable energy sources, implementing water conservation measures, and adopting organic farming practices.

Also, there are ongoing efforts to promote and protect the cultural heritage of tequila, which has deep roots in Mexican history and traditions. We advocate to see greater recognition and protection of tequila's cultural significance, as well as more support for small-scale producers who are preserving traditional methods of tequila production.

Do you have any special releases or limited editions?

Yes, we have a limited-edition line: Silver, Añejo, and Extra Añejo, decorated with Swarovski crystals.

What are your thoughts about the influence of terroir?

The most important thing to take care of in the terroir is the pH, talking about agaves. The terroir in Los Altos de Jalisco is very fertile because it is fed by the volcano that surrounds it. The richer and more fertile the terroir, we will have a better agave production (agaves richer in sugar that will give us a better distillation). At Casa Don Ramón, we expect a minimum of seven years of maturation. Yes, it affects the flavor: the more mature the agave is, the more complex the aromas and flavors will be.

What do you think led to the tequila boom?

Tequila is an emblematic drink of Mexico. The fact that new generations started to appreciate this beverage and move away from the fact that tequila gave hangovers is a big factor. Today, the rise of the premium sector positioned tequila as a sipping drink, rather than a one-shot situation, with some of the biggest brands turning their communication, processes, and products to help drive this trend.

How do you see tequila growing in the next few years?

It will most certainly keep growing at the same speed it has. The main driver in the next years is innovation, like the rising of the *cristalino* trend outside of Mexico (where it is the best-selling category) and the flavored tequilas.

What do you think about using tequila in cocktails?

It depends on the taste of each person; our products have the quality to be enjoyed and to be mixed in exquisite combinations.

What do you think is the proper way to drink tequila?

To taste it and appreciate the liquid, we recommend serving it in a tequila glass, not in a *caballito* (a term for a shot glass that literally means "little horse").

Take a sip to clean the palate, and in the second, take a breath, hold it, take the drink, and release the air through the nose. This is how we appreciate the notes to the fullest.

What do you think is a tradition associated with the production of tequila in Mexico?

The jimadores are a type of farmer originally from Mexico who is dedicated to harvesting agave plants, mainly to produce tequila, sotol, and mezcal, a task that requires the ability to identify the mature agave; that is, the one that takes between eight and twelve years planted.

This work is inherited from father to son, and they use the *coa de jima* as their main work tool, which is like a flat-bladed knife at the end of a pole and is used to remove the flower from the agave.

How are tequila and mezcal seen nowadays?

Tequila and mezcal have evolved to be an emblem of Mexico, and they are being recognized worldwide as such, with exports of these drinks growing continuously every year. They continue to hold great importance in Mexican culture today. They are seen as symbols of Mexican identity and heritage, and are celebrated in festivals and cultural events throughout the country.

Tequila is perhaps the most well-known and widely consumed agave-based spirit, both within Mexico and internationally. It has become a popular drink worldwide, often associated with parties, celebrations, and a festive atmosphere. However, many Mexicans also take great pride in tequila as a symbol of our cultural heritage, and there is a growing movement to protect and promote traditional tequila-making methods. Mezcal, on the other hand, has long been considered a more artisanal and traditional spirit, with a history that dates back centuries. It is still produced using traditional methods in many parts of Mexico and has gained popularity in recent years among bartenders and cocktail enthusiasts for its unique flavors and versatility.

CASA SAN MATÍAS

Casa San Matías was founded by Don Delfino Gonzalez in 1886, during the Mexican Revolution. It is one of the oldest family tequila distilleries in Mexico, operating for more than 130 years.

Around fifteen years ago, they relocated the distillery from Ojo de Agua, Tecámac, to Los Altos de Jalisco.

Today, Casa San Matías is run by Carmen Villarreal Treviño, the only woman in Mexico running a tequila distillery. She took over the business in 1997 after the death of her husband, Jesús López, and from then on she tried to accomplish several of her husband's projects, such as ultra-premium, ultra-aged, Rey Sol Tequila, and Carmesí. A smooth tequila that could appeal to all palates, Carmesí won first place for tequila Reposado from the Mexican Academy of Tequila, as well as the gold medal in the International Review of Spirits.

At Casa San Matías, which is in the top-five biggest distilleries in the Mexican market, they produce Pueblo Viejo (introduced in 1989), Rey Sol (launched in 1998), Tequila San Matías, Orgullo Pueblo Viejo (released in 2006), San Matías Tahona, and Tequila Corazón, which is the only brand that is not owned by Casa San Matías, but by Sazerac.

Casa San Matías uses only the finest blue agave plants and traditional methods. The agave is harvested in the highlands of Jalisco, which are rich in iron and minerals. The agave hearts are cooked in stone ovens for forty-eight hours at 194°F (90°C), then crushed with their original tahona basalt stone wheel from 1886. The juice from the extraction is mixed with natural spring water from the distillery. The fermentation takes place in pinewood vats with native yeast for seventy-two hours, and the double distillation occurs in copper pot stills at very low temperatures.

Besides their Special Editions, Casa San Matías offers the following lines:

- San Matías Gran Reserva: Blanco and Extra Añejo (aged for three years).

- Pueblo Viejo: Blanco, Reposado (aged for three months), and Añejo (aged for twelve months).

- Rey Sol: Extra Añejo (aged for six years).

- San Matías Cristal: an Añejo cristalino tequila.

- San Matías Tahona: Blanco, Reposado (aged for three months), and Añejo (aged for twelve months), produced with the artisanal method.

Casa San Matías was the first tequila distillery to take part in the United Nations carbon footprint program to combat global warming. It is also one of the few to use a biodigester that breaks down organic waste produced in the distilling process, allowing it to operate in an environmentally friendly way.

Casa San Matías has also been recognized with the Gender Equity Model certification by Mexico's National Women's Institute and was the first tequila distillery to be certified as a "Great Place to Work."

A CHAT WITH CARMEN VILLARREAL TREVIÑO

I had the pleasure to speak with Carmen, owner of Casa San Matías. She has a fantastic personality, and she is a strong leader. Here is what she told me.

"When I entered the company, it was a sorrowful time for me. After my husband passed away in 1997, I took over the company, initially thinking it would be temporary. I hired a director, but the team didn't accept him, so I stepped in and took charge myself. Over time, the job became my passion, and I found so much enjoyment in it that I decided to stay."

When I asked about her opinion on the challenges that a woman can face in a male environment, she answered, "I have never personally experienced any significant challenges as a woman in this industry. I never allowed myself to dwell on it; my focus was always on my work. I believe that the success and resilience of women come from their assertiveness and determination."

Then, I tried to understand the secret behind such a successful brand. She told me, "We prioritize four standards: team, quality, environment, and community. What drives us forward in this company, just like my predecessors, is our passion and the people we work with. We want to showcase the best of Mexico to the world. We take care of our employees, who have been with us for years and come from generations of people who have worked for the company. When they are happy, it reflects in the final product. Casa San Matías has won numerous awards for being a company where people are happiest to work. My role is to provide an environment that showcases the talent and capabilities of our team. I have a lot of trust in them. In the future, I want to expand our portfolio. We have plenty of ideas and creativity behind us. It's a dream that is coming true to sell our products worldwide."

I asked her about Rey Sol, and its bottle's lovely and peculiar shape. She replied, "Rey Sol was originally initiated by my husband, but when he passed away, I took it upon myself. My husband wanted to merge art with the art of making tequila. Rey Sol was my first project when I took charge of the company. Rey Sol is dedicated to my husband and means the 'king sun,' to represent his personality. He was a wonderful man, and it has been an honor for me to complete this project."

Finally, about the tequila boom, she said, "The boom of tequila is due to its product versatility and the various ways it can be enjoyed. Tequila cocktails pair well with almost everything, bringing joy to people around the world. As a result, we are even happier to produce it. I am pleased to know that people appreciate drinking tequila, even in the comfort of their own homes."

CASA SAN MATÍAS GRAN RESERVA EXTRA AÑEJO

Casa San Matías Gran Reserva Extra Añejo was launched in 1993 as the first Extra Añejo tequila. It's aged for three years in French oak barrels, and it has won several awards, including the silver at the Los Angeles International Spirits Competition in 2008 and the silver at the San Francisco World Spirits Competition in 2019.

Gran Reserva Extra Añejo is amber in color and presents ripe fruit, chocolate, and nut (such as toasted almond and hazelnut) aromas on the nose. It offers sweet flavors, but also sapidity and a slight acidity. The ABV is 40% (may vary to 38%).

CASA SAN MATÍAS CRISTAL AÑEJO

Launched in 2015, Casa San Matías Cristal Añejo is aged for eighteen months in American oak barrels and goes through a filtration process to extract the color and obtain a clear, silver reflection in the tequila.

On the nose, it presents aromas of vanilla, chocolate, roasted coffee, and nutmeg, while on the palate, it offers sweet agave and olive flavors. The ABV is 40%.

REY SOL

Rey Sol is an Extra Añejo aged for six years and bottled in a decanter designed by Mexican artist Sergio Bustamante. The bottle is sun shaped, a symbol of strength and beauty, to reflect the spirit of Mexico.

Intense amber and bright in color, Rey Sol presents oak, chocolate, vanilla, dried fruit, and nut (such as roasted almonds and hazelnut) aromas on the nose; it offers sweet and oak notes on the palate; and the finish is long-lasting, with chocolate and almond hints. The ABV is 38% (but may vary to 40%).

Casa San Matías Gran Reserva Extra Añejo

Rey Sol

Casa San Matías Cristal Añejo

TEQUILA CORAZÓN

Corazón is owned by Sazerac and produced in Casa San Matías. The name comes from the Spanish word for *heart*, which signifies both the agave heart and the passion invested in crafting the spirit. Tequila Corazón's production process is overseen by Carmen Villarreal.

Tequila Corazón is made from 100 percent blue Weber agave harvested by hand in Los Altos de Jalisco. The agave hearts are cooked in clay ovens for forty-eight hours and then ground. Once crushed, natural spring water is added. The fermentation lasts for seventy-two hours, and it occurs with a proprietary yeast as well as native yeasts present in the air. The distillation process is done slowly and at a very low temperature. The aging takes place in American oak barrels, and before the tequila is bottled, head of operations Mario Echanove and master distiller Rocio Rodriguez Torres check the quality.

Tequila Corazón offers the following expressions:

- Single Estate: Blanco (unaged), Reposado (aged for six to eight months), Añejo (matured for sixteen to eighteen months), and Extra Añejo (aged for at least thirty-six months).

- Single Barrel Tequila: matured in barrels from Sazerac's award-winning charred oak whiskey brands. Single Barrel Reposado rests for eleven months in barrels from Buffalo Trace, Eagle Rare, and 1792; for ten months in Blanton's barrels; and for nine months in Weller's barrels. Single Barrel Añejo rests for eighteen months in Buffalo Trace's barrels, for twenty-four months in Eagle Rare's and 1792's barrels, for twenty months in Blanton's barrels, and for thirteen months in Weller's barrels.

- Expresiones del Corazón: aged in Buffalo Trace's exclusive Antique Collection barrels, which are monitored every two months until the tequila gets the characteristics desired.

Artisanal Blanco is aged for less than sixty days, Buffalo
Trace Old 22 Añejo is matured for at least twenty-two months
in barrels that held whiskey for twenty-two years, Sazerac
Rye Añejo is aged for twenty-four months in Sazerac Rye
barrels, Thomas H. Handy Sazerac Añejo is matured for nineteen months in Thomas H. Handy bourbon barrels, George T.
Stagg Añejo is aged for twenty-two months in George T. Stagg
bourbon barrels, and William Larue Weller Añejo is matured
for fifteen months in William Larue Weller barrels.

TEQUILA CORAZÓN SINGLE-ESTATE BLANCO

Winner of the Best Blanco at the World Tequila Awards in 2019 and of the
gold medal at the Los Angeles International Spirits Competition in 2019,
Tequila Corazón Blanco is an unaged expression.

Silver in color, it presents aromas of baked pineapple, roasted jalapeño,
and tangarine zest on the nose; it offers mineral notes and a creamy texture on the palate; the finish is spicy; and the ABV is 40%.

DEL MAGUEY SINGLE VILLAGE MEZCAL

Ron Cooper, an internationally renowned artist and mezcal vision-
ary, visited Teotitlán del Valle, Oaxaca, during the seventies, and that's
when the dream to open a distillery began. But it was only in 1995 that
Ron Cooper founded Del Maguey, delivering his vision of a 100 percent
organic and artisanal mezcal.

Thanks to a strong relationship with Zapotec Mexican Indian producers in the remote villages of Oaxaca, he combined the original organic
process with technology and embraced the variation of microclimates

and terroir. The result is that each product will have a distinctly rich, sweet, and smoky taste. Every product is handcrafted by individual family *palenqueros* (producers) in old-style towns. Del Maguey is the first to name each product after the village in which the mezcal is made.

In 2017, Pernod Ricard, an international spirits company, bought a majority stake in the company, making it part of a group that includes Jameson Whiskey, Absolut Vodka, and Havana Club Rum.

The distillery has several different artisanal mezcal expressions in its portfolio; below, you will see a list of the villages and the expressions they produce:

- San Luis del Río: Paciano Cruz Nolasco, the village maestro, is one of the first to produce for Del Maguey. Together with his family, he is the maker of San Luis del Río, Vida, Vida de Muertos, and Madrecuishe (limited edition). They all are naturally fermented and twice distilled in wood-fired copper stills.

- San Baltazar Chichicapa: alongside his son, Maximino, Zapotec palenquero Faustino Garcia Vasquez is the maker of Chichicapa. This expression is naturally fermented and twice distilled in wood-fired copper stills.

- Santa Catarina Minas: village maestro Luis Carlos Vasquez is the maker of Minero and Arroqueño, which are naturally fermented and twice distilled in ancestral clay stills with bamboo tubing, and the maker of Pechuga and Iberico (made with wild mountain apples, plums, red plantains, pineapples, almonds, and Ibérico ham), which are distilled three times. This village also produces Del Maguey Barril Mezcal, which is fermented for nearly 30 days before being distilled in ancestral clay pot stills. This unique expression is dedicated to Florencio Lareano Carlos Sarmiento.

- Santo Domingo Albarradas: Espiridion Morales Luis was the village maestro, but nowadays, his legacy continues through his sons, Juan and Armando, and his daughter, Ester. They are the makers of Albarradas, which, like many other Del Maguey expressions, is naturally fermented and twice distilled in wood-fired copper stills.

- Santa Maria Albarradas: Rogelio Martinez Cruz, the master distiller, sold Tobalá to Del Maguey in 1996. With his family, he is the maker of Tobalá, Wild Tepextate, Tobaziche, and Wild Jabalí, all naturally fermented and twice distilled in wood-fired copper stills. In the town, Florencio Carlos Sarmiento, Florendo Carlos Vasquez, and Luis Carlos Vasquez also produce Del Maguey Cuixe Mezcal.

- Las Milpas: made by master distiller Anastasio Luis as per the usual artisanal method.

- San Pedro Teozacoalco: Fernando Caballero Cruz is the maker of this mezcal, which is naturally fermented and twice distilled using a steel pot with a clay condenser and bamboo tubing.

- San Jose Rio Minas: master distiller Roberto Gutierrez, with his sons, is the maker of San Jose Río Minas, produced in the same way as Wild Papalome above.

- Mezcal de Puebla/San Pablo Ameyaltepec: master distiller Aurelio Tobon, alongside his family, is the maker of Mezcal de Puebla. In this area, it is still common to use the French continuous distillation method, which requires up to twenty hours for a single batch.

Del Maguey is very active in initiatives and sustainability, supporting Oaxaca's biodiversity and rich cultural heritage. It is approved organic by the OCIA and USDA, making it one of the first mezcals in the world with organic certification. It works closely with NGOs, and it is currently involved in projects such as the Zapotec Talking Dictionary Program, an online multimedia resource, in collaboration with Swarthmore College, to support language revitalization; an Apiculture Program, to increase biodiversity through bee pollination, a Reforestation Program that is planting trees in areas where Del Maguey is present; and a Digital Library Program that provides computers and tablets for educational purposes.

DEL MAGUEY VIDA CLÁSICO

Launched in 2010, Vida Clásico is an artisanal, organic mezcal and one of the best-selling by Del Maguey. Created alongside the Red Ant River in San Luis del Rio, it's handcrafted. Espadín agave is roasted for three to eight days, followed by an eight- to ten-day wild fermentation; then it is slowly double distilled in small, wood-fired, riverside copper stills. This extra care delivers a natural and complex flavor.

In 2012, Del Maguey Vida won the Ultimate Spirits Challenge Chairman's Trophy, and it was named number one by "The World's 50 Best Bars Brand Report 2015."

It can be sipped, but it is also a highly mixable base for cocktails due to its versatility. The aroma notes are tropical fruit, honey, and roasted agave, while the tasting notes are ginger, cinnamon, and tangerine. The finish is long and soft. The ABV is 42%.

Q & A WITH JON ANDERS FJELDSRUD, BRAND AMBASSADOR FOR DEL MAGUEY

Can you tell us a bit about yourself, your background, and how you became interested in mezcal?

There is a saying in mezcal that you do not find mezcal, but mezcal finds you; that's very much my story. One day it was there in my hand, staring back at me, and I have no idea how it got there.

Maybe it was through my friendship with Pablo "Papi" Hurtado, a longtime bartender at Café Pacifico, or living with Mexicans in London, or maybe me sneaking in whenever the late great Tomas Estes (founder of Tequila Ocho and Café Pacifico/La Perla restaurants) was in town doing staff trainings at Café Pacifico. Maybe it was a combination of all of them. Tomas made such an impact on me, so he was a huge influence, I learned his way of hosting a tequila talk; the way he was telling stories and anecdotes made the tasting alive. I am also an apostle to his notion of being an ambassador maker and not an ambassador, something that's a little funny, because CNIT (the Mexican national tequila chamber) made him the official tequila ambassador to the European Union, but he saw himself as someone who was inspiring others to talk about agave spirits and promote them wherever in the world they were.

I came from Norway to study and stayed. I have been very lucky that I have worked with amazing people at great places, people I have learned a lot from.

I've worked in a long line of different bars, like Salsa, 10 Rooms with Dre Masso, Thomas Gillgren, Marco Li Donni, Giuseppe Santamaria, 10 Tokyo Joe, Sanderson Hotel with the late Henry Besant, Max Warner, Xavier Padovani, Jason Crawley and a host of other great bartenders, Light Bar & Restaurant, Baltic Bar & Restaurant, Jan Woroniecki's restaurant with Robbie Hitchcock, Rockwell Bar at the Trafalgar Hilton Hotel with the late Kester Thomas, Pablo Hurtado, Giovanni Spezziga. Café Pacifico with Darren Brooks and Leo Besant, among others. Charlotte Street Blues, El Camion, and the Pink Chihuahua with the late Dick Bradsell.

I helped the Wahaca group setting up two bars, first Southbank Wahaca and then London's first mezcalería, Wahaca, working with Thomasina Miers and her team, and after this went back to El Camion for another two years.

I started working as a brand ambassador for Amathus and Harry Georgiou in 2014, and worked with Amathus Drinks' portfolio of aquavits and agave spirits with brands like Tequila Calle 23, Tequila Centinela, Tequila Cabrito, Del Maguey Mezcal, Mezcal Alipús, Mezcal Los Danzantes, Mezcal Jaral de Berrio, Mezcal Pierde Almas, Mezcal Siete Misterio, and aquavit from Arcus, Altia, and Spirit of Hven on the UK market. I worked for Amathus for four years.

When Del Maguey was sold to Pernod Ricard, I came with the brand to Pernod Ricard UK and worked there for almost two years, as a brand ambassador for Del Maguey Mezcal, Altos Tequila, and the Swedish-produced Åhus Akvavit.

Work stopped during the COVID global pandemic in 2020, so I started working as a part-time bartender for Tomos Perry's Brat restaurant and for Eric Yu's Fam bar in London. During the same time, I have been working with Dos Hombres mezcal, Bruxo Mezcal, Sin Gusano agave spirits, Casa Lumbre (with brands like Abasolo, Nixta, and Ojo de Tigre), Copenhagen Distillery, and Dangerous Don mezcal, hosting trainings, events, and trade visits and representing these brands in the UK.

What does your role as an agave ambassador involve?

As in any business, the business needs to be profitable, so my main job is to sell the agave spirit, but my role is also to promote and represent the brands, the producers, their villages, and their families—to represent the culture behind it and the traditions that come with it. As well as to educate on what it is, how to use it, and how to drink it in a responsible way.

What are some of the most memorable or interesting experiences you've had while exploring the world of agave?

I would say that's meeting the people making agave spirits, to visit the families and to eat with them—that's been an amazing experience, to talk and to listen to their stories. Without these people, there are no agave spirits—never forget that.

How do you think the increasing popularity of mezcal and tequila will impact the bar industry in the long term?

In some sense it has; bartenders are always looking for new flavor, that next new thing. Agave spirit is that at the moment, and the interest doesn't seem to diminish.

What trends are you currently seeing in the mezcal industry?

As more global actors are getting involved with the industry, we see some changes in the message as well as how it's sold, and to whom it is sold. We see more commercial mezcal (and tequila) and what I feel is a dumbing down of the industry: making products less agave flavor forward and more vodka-like, and the heavy use of filtering, of very modern production methods (column stills and diffusers). But we also see a greater focus on or better understanding of the importance of where the mezcal is from, who makes it, and how it's made. Also, we are seeing more mezcal and agave spirits from other regions, not just from Oaxaca, something that's great. We also see some tequila brands that have changed their production method toward a more traditional tequila production, by removing autoclaves and building brick ovens and putting a focus on tahonas and traditional methods. We also have seen mezcal brands that are made by blending mezcal from more than one village or producer, and we have seen industrial mezcal (made in übermodern distilleries).

What challenges does the industry currently face?

Transparency—there are too many secrets. Like, what is the going rate of mezcal and the agaves? Who benefits when agaves are sold? What happens with the bagasse and vinazas, water issues, wood issues? Agaves, where are they from? What happened with the certification process, the tax on liters produced before export, and health of the product, who is testing it for export, and who is not? What about conejo mezcal?

The NOM (a document that regulates the industry) is not fit for the purpose; it needs to be changed.

In the thirty-two states of Mexico, twenty-two have historical mezcal production; this should be reflected in the NOM. All agave spirits made in Mexico should be allowed to be called mezcal, like alcohol from grapes can be called wine, and not something as obscure as komil. As well, every region has different practices and different methods, and different species of agaves (or subspecies), so that needs to be taken into consideration, and it's currently not. As an example, you can specify state, region, and village, like Mezcal de Oaxaca, village of Santa Catarina Minas, Minero style; this did great for burgundy wine and can work great for agave spirits too.

I don't have any issues with blending mezcal from different villages or producers, but it needs to be done correctly and managed correctly. As well, it must be stipulated on the label and not sold as something it is not.

As mezcal becomes more popular globally, how do you think the industry is addressing the issue of sustainability? Are there any specific initiatives or practices you think are particularly effective in ensuring that mezcal production is environmentally and socially responsible?

There are some really great people out there who are very aware of the shortages in the industry and are working on changing the industry for the better. Education is a key to this, and education needs to be prioritized. Good practices need to be learned, implemented, and encouraged. As well, the NOM needs to be looked at and made sure that it is fit for its purpose. Currently I like that the consumers of agave spirits care and are asking good questions, but there is still a lot of work.

As an ambassador for agave, you have likely had the opportunity to see the spirit being enjoyed in many different parts of the world. How do you think the popularity and perception of mezcal vary from country to country, and what do you think are the main factors driving this variation?

Yes, a little. In the US and Mexico, they enjoy the mezcal a little differently than in the rest of the world. The US consumes a lot both in cocktails and neat. Mexico does not have a great cocktail culture (but it's very exciting that it is catching up on this), so it is drunk neat or with a single mixer. In the rest of the world, it's enjoyed neat or in cocktails, but not in the same volume as in the US, but it's still an industry/bartender enjoyed spirit.

How do you think the global demand for mezcal has changed over the past few years, and what do you see as the future of the industry?

Yes, it has. Mezcal has gone from only being sold in the village where it was made to being sold on a global stage, just in a few short years. Now that's great for the producers, their families, and their villages if it's managed correctly, and I am not seeing this yet; only a few players have been good at this.

I don't know if it was good that some of these brands were snapped up for big money. These global companies buying any random agave spirit brands, what are they buying? They are not buying the villages, the producers, and their agaves, in some cases not even the distillery, so what do they buy? They buy the name, the bottle, and the label, but what does this mean? Maybe this is where it went a little wrong. Are they really understanding the category? That notion that your brand was created in that village by that producer using agaves from that region, with the style and flavor of that hand of the maker, and for you to then move production to another village or region? It is like producing bordeaux wine in Alsace—total nonsense.

Maybe mezcal the way it was made can't be scaled to fit a global scale. Tequila was made in earth pits up to 150 years ago, before they had to change to steam due to demand, but also due to wood depletion. Does mezcal need to do this too? Then you have the issue of agave shortage, wood shortage, bagasse and vinaza problems. Maybe we should be running out of agave spirit, like wine does; you make a certain amount of mezcal (like vintages) for the year, and that's it for that year. Sure, that is not great for the global sales, but maybe it's good for the villages, the land, the people living there, and the Earth.

How do small, artisanal mezcal producers compete with larger, more established brands in the market?

This is a great question: How do you make your brand successful? What does success imply? Is that to modernize your distillery, to sell great volumes of mezcal, or make your mezcal available outside your village? All of them? How do you balance the need for commercial success with artisanal methods, keeping the mezcal production traditional? To answer this, we need to look at the industry. Most mezcals are made in small or medium-sized distilleries, by an extended local family using products from that region, to be sold in that village or district; it was never intended to be exported. The mezcal that was exported was made in larger distilleries that produced mezcal using very modern equipment and methods, or we had mezcal brokers, companies that bought village mezcal and labeled it under their label. We still see that, and that will not change, but we see more local producers or village cooperatives starting their own label, partly due to their children returning or due to increased revenue, and with that they can afford the cost of certification and export their mezcal. We also see this because their children are returning with degrees in sales or marketing and wanting to take part in this.

In your opinion, what are the key factors that consumers should consider when choosing a mezcal brand?

Who made it and where it was made. Without the producers, there is no traditional mezcal; if the brand does not speak about where and by whom it's made, maybe they don't get it, and maybe they are only in it for the money. And then the question should be, what else are they not careful with?

What do you think about using mezcal in cocktails?

Mezcal works great in cocktails; it's incredibly diverse and works with so many other spirits and liquors. It dries up the cocktail, and an overly sweet drink can become drinkable with some mezcal. Sure, there is a debate about using mezcal made from rare and wild agaves in cocktails, but they work too. However, the price the bar needs to charge for the cocktail may become untenable.

Can you tell us about any traditions or cultural significance associated with the production of mezcal in Mexico?

It's still, in local rural areas, part of folk medicine, and it's an integral part of village life, and used in celebrating the big events in life, like funerals, quinceañeras, weddings, and others. I have friends in the mezcal world who have distilled a batch of mezcal to be consumed at their funerals.

What's your thought about aging mezcal?

The tradition of aging mezcal is new, in the sense of aging it in wood, but resting mezcal is as old as the making of it; they used black clay or glass *demijohns*. They did this not to improve the mezcal but to store it. Mezcal changes when you rest it like that; its blends or marries. I like aged mezcals if they are aged well and in barrels that are suitable for aging, but prefer wood unaged mezcal.

Is there any change you would like to see in the industry?

In general, it is a great industry to work in, with a family vibe to it, where a lot of brands work together. That I hope will not change. Maybe a regulatory body not linked to any parties, organizations, or groups.

DERECHITO TEQUILA

Derechito Tequila was founded by Alberto Callejo Torre in 2018. Working in design and marketing, he moved from Madrid to Mexico in 2015 and quickly became fond of tequila. After meeting the Leal family, who were running Tequila Selecto de Amatitán, he decided to create Derechito Tequila (named after the diminutive of "derecho," meaning straight or neat as a reference to a way of drinking).

Derechito Tequila won the gold and bronze medals in 2020 at the third edition of the London Spirits Competition (LSC).

Derechito Tequila is produced at Tequila Selecto de Amatitán (with numerous other brands) in Amatitán, Jalisco. The harvesting process is overseen by captain of jimadores "Filoso" Ralei. The agave hearts are cooked in a stone oven in a process overseen by oven chief El Norber, and then they are crushed with a roller mill with water injection. The fermentation occurs in 30,000-liter stainless-steel tanks with local and organic yeast for about seventy-two hours. The distillation takes place in alembic pot stills.

Derechito Tequila offers the following expressions:

- Blanco: the unaged expression.

- Reposado: aged for nine months in American oak barrels.

- Añejo: matured for up to twelve months in French oak barrels.

- Extra Añejo: aged for thirty-six months in American oak barrels.

- Derechito Rosé: a limited edition.

They also produce Mezcal Cupreata, made with 100 percent *Agave cupreata* harvested in Río Balsas, in the state of Michoacán and Guerrero. Produced using the Mexican Pacific technique, the agave hearts are cooked in an underground stone oven, ground with a miller, and fermented in wood vats with natural yeast. The double distillation takes place in a Filipino copper pot.

Derechito Tequila uses waste fibers as natural fertilizer in their fields. They also adhere to social responsibility programs and environmental conservation programs.

DERECHITO AÑEJO

Brilliant amber in color, Derechito Añejo presents aromas of cooked agave, dried fruits, and oak on the nose; on the palate, it's smooth and silky, and the finish is warm. The ABV is 40%.

DERECHITO EXTRA AÑEJO

Intense bronze in color, Derechito Extra Añejo presents aromas of wood, agave, chocolate, and nuts on the nose; on the palate, it offers flavors of toasted oak and sweet hints. The ABV is 40%.

DERECHITO ROSÉ

This special edition is matured for forty-five days in French oak barrels imported from Sotillo de la Ribera (Burgos, Spain) and previously once used for the wine Parajes de Callejo Tempranillo y Albillo Mayor, Añada 2020.

Pink in color, Derechito Rosé presents aromas of red fruits and wood on the nose and flavors of cooked agave and berries on the palate.

Derechito Extra Añejo

Derechito Rosé

DERRUMBES

Derrumbes was founded by Esteban Morales and Sergio Mendoza in 2012, with the aim of creating mezcals from outside Oaxaca, supporting the family-run producers.

In 2008, Esteban Morales, a former chef, began to sell mezcal as a distributor in Guadalajara, when he started to look for brands to add to his portfolio. In 2011, he founded La Venenosa Raicilla, a native agave distillate. In 2012, he got in touch with his friends who wanted to found a mezcal brand. One of them was Sergio Mendoza, founder of Don Fulano Tequila; the other was his wife's cousin. Together, they established Derrumbes.

Each bottle of Derrumbes mezcal represents a different region, chosen to highlight the traditions, terroir, and organoleptic characteristics of the region. Each mezcalero produces Derrumbes mezcals with traditional methods. Here are their different expressions:

- Oaxaca: produced in Santiago Matatlán by master distiller Javier Mateo, with agaves espadín and tobalá.

- Michoacán: made in Tzitzio by maestro mezcalero Lupe Pérez Toledo, with agaves cupreata and alto. The agave hearts are cooked in an underground stone pit with black oak and ground with a mechanical mill. Fermentation occurs in underground wood and clay vats, and the distillation takes place in Filipino-style stills made of wood staves and copper over direct flame. Finally, the mezcal is matured in glass for a minimum of sixty days.

- San Luis Potosí: produced in Charcas by master distiller Juan Manuel Pérez with *Agave salmiana crassispina*. The agave hearts are cooked in a brick oven with black oak and ground with a tahona. The fermentation occurs in masonry vats with natural yeasts. The distillation takes place in a copper pot still. The mezcal is then aged in glass for sixty days.

- Zacatecas: made in Hacienda de Guadalupe, Huitzila, Zacatecas, by maestro mezcalero Jaime Bañuelos, with blue Weber agave. The agave hearts are cooked in underground stone pits with black oak and ground with a tahona. The fermentation occurs in stainless-steel vats with natural yeasts, and the distillation takes place in a copper pot still. The mezcal is matured in glass for sixty days.

- Tamaulipas: produced in San Carlos by master distiller Cuahutémoc Jaques, with agaves Americana, univittata, and funkiana. The agave heart is cooked in underground stone pits with black oak and ground with a mechanical mill. The fermentation occurs in stainless-steel vats with natural yeast, and the distillation takes place in a copper pot still. The mezcal is then aged in glass for a minimum of sixty days.

- Durango: made in Nombre de Dios by maestro mezcalero Uriel Simental, with *Agave durangensis*. The agave hearts are cooked in an underground stone pit with black oak and crushed by hand with an axe and a mallet. The fermentation occurs in underground wood and clay vats, and the distillation takes place in a hybrid wood and copper still. The mezcal is then matured in glass for a minimum of sixty days.

Derrumbes is committed to socially responsible practices. Their small batches of mezcal are processed outside Oaxaca to allow other regions to produce more and, in the meantime, release the pressure on the Oaxaca ecosystem. In this way, Derrumbes aims to create a market for mezcal from the lesser-known states.

DERRUMBES OAXACA

Produced in Santiago Matatlán by master distiller Javier Mateo, Derrumbes Oaxaca is made with agaves espadín and tobalá. The agave hearts are cooked in an underground stone pit with black oak, and ground with a traditional tahona. The fermentation occurs in wood vats with fibers, pulque as yeast, and water from Mitla. The distillation takes place in a copper pot still, and the mezcal is then matured in glass for a minimum of sixty days.

Clear in color, Derrumbes Oaxaca is a full-bodied mezcal that offers citrus, fruity, and smoky flavors on the palate. The ABV is 48%.

DON JULIO

Don Julio's story starts with Don Julio González-Frausto Estrada in Atotonilco el Alto, in the highlands region of Jalisco. Don Julio started to work at ten years old, distributing tequila by horse to support his family of eight. In 1942, he approached a wealthy local businessman for a loan of 20,000 pesos to open his own distillery. The man granted the loan, and Don Julio opened La Primavera (The Springtime), where he started to produce Tres Magueyes. However, it was another forty-three years until the brand Don Julio was officially born. In fact, in 1985, to celebrate Don Julio's sixtieth birthday, his sons commemorated the date by creating a tequila in his name, Don Julio. Following its popularity, Don Julio and his family decided to launch the tequila on the market in 1987, and it became the first luxury tequila.

In 2012, Don Julio passed away, and today his company is run by his protégé, Enrique de Colsa, who trained with him for five years and took the reins of the company in 2004. To celebrate the seventieth anniversary of the brand in 2012, de Colsa, inspired by Don Julio's innovative playbook, created Don Julio 70, the world's first clear Añejo.

In 2014, British beverage company Diageo acquired Don Julio and La Primavera distillery. Don Julio is still produced and distributed by Tequila Don Julio, S.A. de C.V. from La Primavera in the Colonia El Chichimeco district, in Atotonilco El Alto.

Don Julio is known to have revolutionized the world of tequila. He chose quality over quantity, meaning that he planted each agave farther apart to allow proper room to grow and fully mature before harvesting, a practice that would later become an industry standard. He also introduced a new design for tequila bottles. They used to be tall and were typically hidden under the tables. Don Julio redesigned a shorter bottle for his guests to pass around the table while still being able to see each other. In this way, he also wanted to state that his tequila deserved a place on the table.

At La Primavera, the tequila is made with 100 percent pure blue Weber agaves, each handpicked from the highlands of Jalisco. Once harvested, the agave hearts are steam cooked in a traditional brick oven for three days, and then they are crushed and fermented with water and wild yeasts. The distillation takes place in copper pot stills, and the tequila is aged in temperature- and humidity-controlled white oak barrels. Each small batch is numbered. Finally, the tequila is bottled in handblown, numbered bottles.

Don Julio offers six main expressions (besides the limited editions):

- Blanco: double distilled, unaged expression.
- Reposado: matured for eight months in American white oak barrels.
- Añejo: aged in smaller batches for eighteen months in American white oak barrels.
- 70 Añejo Cristalino Tequila: twice distilled and matured for eighteen months in American white oak barrels, then charcoal filtered.
- 1942 Tequila: small batches and aged for a minimum of two and a half years, a tribute to when Don Julio started his distillery.
- Alma Miel: a blend of Blanco tequila distilled with oven-roasted agave honey and Añejo Tequila aged for at least 14 months and finished in Crémant du Limoux barrels.
- Primavera: an homage to the La Primavera distillery, it's a Reposado finished in highly coveted European casks (which held wine infused with macerated orange peels).
- Rosado: Reposado tequila finished in ruby port wine casks.
- Ultima Reserva: rested in former bourbon barrels, and finished in Madeira wine-seasoned casks.

In terms of sustainability, Don Julio was the first agave plantation to receive a perfect score from the Farm Sustainability Assessment.

Don Julio also partners with nonprofit organizations, such as the Restaurant Workers' Community Foundation, dedicated to making the restaurant industry more hospitable to everyone, and No Us Without You LA, which aims to provide food security for Mexican hospitality industry workers in the Greater Los Angeles area.

The Tequila Don Julio Fund is also a donor to the Association of Latino Professionals For America (ALPFA) to empower Hispanic entrepreneurs all across the US.

DON JULIO BLANCO

Made with 100 percent blue agave and bottled straight after the distillation, Don Julio Blanco can be enjoyed neat, on the rocks, or in cocktails. Crystal clear in color with a medium viscosity, on the nose it presents citrus and fruity aromas, such as lemon, lime, and grapefruit; on the palate, it offers light, sweet agave flavors. The ABV is 38%.

PENSADOR MEZCAL

Ben Schroder is the founder of Pensador (the name comes from the phrase *El camino del pensador*, "The path of the thinker"). The first time he tried mezcal was back in 2015, when he visited Mexico. He spent two months traveling around and learning everything involved in the process of making artisanal mezcal. Once he returned to England, where mezcal was still a new product, he decided to go back to Oaxaca with the idea to found a brand. He drove through several regions until he found Atenogenes and Jose García, father-son grower-producers, who had been making quality mezcal for decades in an agave field right off the Calle

Pensamientos (Thoughts Road) in Miahuatlán, southern Oaxaca. They started to work together to bring out their first product, an Ensamble mezcal made of espadín and madrecuishe. When the sales increased to the point that Garcia's distillery production capacity reached its maximum, José introduced Ben to another pair of grower-producers, Alberto and Onofre Ortiz, who started to help supply the espadín and assist with the bottling process.

All the mezcal produced from Pensador comes from Miahuatlán, which heavily influences the product. The agaves used in their expressions reflect the varietals found in the area. Miahuatlán has an especially distinctive terroir. It's very dry and classified as "semiarid," and it has chalky soil with a high limestone content. The most prevalent agaves are espadín and madrecuishe. The result is bright, mineral, and fruit-forward mezcal.

During the production, which is artisanal, agave hearts are hand harvested, halved, and placed in a fire-powered pit oven made from local woods. The cooking process lasts for six days. Once cooked, the *piñas* (hearts) are crushed by a traditional tahona and then placed into open-top wooden barrels for natural fermentation. Water is added at regular intervals after a few days. The double distillation takes place in a small, fire-powered copper alembic still. Besides locally sourced water, nothing else is added during this process, which is carried out by fire, sun, and hand. No electrical equipment is used.

Pensador's main expressions are Ensamble and Espadín, but it also offers special limited editions. One of them is Especial, which contains *destilados de agave* (uncertified mezcal). Each batch features rare and exciting agave with mind-bending, face-melting flavor profiles. One example is a batch made with *cucharilla*, a plant used in the production of sotol.

In terms of sustainability, Pensador uses cultivated varietals for 90 percent of the mezcal they produce. Only in the case of the Especial series, Ben said, "We use different wild varietals for each batch, depending on availability, to ensure that we don't deplete any individual varietal." Plus, he added, "We donate 10 percent of proceeds from each bottle sold to environmental projects in the communities where our mezcals are made. Our first project is addressing water sustainability in the village of San Isidro Guishe, which has experienced hotter weather and lower rainfall in recent years. We are building a well and running workshops with the local farmers to develop sustainable agricultural practices."

A QUICK CHAT WITH BEN SCHRODER, FOUNDER OF PENSADOR

I asked Ben a few questions about mezcal and what he thinks of some common practices. I got very interesting answers. As explained in previous chapters, a few years ago, mezcal had negative connotations. Either it was the spirit with the worm or it was very bad to drink. Ben added that people couldn't see past the smoky flavors and that mezcal became a kind of easy way to make money.

But, luckily, the misconceptions around mezcal changed so much that not only is it one of today's most appreciated spirits, but it has also arrived behind many bars. As Ben said, "Mezcal (and tequila) are a national icon and a symbol of immense pride." People can finally see it.

Along with many others, Ben agreed that using mezcal in cocktails can definitely benefit the industry, despite the fact that for him the traditional way of drinking it is still neat and at room temperature. Aging mezcal is a different story, though: "I'm not really interested in aged mezcals. It's not a traditional process, but I don't think that makes it heretical or offensive. I just think there's a whole world of delicious aged spirits out there, so why make mezcal taste more like them, when its unaged flavor is completely unique and completely delicious."

In regard to the future of mezcal, Ben opined, "It will continue to grow slowly and steadily. It's not a boom-and-bust trend."

PENSADOR ENSAMBLE

Made following the artisanal method, Pensador Ensamble is made with espadín and madrecuishe. After being ground-oven cooked together, the hearts are crushed by the tahona, then naturally fermented and double distilled in a copper alembic still by the Garcia family.

Ensamble is a complex and complete sipping spirit. On the nose, it has strong notes of cracked black pepper, vegetal fibers, earth, flint, and green vines. On the palate, it has caramelized agave, earthy minerals, and smoked cucumber notes. It's sweet and refreshing, and the ABV is 48%.

PENSADOR ESPADÍN

A classic Miahuatlán expression designed for a different context, Pensador Espadín is perfect as an everyday sipper or as a base for cocktails. It is 100 percent espadín mezcal with notes of earthy minerals, herbs, floral nectar, and a gentle smoke. The ABV is 47.5%.

PENSADOR ESPECIAL BATCH PA1

A limited series classified as destilado de agave, this mezcal is made with wild tepextate agaves sourced from several producers and ground-oven cooked, fermented naturally, and double distilled in a refrescador still (one distillation occurs in a water-cooled alembic still).

Pensador Especial Batch PA1 offers a unique umami flavor, with notes of green pepper, fresh coriander, jalapeño, and seaweed. The finish is long, and the ABV is 47%.

EL CAMINO DEL

PENSADOR

· MEZCAL ·

48% ALC.VOL	ENVASADO DE ORIGEN
HECHO EN MÉXICO	MEZCAL ARTESANAL
OAXACA	JOVEN	100% MAGUEY

DENOMINACIÓN DE ORIGEN PROTEGIDA

EL CA

PEN

M

48% ALC.VOL

HECHO
EN MEXICO

OAXACA

DENOMINACIÓN

ENSAMBLE

ESPECIAL

INO DEL
SADOR
ZCAL

EL CAMINO DEL
PENSADOR
· AGAVE ·

NVASADO DE ORIGEN

DESTILADO DE AGAVE ARTESANAL

MEZCAL
ARTESANAL

HECHO
EN MÉXICO

LOTE
PEQUEÑO

OVEN | 100% AGAVE

OAXACA | JOVEN | 100% MAGUEY

E ORIGEN PROTEGIDA

BOTELLAS LIMITADAS ESPECIALES

EL TEQUILEÑO

In 1959, El Tequileño was founded by Don Jorge Salles Cuervo, who named it to honor the birthplace of Tequila. In 1970, his son, Juan Antonio, joined the family business, and he took the reins after Don Jorge passed away in 2000.

In 2008, Jorge Antonio Salles, Juan Antonio's son, started to run the distillery and became the master distiller. In 2017, El Tequileño was acquired by Paradise Spirits, and in 2018 the brand created the first Reposado Rare, while Juan Antonio Salles received the title of Gran Tequilero by the National Chamber of the Tequila Industry for his lifetime achievement. In 2019, El Tequileño opened Casa Salles Hotel Boutique, where visitors can learn more about tequila and visit the distillery.

Today, El Tequileño is still produced at La Guarreña distillery, located in Tequila. The brand has won several awards, such as double gold at the San Francisco World Spirits Competition in 2020 for Reposado Rare and gold in the Spirits Business in 2022 for Platinum Blanco.

El Tequileño is produced with blue agave harvested in the highlands of Jalisco. The agave hearts have been cooked in autoclaves since 1959 and ground with a roller mill with the addition of spring water directly from the Volćan de Tequila. The fermentation occurs with airborne yeast, and it's influenced by the 150-year-old mango trees that grow near the distillery. The distillation takes place in copper pot stills.

El Tequileño offers the following main expressions:

- Blanco: aged for fourteen days in American oak barrels.
- Reposado: 100 percent agave tequila matured for three months in American oak barrels.

- Cristalino: Reposado tequila rested for four months in American oak barrels and filtered to remove the color.
- Platinum Blanco: made with 100 percent estate-grown agave and rested for fourteen days in American oak barrels.
- Reposado Gran Reserva: matured for a minimum of eight months in American oak and blended with 18-month Añejo.
- Añejo Gran Reserva: 100 percent premium grown blue agave and aged for a minimum of eighteen months in American and French oak before being blended with Extra Añejo.
- Reposado Rare: an exclusive limited release, made with 100 percent blue agave and aged in a large American oak barrel, for six years.

El Tequileño converts 98 percent of its production residuals into organic compost used as fertilizer, and the brand also works to preserve the local water sources.

EL TEQUILEÑO PLATINUM BLANCO

Winner of the gold medal at the Spirits Business in 2022, silver at the International Spirits Challenge in 2021, and silver in the Spirits Selection at Concours Mondial de Bruxelles in 2020, El Tequileño Platinum Blanco is made from 100 percent estate-grown agave in the highlands of Jalisco, and it's left to rest for fourteen days in American oak barrels before being bottled.

On the nose, it presents cooked agave, herbal, anise, and black pepper aromas; on the palate, it offers spices and savory flavors, with a delicate finish. It can be enjoyed on the rocks or mixed in cocktails. The ABV is 40%.

El Tequileño Platinum Blanco

El Tequileño Reposado Gran Reserva

EL TEQUILEÑO REPOSADO GRAN RESERVA

Reposado Gran Reserva is aged for a minimum of eighteen months in American oak barrels and then blended with a small amount of Añejo also aged in American oak.

On the nose, Reposado Gran Reserva presents aromas of banana, caramelized pear, nutmeg, vanilla, and caramel; on the palate, it offers notes of oak, vanilla, spice, toffee, and macadamia nuts. It can be enjoyed on the rocks or in cocktails. The ABV is 40%.

EXCELLIA

Excellia was founded in 2011 by Jean-Sébastien Robicquet, founder of EWG Spirits & Wine and brand creator and producer of G'Vine gin and Esprit de June liqueur, and Carlos Camarena. The tequila is produced at the Tequila Orendain factory in Jalisco.

Excellia was awarded Best in Class at the 2011 International Spirits Challenge, a gold medal at the San Francisco World Spirits Competition in 2011, a silver medal at the International Spirits Challenge in 2011, and a silver medal at the International Wine & Spirits Competition in 2011.

Excellia is made from 100 percent agave Tequilana Weber blue. The agave hearts are slowly cooked in traditional brick and stone ovens, then shredded. They are fermented in wooden vats and twice distilled in copper stills. Finally, the tequila is bottled and labeled by hand.

During the aging process, Excellia uses vintage grand cru Sauternes wine casks that have been used for two or three years, imparting sweet and fruity notes to the tequila. They also use twenty-year-old cognac barrels that have been used for more than twenty years.

That makes Excellia tequila influenced by three different regions: Los Altos, with a rich clay soil that grows sweet and fruity agaves; the Sauternes region in France, where the grand cru wine casks are from; and the Cognac region of France, where the cognac casks are made.

Excellia offers the following expressions: Blanco rests for a few weeks, Reposado is aged for nine months, and Añejo rests for eighteen months.

EXCELLIA BLANCO

Excellia Blanco rests for a few weeks in grand cru Sauternes wine casks and cognac barrels. Clear in color, on the nose it presents aromas of roasted pineapple, guava, peppers, and honeycomb; on the palate, it gives herbaceous and citrus notes; and the finish is long and warm, with fig, nut, and tobacco hints. The ABV is 40%.

TEQUILA FORTALEZA

Tequila Fortaleza was launched in 2005, but its story goes back to the 1800s, beginning with Don Cenobio Sauza.

He founded his first distillery in 1873, La Perseverancia, in Tequila, Jalisco. He is recognized as the first to export mezcal de tequila to the US, the first to state that blue agave was the best for the production of tequila, the first to use steam to cook agave, and (possibly) the first to change the name of *vino de tequila* to just tequila. When he passed away, his son Eladio took over, founding the distillery La Constancia and then leaving the family business to his son Francisco Javier, who made the family's tequila, Sauza, well-known in the world. Don Javier also bought a piece of land in Tequila and started a small distillery that he called La Fortaleza.

Don Javier's family started to produce tequila at La Fortaleza with a small brick oven, a tahona pit, a few wood fermentation vats, and two small copper pot stills. But since the distillery wasn't producing much tequila, it was closed down and converted into a museum to show the traditional tequila-making process. Don Javier sold the business in 1976 but kept the land with the distillery. In 1999, Don Javier's son, Don Guillermo, decided to run the distillery again, and after several years of renovation, La Fortaleza resumed production, making tequila in the same way Don Cenobio used to make it. This tequila was named Los Abuelos (The Grandfathers), but due to trademark issues, he had to change it to Fortaleza (Fortitude), which was the name Don Javier gave to the distillery.

Fortaleza harvests blue agave in the Tequila Valley, allowing it to grow for eight years. The agave hearts are cooked in an old stone oven for thirty-six hours and then crushed by a tahona pulled by an electric tractor (which took the place of the family's mule after he died). The fermentation occurs in open-air tanks with natural yeast, without adding any sugars or chemicals, for about four days. The distillation takes place in traditional copper pot stills. The tequila is then aged in American oak barrels that are chipped and reburned multiple times, bottled in hand-blown bottles, and finished with a hand-painted agave piña stopper on top, in a small bottling station inside the distillery. Fortaleza's main expressions are Blanco, Blanco (still strength), Reposado (the aging statement is on the bottle), and Añejo (matured for 18 months).

FORTALEZA BLANCO

Fortaleza Blanco is a 100 percent blue agave, unaged tequila that can be enjoyed neat or on the rocks. Silvery clear, on the nose it offers aromas of citrus, rich cooked agave, butter, olive, and black pepper; on the palate, it presents citrus, cooked agave, vanilla, basil, olive, and lime flavors. The finish is long and deep. The ABV is 40%.

GRACIAS A DIOS MEZCAL

In 2010, Pablo López, Enrique Jiménez, and Xaime Niembro opened a *mezcalería* in Querétaro, Mexico. They sold mezcal from different maestros mezcaleros and regions from Oaxaca. But, two years later, during a tour in the Oaxacan region, they met Oscar Hernández, a fourth-generation maestro mezcalero and magueyero, and together they founded Gracias a Dios (Thank God).

Oscar Hernández was born in Matatlán and learned how to make mezcal from his mother when he was fourteen years old. The distillery is located in Santiago Matatlán. At Gracias a Dios, they cultivate agave espadín in a greenhouse, growing it for two years before moving it into the fields. Once the plant is harvested, the agave hearts are removed and cut into four sections, then cooked for four days in a conical oven. The grinding process is carried out by a tahona turned by La Gaviota, a mare who lives at the distillery. The fermentation and distillation are overseen by Hernández. The fermentation takes place in 1,000-liter pine tubs with wild yeast, for ten to fifteen days. A double distillation happens in a 250-liter copper alembic still. The labeling and bottling are carried out by the Shin Dobb cooperative.

The main expressions are:

- Espadín, which can be found both as Blanco and Reposado, and is aged for three months in new American oak barrels.

- Tobalá, with its vegetal and aromatic notes.

- Cuishe, with clove, white pepper, cinnamon, and apple flavor.

- Tepeztate, which has mineral, lime, and dried fruit notes.

- Mexicano, with a predominant tobacco aroma.

- Cupreata, with notes of citrus and spice.

They also offer limited and special editions, such as:

- Arroqueño, which has herbal and fruit notes.

- Madrecuishe, with a predominant herbal character.

- Mezcal de Pechuga, made with local fruits, such as banana, apple, pineapple, and raisins.

At Gracias a Dios, they ecologically manage the land and replant agaves. They are 100 percent powered by solar panels, and 60 percent of the water comes from rain. Buildings are constructed with adobe bricks, using leftover maguey from the mezcal process. They also plant around 3,000 trees every year.

GRACIAS A DIOS ESPADÍN BLANCO

This is an unaged mezcal made with 100 percent artisanal, handmade espadín agave, and it is twice distilled in copper stills. The nose presents a light smoke balanced with an herbal character and bell pepper; on the palate, it is very fresh and mild, with herbal notes such as lemongrass and cooked agave; and the finish is dry and spiced (anise, ginger, and salty caramel). The ABV is 45%.

G4 TEQUILA

G4 Tequila was founded by Felipe Camarena, after he had worked most of his life at the family's distillery La Alteña in Arandas, Jalisco. Felipe decided to open his own distillery in 2007. Work finished in 2011, creating El Pandillo (named after Felipe's grandfather's favorite bull), where the old tahona stone from the family distillery, which burned during the Mexican Revolution, is displayed. Today, he runs the distillery with his sons, Luis and Alan. They wanted to honor the history of their family, which started to produce mezcal in 1937, by naming the company G4 after the fourth generation of master distillers.

G4 Tequila has won several awards, such as the platinum medal for Añejo and Extra Añejo and the gold for Reposado and Blanco at the Global Spirits Awards in 2022.

At El Pandillo in Arandas, they use 100 percent blue Weber agave. The agave hearts are cooked for twenty-two hours in traditional stone ovens, which have been modified by placing steam jets at the bottom and top of the oven so the agave can be cooked evenly. Then the agave hearts are crushed by Igor, a mechanical shredder hand built by Felipe, with special steel blades that can grind large agaves quickly to lower the operating costs. After being shredded, the agave passes by Frankenstein, a mechanical tahona. Then, before the distillation, the fermented agave obtained from the natural fermentation is left to sit in warming tanks, allowing it to preheat for a faster distillation. The distillation takes place in traditional copper stills with 50 percent harvested rainwater and 50 percent natural spring water. Finally, the tequila is placed in bourbon barrels to mature.

Besides the special editions, G4 Tequila's main expressions are:

- Blanco: the unaged expression, bottled straight after the distillation.

- Reposado: aged for at least six months.

- Añejo: matured for eighteen months in American oak bourbon barrels.

- Extra Añejo: aged for three years in old Tennessee whiskey barrels.

- Blanco 108: high-proof unaged Blanco.

The Camarenas are very attentive to the environment and practice sustainable methods. They only use natural ingredients and no chemicals or anything artificial. El Pandillo's roof is a rainwater collection system that leads to a 200,000-liter underground storage tank. This allows the family to use rainwater alongside spring water for their production. They also plant cinnamon trees, strawberry guava trees, fig trees, and citrus trees to attract birds, so they will pollinate the surrounding agave fields. Finally, they use the vinaza (tequila production toxic waste) to fertilize the soil. Since it is a toxic substance, the family adds calcium carbonate to bring the alkaline level to normal before use.

G4 TEQUILA REPOSADO

G4 Tequila Reposado is aged for at least six months in old George Dickel Tennessee whiskey barrels. Light amber in color, it presents notes of cooked agave and black pepper on the nose; on the palate, it offers light notes of pepper and licorice, with a light and warm finish. The ABV is 40%.

CASA HERRADURA

Casa Herradura produces Tequila Herradura and El Jimador (1994), as well as Antiguo de Herradura, Don Eduardo, Hacienda del Cristero, Pepe Lopez Tequila, Gran Imperio, and Suave 35.

Their story begins with Félix López, who worked as a distillery administrator at the Hacienda de Padres for Josefa Zalazar and her sons in Amatitán, Jalisco. In 1870, López took over the distillery and the agave fields and registered them as Hacienda San José del Refugio. With his wife, Carmen Rosales, he modernized the production of tequila and the facility, which remained in use until 1963.

When he died in 1878, his wife and her brother, Ambrosio Rosales, took over the business, until it was inherited by López and Carmen's sons, Aurelio and María de Jesús. Aurelio decided to change the name to Herradura, meaning "horseshoe," because, it is said, he found a horseshoe on the property and kept it as a sign of good luck.

During the Cristero War (in the 1920s), both Aurelio and María de Jesús, who were sympathizers with the rebels that fought against the restrictions imposed by the Mexican government, had to escape. The distillery passed to the siblings' cousin, David Rosales, who, in 1928, registered the Herradura brand in Mexico City, with a horseshoe as its logo. In 1960, Doña Gabriela de la Peña and her sons, Pablo and Guillermo Romo, took over the family business. They transformed the distillery into a museum and built a new, modernized distillery on-site in 1963. Under Doña Gabriela's supervision, Herradura claimed to be the pioneer of the first Reposado in 1974 and the first Extra Añejo in 1995.

In 2007, Casa Herradura was sold to the US-based company Brown-Forman and was also named Best Distillery of 2007 by *Wine Enthusiast* magazine.

At Casa Herradura, they use waste agave fibers to improve the soil and biogas to supplement the oil-powered boilers. They are reducing their environmental footprint and have adopted sustainable practices such as minimizing waste, purifying water, and maximizing energy efficiency. In 2015, they received the Environmental Excellence Award from Mexico's Federal Attorney for Environmental Protection (PROFEPA), and, since the area surrounding Casa Herradura has been designated a UNESCO World Heritage Site, they introduced sustainable and environmentally sound practices.

TEQUILA HERRADURA

Today Tequila Herradura is sold in 136 countries in Europe, South America, North America, and Asia.

Encompassing all the tequila produced at Casa Herradura, Tequila Herradura is made with 100 percent blue agave harvested by hand in Amatitán, Jalisco, where they have an herbaceous and spicy aroma, but also in the highlands, where they are more floral and sweet. (Casa Herradura keeps its fields full with more than twenty-five million agave plants.) The agave hearts are cooked in traditional brick ovens for twenty-six hours, cooled down for twenty-four hours, and then crushed by a mill. The fermentation, occurring in open stainless-steel tanks, relies on airborne wild yeast coming from different species of fruit and citrus trees growing on the property. Fermentation lasts for seventy-two hours in summer and seven to eight days in winter. The distillation takes place in stainless-steel pot stills at low temperatures for up to nine hours. The aging process occurs in charred American white oak barrels made by the Brown-Forman Cooperage and stored lying on their sides in warehouses. Finally, the tequila is bottled on-site, and the horseshoe is applied by hand on every bottle.

Tequila Herradura Reposado

Tequila Herradura offers the following main expressions:

- Silver: rested for forty-five days before bottling; winner of thirty-one competitions and nine golds (since 2006), such as the Fifty Best gold medal.

- Reposado: aged for eleven months (longer than the industry standard).

- Añejo: matured in American white oak barrels for twenty-five months (thirteen months more than the standard).

- Ultra: Añejo tequila in which a hint of pure agave is added and then filtered to remove the color and highlight the smoothness.

- Double Barrel Reposado: aged in charred American white oak barrels for eleven months, then moved into new charred barrels for a further thirty days.

- Selección Suprema: ultra-rested Extra Añejo matured in American white oak barrels for forty-nine months.

- Legend: Añejo tequila matured in heavily charred, new American white oak barrels for twelve months.

TEQUILA HERRADURA REPOSADO

Introduced in 1974, Tequila Herradura Reposado is aged for eleven months in charred American white oak barrels.

Amber in color, it presents aromas of toffee and spices such as cinnamon on the nose, and it offers flavors of cooked agave, vanilla, and butter on the palate. The finish is sweet, with a hint of spice. The ABV is 40%.

EL JIMADOR TEQUILA

El Jimador was founded by Pablo and Josè Guillermo Romo de la Peña, owners of Grupo Industrial Herradura, and it was named to honor the hard work of the farmers who harvest the agave plants.

The blue agave plants are hand harvested and cut by *jimadores*, using a *coa* (a long, sharp knife). After the agave hearts are slowly crushed, the fermentation occurs in open-air tanks with wild yeast floating on the property, and the double distillation takes place in a column still. Finally, the tequila is aged in American white oak barrels.

El Jimador offers the following expressions:

- Silver: bottled straight after the distillation, and winner of more than twenty-two awards since 2010, including the silver medal in the San Francisco World Spirits Competition in 2013.

- Reposado: aged for two months.

- Añejo: matured in American oak barrels for twelve months, and winner of more than thirty-one awards since 2010, including the gold medal for Spirit of the Americas in 2014.

- Premium Malt Beverage: El Jimador's mixed cocktails line. All tequila based, they are Lime Margarita, Grapefruit Paloma, Piña Coconut Margarita, and Orange Sunrise.

EL JIMADOR REPOSADO

Winner of the double gold medal at the San Francisco World Spirits Competition in 2012, and winner of over twenty-five awards since 2010, El Jimador Reposado is aged for two months in handmade American oak barrels.

Golden in color, it presents aromas of vanilla, toasted wood, fruits, and spices on the nose, and it offers spice, fruit, wood, vanilla, and toasted hazelnut flavors on the palate. The finish is long and warm, with vanilla hints and a subtle spice note. The ABV is 40%.

ILEGAL MEZCAL

Ilegal was founded by New York–born John Rexer in 2006, but its story started in 2004. At that time, Rexer, who had moved to Guatemala, was the owner of Café No Sé, a bar in Antigua, and he used to smuggle unbranded mezcal from several villages in Oaxaca, such as Tlacolula de Matamoros, San Lorenzo, Villa Sola de Vega, Santa Catarina Minas, Hierve el Agua, and Santiago Matatlán. To avoid having to smuggle mezcal across the border, he eventually decided to distill his own mezcal; hence, Ilegal. In 2016, Ilegal Mezcal sold a minority stake to Bacardi, which made it possible for Ilegal to distribute in the US.

Ilegal distills its mezcal in Santiago Matatlán Valley in Oaxaca and is made from sustainable raw materials and processes.

At Ilegal, they use agave espadín, which is cooked with mesquite and eucalyptus wood, then ground with a horse-drawn tahona. The natural fermentation takes place in pine vats for around seven to ten days.

Ilegal Mezcal is distilled in small batches, and each bottle is hand corked, labeled, and numbered. The mezcaleros never cook and distill at the same time, so that they can maintain the light smoke in Ilegal's flavor profile.

Ilegal Mezcal offers three different expressions:

- Joven: bottled without being aged.

- Reposado: matured in a combination of used and new American oak, medium-char barrels for six months.

- Añejo: aged for thirteen months in a mix of new and used American oak, medium-char barrels. All their barrels come from a family-run business, Kelvin Cooperage, which has operated since 1963.

Ilegal has also partnered with Bronx Brewery to create a new kind of hard seltzer, Side Hustle Seltzerita. It is aged using Ilegal Mezcal oak staves, and it's bursting with grapefruit, mezcal flavor, and lime.

Ilegal is 100 percent natural, with no artificial colors, yeasts, flavors, or additives used during the process of making the mezcal. Wastewater is treated and then reused for distillation, and the agave fiber waste is transformed into adobe-style bricks used at the distillery.

To reduce the impacts of deforestation, all the wood used by Ilegal comes from certified farmers. Since 2022, due to the recent global glass shortage, Ilegal has started to use recycled bottles. They are all made by a family-run company, Fusión y Formas, that recycles 10,000 tons of glass each year at its facility in Jalisco. The company emits fewer CO_2 emissions and saves energy during the smelting process.

Ilegal also supports several organizations and communities that deal with climate change issues, immigration, the refugee crisis, gender discrimination, racism, and xenophobia.

Ilegal Joven

ILEGAL JOVEN

Ilegal Joven is an unaged mezcal made with 100 percent espadín agave. On the nose, it has the distinctive flavor of roasted agave and earthy tones. On the palate, it has a complex herbal character, such as eucalyptus, followed by caramel and raisin flavors, with a hint of black pepper. The finish is floral and lightly smoky. The ABV is 40%.

LOS DANZANTES (LOS NAHUALES)

Twin brothers Jaime and Gustavo Muñoz were the owners of Los Danzantes restaurant in Coyoacán (nowadays they own five restaurants), wanting to showcase the quality of fine Mexican cuisine through the best food and the best tequilas. In 1996, they went to Jalisco to find a product to sell at their restaurant, but they couldn't find anything they were both happy with. So they headed to Oaxaca instead, and in 1997 they purchased a distillery and began to distill their own mezcal, Los Danzantes (Los Nahuales in the US, due to a trademark issue with the Danzantes name). In the beginning, they meant to supply only their restaurants, but due to growing demand, they ended up producing both for local and international markets.

In 1999, Los Danzantes opened Mezcal Alipús, and it has bottled Mezcalero since 2009. In 2004, Hector Vasquez de Abarca started to run the Los Danzantes distillery, developing a blend of traditional production methods and modern distilling innovations. For example, while studying chemistry, he realized that the wood-fired stills at the distillery could be changed to gas to maximize control of the process. When he moved to Italy, Karina Abad Rojas, a trained chemist, took over the management position.

In 2013, the distillery was awarded the annual National Quality Award by the president of Mexico, Enrique Peña Nieto.

Los Danzantes Joven

Los Danzantes has its own laboratory to carry out experimental productions, without abandoning traditional and artisanal methods.

MEZCAL LOS DANZANTES (LOS NAHUALES)

This distillery is located in Santiago Matatlán, Tlacolula de Matamoros, Oaxaca, and combines traditional methods with a modern technical approach.

Agave is purchased from growers in the region; Los Danzantes works primarily with espadín and tobalá. The agave hearts are cooked in a conical wood-fired oven underground with white oak for three days, then crushed with a tahona pulled by a horse named Sansón. The fermentation occurs in open-air pine vats with natural yeast for six days, and the distillation takes place in small copper pot stills. Finally, the mezcal is bottled by hand (machine bottling is avoided).

The Los Danzantes' classic expressions are Joven, Reposado (rested in American and French white oak barrels for nine months), and Añejo (rested for sixteen months). They are all made with 100 percent espadín agave, cultivated in the region of the Valley and the Sierra Norte of Oaxaca, and produced by mezcalera Karina Abad Rojas.

Then, depending on the availability of agaves, Los Danzantes offers limited editions:

- Joven Tobalá: agaves are cooked with white encino (holm oak) and mesquite, then fermented for five days.

- Joven Arroqueño: agaves grow in Miahuatlán de Porfirio Díaz, Oaxaca, and are cooked with white encino and mesquite, then fermented for six days.

- Joven Sierra Negra: agaves from San Juan Lajarcia, Yautepec, Oaxaca, is cooked with encino and mesquite, then fermented for six days.

- Pechuga: made with espadín. During the third distillation, seasonal regional fruits and a chicken breast from the ranch are added, and finally, it is stained with Grana Cochinilla (*Dactylopius coccus*—an insect used to color food and drinks).

- Still Proof: espadín agave is cooked with white oak, fermented for six days, and aged in glass.

- Joven Coyote: agave is cultivated in the Río Flor in Zimatlán de Álvarez, Oaxaca, then fermented for eight days.

- Reposado: made with espadín harvested in Oaxaca. Fermented for six days and rested in American oak and French oak barrels for nine months.

- Anejo: made with espadín harvested in Oaxaca, fermented for six days and aged in American and French oak barrels for sixteen months.

Since 2014, Los Danzantes has been running the Proyecto Maguey, or Maguey Project, alongside the Centro de Investigación Científica de Yucatán (CICY) and the University of Chapingo, which aims at helping the reproduction of wild agaves by planting natural germplasm plants.

LOS DANZANTES JOVEN ESPADÍN

Made with 100 percent espadín agave, Los Danzantes Joven Espadín is fermented for six days in 800-liter wooden vats with native yeasts, then double distilled in 250-liter copper stills. It is clear in color, and, on the nose, the aroma is cooked agave and a mix of green herbs; on the palate, it presents flavors of fresh fruit, green herbs, and cooked agave. The finish is long, with wood and smoke notes. The ABV is 47%.

MEZCAL ALIPÚS

Alipús was born in 1999 from the Los Danzantes distillery. Don Joel Antonio Cruz and his sons were the first producers, in San Juan del Río. Today, Alipús works with several Oaxacan families from six different regions: San Juan del Río, Santa Ana del Río, San Baltazar Guélavila, San Andrés Miahuatlán, San Luis del Río, and San Miguel. The mezcals are then bottled at Los Danzantes in Santiago Matatlán.

In 2004, Jaime Muñoz from Los Danzantes met Ansley Coale, cofounder of Germain-Robin and founder of Craft Distillers, who later would be the one to import Alipús in the US.

Alipús was born with the intent to provide small distilleries with a wider market, so they could stay in business.

The agaves used in Alipús typically come from each producer family's own plantings. To be considered Alipús mezcal, the product needs to be artisanal or ancestral and come from 100 percent agave. Each palenque has its own method, but generally, the agave hearts are cooked in below-ground ovens, crushed with horse-drawn wheels on a stone floor, fermented slowly in open wooden vats using native yeasts, and double distilled in small wood-fired copper pot stills or clay pot stills. Each edition takes its name from the village in which it is distilled and reflects the characteristics of the terroir.

Alipús' main expressions are:

- Alipús San Juan: produced by the Joel Antonio Cruz family since 2000 and by Don Rodolfo Juan Juárez since 2013 in San Juan del Río, Oaxaca, it is made from nonirrigated, 100 percent espadín by Don Joel Antonio Cruz and his family. It is cooked with mesquite wood, fermented in pine vats, and twice distilled in copper pot stills by Don Rodolfo

Juan Juárez in the Cruz family distillery along the river from agave growing at 4,600 feet (1,400 meters) in iron-rich soil.

- Alipús Santa Ana: made by the Hernandez Melchor family since 2001 in Santa Ana del Río, Oaxaca, it is fermented in slender pine vats from agave espadín growing at 4,000 feet (1,219 meters) in mountainous, sandy soil.

- Alipús San Baltazar: produced by Don Cosme Hernandez and his son Cirilo since 2007 in San Baltazar Guélavila, Oaxaca, it is fermented in very old pine vats from agave espadín growing at 4,100 feet (1,250 meters) in rocky soil.

- Alipús San Andrés: made by Don Valente Ángel García Juárez since 2009 and also by Don Atanasio Aragón Martínez since 2018 in San Andrés Miahuatlán, Oaxaca, it is distilled in cypress vats from agave espadín growing at 5,000 feet (1,500 meters) in ferriferous, or iron-rich, soil, but the local practice is to also add agave madrecuishe in the roasting process.

- Alipús San Luis: produced by Don Baltazar Cruz Gómez since 2014 in San Luis del Río, Oaxaca, it is fermented in pine vats from agave espadín growing at 4,100 feet (1,250 meters) in sandy soil.

- Alipús San Miguel: made by Tío Jesús Ríos, Tío Leonardo Rojas, and Tío Félix García since 2013 in El Potrero, Sola de Vega, Oaxaca.

As part of Los Danzantes, Alipús is also part of the Proyecto Maguey, or Maguey Project, launched in 2012 to help the preservation and reproduction of wild agave. Los Danzantes and craft distillers take lower-than-normal markups so that the distillers they work with can be better paid.

Alipús San Miguel Sola by Tío Jesús Ríos

ALIPÚS SAN MIGUEL SOLA BY TÍO JESÚS RÍOS

Alipús San Miguel Sola by Tío Jesús Ríos is produced in El Potrero, Sola de Vega, Oaxaca, from 80 percent agave espadín and 20 percent semiwild arroqueño that grows at 3,200 feet (970 meters) in ferriferous soil. The agave hearts are crushed by hand in an oak canoa (type of vat used to crush the agave hearts) and fermented in oak vats. It's distilled in small clay pot stills.

Clear in color, Alipús San Miguel Sola by Tío Jesús Ríos presents smoky aromas, together with tobacco and cocoa notes, on the nose; on the palate, it offers flavors of tropical fruit, pepper, and citrus. The finish has fruity and earthy notes. The ABV is 47.5%

MEZCALERO MEZCAL

Mezcalero was founded as a collaboration between Ansley Coale of Craft Distillers, the Los Danzantes distillery, and a handful of individual artisan distillers in 2009.

Each batch is often only composed of 800 to 1,000 bottles. That's because Mezcalero wants to preserve the work of individual artisan distillers who are located in remote villages and run tiny palenques.

Mezcalero produces mezcal with traditional techniques. They cook agave hearts in open firepits and crush them with long-handled wooden mallets. Then they ferment in small wooden vats with native yeast, and double distill in small pot stills made from copper or clay. Finally, the mezcal is delivered to the Los Danzantes distillery, where it is bottled. Mezcalero mezcales are numbered, and the labels specify the agaves, the distiller, and the number of bottles in the batch.

Mezcalero distills agaves that are at least 50 percent wild or semiwild, such as arroqueño, bicuishe, madrecuishe, dobadàn, sierra negra, tepeztate, papalote, Mexicano, and tobalá. These kinds of agaves require a lot of work for harvesting.

The current five expressions from Mezcalero are:

- Mezcalero No. 25: released in 2021, it is made with wild tobalá and was distilled in 2013 by Don Cosme Hernandez and his son Cirilo of San Baltazar Guélavila.

- Mezcalero No. 26: released in 2022 by Don Valente Ángel Garcia in Santa Maria la Pila and distilled in 2018 from agave arroqueño.

- Mezcalero No. 27: made from wild jabalí, tepeztate, and cultivated espadín, it was distilled in 2019 by Rodolfo Juan Juárez in San Juan del Río and released in 2022.

- Mezcalero No. 28: made from wild bicuishe, semiwild madrecuishe, wild Mexicano, and cultivated espadín, it was released in 2017 and hand distilled in 2013 by Don Valente Ángel Garcia in Santa Maria la Pila in Miahuatlán. It is aged five years in glass.

- Mezcalero No. 29: released in 2022 and hand distilled in 2019 by Octavio Jiménez Méndez in Santiago Matatlán from wild tepeztate.

MEZCALERO NO. 26

Hand distilled in April 2010 from agave arroqueño by Don Valente Ángel Garcia in Santa Maria la Pila, Mezcalero No. 26 has a clean and distinct flavor, thanks to the intensity and minerality coming from the ferriferous clay soils in Miahuatlán. In total, 960 bottles of No. 26 have been released, with an ABV of 47%.

Mezcalero No. 26

LA ALTEÑA

La Alteña was founded by Don Felipe Camarena Hernández. His family had distilled tequila since the early 1800s, but during the Mexican Revolution, their distillery was destroyed, so the family abandoned it. Growing up, Don Felipe kept growing and selling agave to other distilleries, until in 1937 he opened La Alteña distillery in the highlands of Los Altos, close to Arandas. In 1940, he started selling tequila made from 100 percent blue agave, with the name Tapatío. Eventually, Don Felipe passed the business to his son, Felipe J. Camarena Orozco, and from him it was passed to his daughters, Lilianna and Gabriela, and his son, Carlos, who is now a third-generation tequilero and master distiller.

In 1990, Carlos Hernández launched El Tesoro de Don Felipe, designed for international markets. In 2008, he founded Tequila Ocho with Tomas Estes to highlight the importance of terroir in tequila, but in 2021, Tequila Ocho's production was moved to the Los Alambiques distillery.

At the distillery, they still use the same old production method the Camarena family used for centuries: traditional brick ovens, a tahona to crush the agave hearts (in the case of El Tesoro), wood fermentation vats, and small copper stills.

La Alteña was one of the early participants in the Bat Friendly Project, which aims to reintroduce genetic diversity into blue agave. The idea is that bats will help cross-pollinate the plants, reintroducing genetic diversity.

All of La Alteña's organic waste, such as the pulp from the cooked agave and the weeds growing during the rainy season, is used for compost. The water used in the production is also recycled. In the field, they use only natural herbicides, fertilizers, and biological pest control.

TEQUI
CAP. 920

TEQUILA TAPATÍO

Today, Tapatío is still owned by the Camarena family. The tequila is made through the artisanal, handmade process. Gabriela Flores, head of hospitality at La Alteña, explained during my visit to the distillery that they harvest their agaves from a red soil which "is full of iron and calcium that help the agave develop different characteristics, compared to the one that grows in the valley. Fruity, floral, herbal, and spiciness are the four characteristics that agave can have when we talk about flavors and aromas. It depends on the characteristic of the soil which flavor and aroma characteristics the agave will develop more. Here in the red soil, we have more floral and fruitier notes. It will be with less fiber and juicier, and sweeter."

The agave hearts are cooked in a brick oven for forty-eight hours, and they rest for a further twenty-four hours. "In here, as we are having a slow cooking process, flavors will develop more. Some flavors and aromas come from the bricks and the flames, like some earthiness and minerality," Gabriela said.

Then the agave hearts are grounded mechanically, fermented in open-air oakwood and pinewood vats with fibers, and double distilled. The tequila is filtered to get rid of any impurities, then bottled and labeled by hand.

Tapatío has won several awards, such as Best Tequila at the Bartender's Best Awards in 2014 and Tequila of the Year at the *Drink Me* Magazine Elite competition in 2014.

Tapatío expressions are the following:

- Tapatío Blanco: bottled straightaway, at 40% ABV.

- Tapatío Blanco 110: distilled at 55% ABV, the maximum alcohol content allowed by regulations.

- Tapatío Reposado: aged for four to six months in American white oak barrels, previously used in aging bourbon.

- Tapatío Añejo: aged for eighteen months in American white oak barrels, previously used in aging whiskey.

- Tapatío Excelencia: aged for four years in first-use deep-charred American white oak barrels.

TAPATÍO BLANCO

Using 100 percent Weber agave, the agave hearts are cooked in brick ovens and then ground with a roller mill. The fermentation occurs in open-air wood vats, and the double distillation takes place in a copper pot still. Bright crystalline in color, it has raw agave, white pepper, citrus, and mint aromas on the nose. It presents cooked agave, pepper, and spice (anise and cinnamon) notes on the palate. The finish is long and spicy. The ABV is 40%.

Tapatío Blanco

Q & A WITH GABRIELA FLORES,
HEAD OF HOSPITALITY AT LA ALTEÑA

Who is Tapatío?

This is a family-operated business; we are currently on the fourth generation of Camarenas at La Alteña, but it is also not only our family—many of the workers here are also the third or fourth generation of their own families working here. We believe the fact that people who have been working here before keep bringing their family members must say something good about the environment and the company. They are no longer just workers in the distillery; they are part of our Alteña family.

How do you choose the type of agave you use?

There are more than two hundred species of agaves in Mexico, but by law, we are only allowed to use the variety blue Tequilana Weber (or as we know it, blue agave) to produce tequila.

Nowadays it takes blue agave around five years to reach maturity; it used to take from ten to twelve years (we believe this has been changing because of climate change and because agave has been forced to mature faster because people have been harvesting it younger each time).

We are using only agave that is completely mature, and that would be from six to eight years. The reason we choose mature agave is because it will develop more sugar and some acidity that is going to help us develop more complex flavors and aromas, and not just alcohol.

How can the terroir influence the production of tequila?
And does it affect the flavor of a singular batch?

A lot! Agave is just like any other crop: the soil, the weather, altitude, water, etc., are going to influence the way agave is going to express itself. Flavors, aromas, and textures may change, depending on where and how that agave grew.

Is there anything that makes your production different from others?

Absolutely. We take our time making tequila; we don't like to cut corners or accelerate the process just to have faster production. What we are looking for is to keep our quality and to do things by the heart, and not just for money.

What do you think about using tequila in cocktails?

I'm okay with that! There are many good cocktails, but it depends on the profile of each tequila brand on which kind of cocktail is the right one.

What is the proper way to drink tequila?

What I like to say is that the best way to drink tequila is the way that you enjoy it the most. I personally like to drink it neat and very slowly and at room temperature, because I like to find everything that the agave has to show me. I would recommend not to drink it by shooting it with lime and salt, because that only hides the flavor and aromas. But again, that is up to you.

What do you think were the main factors that contributed to the tequila boom?

I believe that people were interested in knowing what they were consuming. There used to be a belief that tequila was not a good product and it lacked quality, but that is not true; tequila is the most regulated spirit in the world, and is such a complex spirit because of its main ingredient that naturally is never going to be exactly the same. Each time you try tequila, you are going to find something new. You may like it or not, but it's worth trying it.

How do you see tequila growing in the next few years?

Hopefully it will keep growing, but something I perceive as more important is that people are not only drinking more tequila, they are also consuming information; they are learning about the processes, the quality, and the whole industry, and they are liking it.

Can you tell us about any initiatives or efforts being taken to reduce the environmental impact of tequila production?

Sure! The one that I find most interesting and important at the moment is the Bat Friendly Project, a project created by the UNAM, in which we are trying to save two different species: the bats that pollinate agaves, whose population has been reduced because of lack of food (agave flowers); and the blue agave that has lost most of its genetic diversity because of the main propagation way that has been used for decades to avoid pollination, making the agave more susceptible to plagues or diseases.

This project is promoting bat-friendly practices in agave propagation by allowing 5 percent of the agave population to flower, to ensure there is food for the nectar-feeding bats, causing at the same time the pollination that will help increase the genetic strength and diversity of the agaves.

EL TESORO

Robert Denton used to be the importer of Chinaco Tequila in the US, but when the distillery closed down, he went to Jalisco to look for a high-quality tequila to import. So he headed to the Camarena family, but he didn't like Tapatío because he believed the brand would have been unattractive for the US market—plus there was no translation for the name, and it would be mispronounced. Therefore, in 1988, Felipe J. Camarena offered to create a new brand for the US and called it El Tesoro de Don Felipe. It officially launched in 1990.

Denton's was a small company, so at the beginning, the new brand only produced a few cases and it was only exported. But when the production increased, Denton got a distribution contract with Jim Beam bourbon, which eventually bought Denton's ownership and become the importer, distributor, and partner of El Tesoro. Today, Jim Beam owns El Tesoro, but the Camarena family is the sole producer of the brand, according to the K & L Spirits Journal website.

El Tesoro has won several awards, such as the double gold medal at the San Francisco World Spirits Competition in 2021.

El Tesoro produces its tequila through traditional methods. The agave grows on the Camarena family estate, and they use only 100 percent blue agave. They slowly cook the agave in brick ovens, then crush it using a two-ton volcanic stone tahona. The fermentation occurs in open-air pine and oak vats where the pulp and fibers are put together, rather than being separated. The double distillation takes place in small copper pot stills. El Tesoro is double distilled to proof to avoid watering down the agave flavor. Finally, the tequila undergoes a simple cellulose filtration, then is bottled and labeled by hand.

El Tesoro's main expressions are:

- Blanco: bottled immediately after the distillation.

- Reposado: aged in former bourbon barrels for nine to eleven months.

- Añejo: aged in former bourbon barrels for two to three years.

- Extra Añejo: slowly aged in former bourbon barrels for four to five years.

- Paradiso: an Extra Añejo tequila, slowly aged for five years in former cognac barrels and created by Don Felipe Camarena in collaboration with Alain Royer of A. de Fussigny Cognac.

- Single Barrel: handpicked by Carlos Camarena to create a unique selection of products, each one influenced by the particular combination of the season in which the agave is harvested and the cellar location where the tequila ages.

- El Tesoro 85th Anniversary Edition: Gabriela Flores said, "Last year we turned eighty-five years old! We just released the El Tesoro 85th Anniversary Edition. It's going to be a limited edition; it is already out and is worth it to try it. It is a three-year-old Extra Añejo aged in Booker's Bourbon thirtieth-anniversary barrels, so it is something."

- El Tesoro Mundial Collection: a limited-edition series created by master distiller Carlos Camarena to celebrate the craftsmanship behind El Tesoro. For this collection, El Tesoro partnered with renowned distilleries from around the world.

El Tesoro Añejo

EL TESORO AÑEJO

El Tesoro Añejo is the winner of several awards, such as the double gold medal at the San Francisco World Spirits Competition in 2021. It received 94 points at the Ultimate Spirits Challenge in 2021. It is slowly aged for two to three years in American oak bourbon barrels.

Gold in color, El Tesoro Añejo presents floral jasmine and oaky notes on the nose and sweet agave, pepper, oak, and floral flavors on the palate. The finish has light green and vanilla hints. The ABV is 40%.

LA ROJEÑA

In 1758, José Antonio de Cuervo y Valdés y García de las Rivas obtained a landownership decree that recognized him as the owner of the *"Solar de las Ánimas,"* where he could cultivate agave and start the production of tequila.

His older son, José Prudencio de Cuervo y Montaño, acquired the land through small purchases and expanded their production.

In 1795, José María Guadalupe de Cuervo y Montaño, the youngest son, obtained from the king of Spain the authorization to distribute mezcal wine in Mexico and the Royal Certificate. He also built the first distillery, named Taberna de José Cuervo.

Later on, María Magdalena de Cuervo y Carrillo, inheriting La Taberna and other properties in Tequila, married José Vicente Albino Rojas y Jiménez, who became the manager of the estate and changed the name of La Taberna to La Rojeña (1812).

During the second half of the 1800s, La Rojeña started to export its products to San Francisco. At that time, Jesús Flores y Ponce became the distillery administrator, and after María Magdalena de Cuervo's and José Vicente Albino's deaths, he became the owner of the entire estate, buying the agave field, the ranches, and the distillery. He also began packing the tequila in glass bottles instead of the traditional barrels and changed the distillery's name to La Constancia.

His second wife, Ana González-Rubio, inherited the business after he died. She married José Cuervo Labastida y Flores, who was, at the time, the manager of La Constancia. Together, they sponsored several community initiatives, such as providing running water to houses and repairing schools. They also recovered the original name of the distillery, La Rojeña, and registered Jose Cuervo as a trademark.

After José Cuervo Labastida died (1921), Ana González-Rubio invited her sister's daughter, Guadalupe Gallardo, to live with her and help her in the business. When Ana González-Rubio died in 1940, her niece inherited La Rojeña.

Guadalupe Gallardo invited her sister, Virginia Gallardo, who prematurely lost her husband, Juan Beckmann y Wilkens, to live with her in Tequila.

Juan Beckmann Gallardo, one of Virginia's children, started to work at the distillery at a very young age (at the time Guillermo Freytag Schreir, Guadalupe's sister's husband, was put in charge of the distillery) and later on was sent to Tijuana to promote exports in the US market. He also inherited the family business after Guadalupe Gallardo died in 1964.

Juan Beckmann Gallardo's son, Juan Beckmann Vidal, introduced Reserva de la Familia tequila, and in 1996, his son, Juan Domingo Beckmann Legorreta, joined the company and started to run it in 2013.

Today, José Cuervo's descendants, the Beckmann family, still run the distillery where several brands are produced, such as Jose Cuervo, Maestro Dobel, and 1800 Tequila.

JOSE CUERVO

Jose Cuervo is one of the oldest family-owned distilleries in Mexico and harvests blue agave from Jalisco, Guanajuato, and Michoacán. To cook the agave, they use different methods—oven, autoclave, and diffuser. They distill in either pot or column stills and mature the tequila in barrels coming from World Cooperage in Napa, California. Water is added post-maturation to proof down the tequila, and the bottling takes place in Guadalajara.

Besides special and limited editions, Jose Cuervo offers the following main expressions:

- Tradicional Tequila: this line includes Plata (100 percent blue agave, unaged), Reposado (matured in oak barrels for a minimum of two months), Añejo (aged in charred American oak casks for at least one year and then finished in single malt Irish whiskey barrels), and Cristalino (Tradicional Reposado aged in new American oak and then blended with the Reserva de la Familia Extra Añejo, aged in French and American oak, and finally filtered to get a crystal-clear color and more intense flavor).

- Especial: this line includes Silver (unaged) and Gold (blend of young tequilas).

- Reserva de la Familia: ultra-premium, small batches of tequila made with the artisanal process, including Platino (unaged), Reposado (matured in heavily toasted American oak and then in a French Limousin oak cask), and Extra Añejo (aged in oak barrels for at least three years).

- Añejo Cristalino Organico: aged in American oak, finished in Pedro Ximénez sherry casks, and then filtered.

Jose Cuervo has been involved in sustainability and community projects for the last twenty-one years. In 2009, with the initiative the Agave Project, they started to use the fibers of agave as compost and create biodegradable, agave-based drinking straws (in partnership with BioSolutions Mexico and Penka) which allow the replacement of up to 30% of the plastic present in the straw. They also use agave by-products to create bricks and car parts.

They are currently working on a new project, the House that Tequila Made. Partnering with ITESO (Instituto Tecnológico y de Estudios Superiores de Occidente) University in Guadalajara, they are creating 100 percent sustainable houses for the people in Tequila.

JOSE CUERVO ESPECIAL GOLD

Jose Cuervo Especial Gold is made from a blend of Joven tequilas.

Gold in color, it presents spicy and sweet aromas, with baked agave and leather hints on the nose, and it offers vanilla, mixed spices, oak, cooked agave, and a subtle sweetness on the palate. The finish has hints of cinnamon, black pepper, and vanilla. The ABV is 40%.

MAESTRO DOBEL TEQUILA

Maestro Dobel was founded by eleventh-generation tequila producer Juan Domingo Beckmann Legorreta (Dobel is formed by the first syllables of Domingo Beckmann Legorreta) and Alex Coronado, technical director of Jose Cuervo, in 2008, with the idea of creating something new. That's why they came up with Maestro Dobel Diamante (or Diamond), the first-ever Cristalino tequila, and, in 2016, with the first smoked tequila, Humito.

Maestro Dobel tequila is made with single-estate 100 percent blue agave coming from the volcanic lowlands of the western state of Jalisco. The making of Maestro Dobel tequila starts with the agave hearts being cooked in steam ovens for thirty-six hours and then ground with a mill. The fermentation, in stainless-steel vats, uses a harvested and selected yeast developed in their laboratory, and the distillation takes place in copper alembic stills.

Maestro Dobel offers the following main expressions:

- Silver: unaged, bottled straight after the distillation.

- Reposado: aged for six months in new American white oak barrels.

- Añejo: matured in roasted white oak barrels.

- Diamante: made with 100 percent blue agave, a blend of Reposado, Añejo, and Extra Añejo tequilas. After being aged, it goes through a filtration process to remove the color, preserving the complexity and smoothness of the tequila.

- Humito: a silver tequila in which the agave is smoked with steamed mesquite during the cooking process.

- Pavito: distilled twice in a copper pot still, then for a third time with a fruit and spice maceration and a *pechuga* (chicken breast) placed on the top of the tank.

- 50 Cristalino: Extra Añejo aged in American and Eastern European oak barrels for a minimum of three years and filtered to remove the color.

MAESTRO DOBEL AÑEJO

Winner of Tequila of the Year at the 2020 Bartender Spirits Awards in San Francisco, Maestro Dobel Añejo has a dark amber color with a bright golden tone. On the nose, it presents aromas of wood, agave, and sweet notes, such as caramel, almond, and cinnamon, with hints of pineapple and apple. On the palate, it presents flavors of wood, nuts, and vanilla, together with agave and fruitiness. The finish is long, and the ABV is 40% (may vary to 38%, according to the market).

1800 TEQUILA

1800 Tequila takes its name from the first year, it is believed, tequila was aged in oak casks. It was founded by Juan Domingo Beckmann in 1975. 1800 Tequila won the silver medal (for Reposado and Cristalino) for the Best Agave/Tequila and the gold medal (for Añejo) at the 2021 New York International Spirits Awards Competition.

1800 Tequila is made with 100 percent blue agave, and the agave hearts are mainly steamed in stone ovens and ground with a roller mill. The fermentation occurs in stainless-steel vats and the distillation in copper pot stills and aged according to the expression. Both the bottle's triangular shape and the logo aim to symbolize the Mayan pyramids, while the initials JB printed on the label are meant to honor Juan Domingo Beckmann.

Besides the limited editions and the ready-to-serve margaritas, 1800 Tequila's main expressions are:

- Classic: Blanco, Reposado (a blend of silver tequilas aged in American and French oak barrels for at least six months), Añejo (aged for more than a year in American and French oak).

- Luxury: Cristalino (Añejo finished in port wine casks) and Milenio (Extra Añejo aged for a short period in French oak cognac barrels).

- Flavors: Coconut (100 percent blue agave silver tequila infused with natural coconut flavor) and Cucumber & Jalapeño (1800 Blanco infused with natural cucumber and jalapeño flavors).

1800 AÑEJO

1800 Añejo is made with 100 percent Weber Blue agave and aged in new American and French oak barrels for more than a year. Dark amber in color, it presents oaky vanilla notes on the nose; on the palate, it offers flavors of nuts and toffee; and the finish is peppery and spiced. The ABV is 38% (may vary).

CASA NOBLE TEQUILA

Casa Noble, which means both Noble House and House of Agave (the word *agave* comes from the Greek word for "noble"), is a relatively new brand, but its story dates back to the 1700s. Founded by master distiller Jose "Pepe" Hermosillo in 1997, Casa Noble is produced at La Cofradía distillery (just outside the town of Tequila), where at least forty brands are produced, such as Storywood Tequila.

Jose "Pepe" Hermosillo is a seventh-generation master distiller. His family bought an estate in Tequila in the 1700s and started to produce tequila.

Casa Noble has won numerous awards, such as the gold medal at the San Francisco World Spirits Competition in 2007 and 2009. Jose "Pepe" Hermosillo developed the Single Barrel category.

Casa Noble is made from estate-grown agaves that are harvested at high altitude. The hearts are slow cooked in traditional stone ovens for between thirty-six and thirty-eight hours, then milled using a proprietary corkscrew milling technique. The fermentation lasts five days and relies on native airborne yeast. The distillation is a triple distillation, done slowly in a pot still to maintain the best possible aromas and create a complex tequila. The maturation takes place in new, lightly toasted French oak barrels. Casa Noble was the first to use this kind of barrel for the aging process. In the end, each bottle is signed and numbered.

Casa Noble offers the following main expressions:

- Blanco: bottled straight after distillation.
- Reposado: matured in French white oak barrels for one year. The reposado barrels are used seven to eight times before being disposed of.
- Añejo: aged in French white oak barrels for two years.

Since 2009, Casa Noble Tequila has been certified organic by both the USDA and California Certified Organic Farmers (CCOF). It is also kosher certified and has been given Green Certification for its efforts in energy conservation, environmental awareness, and product integrity by the Mexican government.

Casa Noble has a composting program. All waste and used agave are converted into compost and used as a natural fertilizer. No chemicals are used, and the brand has zero spillage during production, meaning no product is ever wasted.

CASA NOBLE BLANCO

Triple distilled before being bottled, Casa Noble Blanco is made with 100 percent Weber blue agave. On the nose, it offers smoky, herbal, and citrus notes. On the palate, it presents flavors of honey and sweet cooked agave and a hint of citrus. The ABV is 40%.

STORYWOOD TEQUILA

Scottish-born Michael Ballantyne founded Storywood, after meeting master distiller Luis Trejo at the distillery La Cofradía in Jalisco. At the time, Ballantyne was spending time in Mexico and was starting to be intrigued by the flavor of tequila. But as a whisky lover, he was planning to open a whisky bar in San Miguel de Allende, Mexico, so he started to do some research. That was when he met Luis, whose distillery had been producing tequila for fifty years. Michael then decided to combine his experience in understanding oak aging flavor with Luis's experience in making the finest 100 percent blue agave.

Back in Scotland, with the idea of aging tequila in malt whisky casks, he started to work with Speyside Cooperage in Dufftown, which supplies all the barrels for Storywood Tequila. Those barrels are made of American oak and filled with bourbon in America, and then are sent to Scotland, where they are used for Scotch whisky. Then they are sent to Mexico, so Storywood tequila can be aged and bottled.

Michael Ballantyne explained, "Storywood is 100 percent Mexican made, created from a traditional production process and a creation of two minds (myself and master distiller Luis) and two cultures to create something special. The whole idea was to help consumers look past tequila being a shot and see it as how amazing it can be, enjoyed like a fine whisky. My intention from the very beginning was to stay true to tequila's roots, yet find a way to bridge the gap between two fantastic national spirits and combine them as one, to show people what can be done when you think a little different."

When Storywood was founded, none of the tequila on the market was ever fully matured in anything other than bourbon barrels. Storywood is the first to fully mature in upcycled, second-fill (bourbon first, whisky after), single malt whisky casks, as well as fully maturing in oloroso sherry casks. "We are of 1 percent of nearly 3,000 brands to create tequila from the ground up, rather than selecting 'preaged' tequila from a distillery that's already been created. We're very proud of that," Michael said.

All the expressions from Storywood have won multiple tasting awards, such as the gold at the International Spirits Challenge in 2020, double gold at the San Francisco World Spirits Competition in 2020, and the chairman's trophy at the Ultimate Spirits Challenge in 2021.

Storywood makes tequila from ten-year-old mature 100 percent blue agave, harvested from the lowland region of Jalisco. The agave hearts are cooked in traditional brick ovens for seventy-two hours and then crushed with a corkscrew mill. The fermentation occurs with the distillery's wild yeast strains, and the double distillation takes place in copper pot stills. The tequila is then aged in Speyside whisky barrels, which are quite sweet barrels to age with; hence, as Michael said, "We decided to use lowland agave to bring in the earthiness of the tequila with the sweeter barrel. Storywood was created to enhance the flavor of the agave rather than fully transform it."

Storywood focuses on the oak to bring a point of difference to their tequila. Michael explained, "All our tequila is 'fully matured' rather than 'finished' in our own casks. It's a lot longer process for us, rather than just buying off-the-shelf preaged tequila, but it really shows when you've tried it. Where Storywood is different is the quality of our wood and the flavor that it brings to the tequila. I personally select all the casks myself and am a part of the process from manufacturing to bottling. It must be perfect; otherwise it doesn't leave the distillery."

They offer the following expressions:

- Speyside 7 Reposado: aged for seven months in Speyside single malt whisky barrels.

- Speyside 14 Añejo: aged for fourteen months in Speyside single malt whisky barrels; limited release, bottled at cask strength.

- Speyside 7 CS Reposado: aged for over seven months in Scotch Speyside whisky barrels, and bottled at 53% ABV.

- Sherry 7 CS Reposado: aged in oloroso sherry (fortified wine) casks for seven months, with the barrels coming from Jerez, Spain.

- Añejo Double Oak CS: a 60/40 blend of Speyside and oloroso cask tequila, both fully matured for fourteen months and then blended together. "My love for Macallan whisky was really the inspiration for the Oloroso Limited Releases," Michael said.

A QUICK CHAT WITH MICHAEL BALLANTYNE, FOUNDER OF STORYWOOD

I asked Michael his opinion on tequila used in cocktails and the proper way of drinking it. The following is what he told me:

> I think tequila can be enjoyed in many ways on many occasions. For example, in the wintertime I love sipping one of our "cask strength" tequilas, as it brings a lovely warmth to the body, or an old fashioned with our Speyside 14 is fantastic. In the warmer months I'm all about simple serves, so a good paloma or a tequila and tonic really hits the spot. At the same time, who doesn't love a good margarita, right?! I'm drinking mine "spicy," though, with our Speyside 7 Cask Strength. It's just the right amount of kick, between spicy jalapeño and the high-strength flavor from the 53% ABV tequila.
>
> I've been submerged in the tequila category now for almost ten years, and I don't really think there is one right way to drink it. For me it's about educating people on quality tequila. The real reason why salt and lime were introduced

to tequila shots was because of the horrible quality the tequila had at that time. When I started, there were about 1,700 tequila brands, and today there are nearly 3,000 all fighting for the space. So, to answer your question, I think tequila can be enjoyed any way you like it, but just make sure you pick a bottle with the right quality.

I also asked him his opinion on the tequila boom and its consequences:

Well, it's pretty apparent that the celebrity brands and high-level M&As (mergers and acquisitions) have definitely shed light on the industry. There are pros and cons to this level of attention the tequila space is getting, though. Celebrity brands have the ways and means to draw attention to the space, which is fantastic for all brands, small or big, in my opinion. However, the negative on this is that we've seen huge increases in agave prices, which really puts pressure on small brands, especially for brands like Storywood that are staying true to their "handcrafted" roots. At the same time, we're seeing tequila being pushed more and more on cocktail menus from fantastic bartenders who are really thinking outside the box with combining fascinating flavors, and this really helps from a consumer-education point of view. At the end of the day, tequila's been having quite a moment for some time, and to see other big brands experimenting with barrel aging is a true testament to how Storywood trailblazed that space for further growth.

To conclude, I asked him how he sees the future of tequila:

I think it will continue to grow and outpace most spirits, due to the celebrity status and the influx of brands that are out there today. I do think that a lot of smaller brands will be pressed for finding shelf space, though, so point of difference is key. There comes a point, though, where brands need to align with key industry players to continue to grow, and I think that will be the rise or fall of any brand going forward. For myself, Storywood is a passion and love for the culture and a way to bring new flavor to the agave space through focusing on our oak aging techniques. The reality is that I'll never shoot hoops like Michael Jordon, or be as suave as George Clooney, as witty as The Rock, or as funny as Kevin Hart, but as long as I'm educating people and seeing them enjoy what Storywood has to offer, then I won't be going anywhere.

STORYWOOD SPEYSIDE 7 REPOSADO

About Speyside 7 Reposado, Michael said, "All five [of Storywood's] products have won multiple tasting awards, and each in their own right serves a purpose, but if I were to choose one for someone who hasn't had Storywood before, then I'd say the Speyside 7 is a great starting point. It's extremely versatile in cocktails, yet you can sip it neat, on the rocks, or with a dash of water."

Aged over seven months in Scotch Speyside whisky barrels coming from Dufftown, Scotland, Speyside 7 Reposado is pale golden amber in color. On the nose, it presents a caramel, cooked agave, and oak aroma. On the palate, it has vanilla, honey, and earthy flavors, with a lingering earthy and vanilla finish. The ABV is 40%.

LOS AMANTES

Los Amantes (or "The Lovers") was founded in Tlacolula de Matamoros, 18 miles (30 kilometers) outside of Oaxaca City by Ignacio Carballido and Guillermo Olguín, a well-known Mexican artist, with the help of master distiller Eric Hernandez. The brand was inspired by the Aztec legend of Mayahuel, who fell in love with the great god Quetzalcoátl.

At the distillery, the agave hearts, after being harvested in Tlacolula Valley, Oaxaca, are cooked in a traditional pit oven for seventy-two hours and then crushed with a horse-drawn tahona. The fermentation occurs in 100-liter wooden vats. The first distillation takes place in 500-liter stainless-steel pots, and then the mezcal is double distilled in a 300-liter copper pot still. In the case of the Los Amantes Espadín Joven, a third distillation is done to create a product that is as smooth as possible. Los Amantes won several awards, such as gold medal for the Reposado and platinum for the Anejo at the Beverage Testing Institute in 2019.

Los Amantes offers the following expressions:

- Blanco: bottled straight after distillation and made with agave espadín.

- Reposado: made with agave espadín and aged for six months in American oak barrels.

- Añejo: made with agave espadín and matured for twenty-four hours in French oak barrels.

Q & A WITH IGNACIO CARBALLIDO, OWNER AND COFOUNDER OF LOS AMANTES

Let's talk about mezcal. Is there a traditional way to drink it?

Sipping it and chasing with water.

What do you think about using it in cocktails?

Mezcal is a perfect cocktail spirit; it marries perfectly with other spirits.

And what about aging it?

The NOM recognizes and categorizes aged mezcal. There is nothing that prohibits the aging of mezcal. It's an additional element that makes it special and brings another layer.

Is mezcal tied to Mexican traditions and culture?

Mezcal making goes very far back for centuries and has been linked to the farmers in the mountains, and it has become part of their culture and traditions.

What are the misconceptions about mezcal?

That it is a low-quality, gimmicky spirit, because of the worm. We are all staying away from the worm.

What do you think are the main factors that contributed to the mezcal boom?

Some higher-quality boutique mezcals that were marketed as such. More exposure in restaurants and bars and in cocktails.

How do you see mezcal growing in the next few years?

Mezcal, agave spirits will become the wine of spirits. An everyday sipping spirit in the next fifty years or so.

Is there any change you would like to see in the industry?

Yes—people, bartenders have to stop saying that mezcal should not be aged. Especially if they are not well-informed.

What do you think about the environmental impact of mezcal production?

We have to be conscious of the agave growth, take care of resources and the environment. And be conscious about using and harvesting wild agaves. It should not become a competition of which brand is bringing wild agaves to the market.

Is there anything that makes your production different from others?

Yes: the Joven is three times distilled to take all impurities away, leaving us with a fine, elegant product. We also have a unique method of production, a different oven design, and a family trade secret that gives a unique and very specific flavor profile. At the end of the day, we call it our own formula.

LOS AMANTES JOVEN

Made with 100 percent agave espadín harvested when fully ripe at ten years old in Tlacolula Valley, Oaxaca, Los Amantes Joven is triple distilled: the first distillation takes place in a stainless-steel still, the second one in a copper still, and the third one again in a stainless-steel still.

Winner of the gold medal at the Beverage Testing Institute (BTI) in 2019, Los Amantes Joven offers aromas of light cucumber on the nose and salty flavors and citrus notes on the palate. The ABV is 40%.

LA TEQUILEÑA

La Tequileña is a distillery founded by master distiller Enrique Fonseca. A descendant of Portuguese immigrants, he was part of the fifth generation of well-known agave growers. In the 1800s, the Fonseca family was already planting agave to supply the first tequila distilleries in the region of Atotonilco El Alto in the highlands of Jalisco. The Fonsecas' estate grew until it became a major agave farm that was able to supply the top tequila distilleries of the time.

In the 1980s, Enrique decided to buy a distillery, La Tequileña, in the heart of Tequila town. Not knowing much about how to make tequila, Enrique started to study, and then he flew to Europe to study even more. In France, he learned the importance of the wine; in Scotland, he managed to meet several single malt producers and learned from them the effect of copper on a spirit, the art of distillation using pot and column stills, and the sourcing of excellent oak casks.

Once back in Mexico, he started to produce his own tequila, Fuenteseca, by using the alembic still and the column still to make a tequila that could maintain the agave character and, at the same time, be lighter and more refined.

Today La Tequileña produces daily 25,000 liters of tequila (or 15,000 liters of 100 percent blue agave tequila), and they are the home of different brands: Fuenteseca, Xalixco, Cimarrón, Zapata, Purasangre, Tequila Lapis, Arquitecto Tequila, Cierto Tequila, Don Fulano, Casa Don Lorenzo, Tears of Llorona, and Tres, Cuatro y Cinco.

After harvesting the blue agave, La Tequilena plants two cycles of other crops, especially legumes, before planting agave again, so the soil and its nutrients will be restored.

CIMARRÓN TEQUILA

Cimarrón Tequila is owned by Enrique Fonseca. It is made with 100 percent blue agave that is cooked in low-pressure autoclaves for thirty hours. Then, it is crushed by a large screw press that squeezes the juice out of the agave. The fermentation occurs in stainless-steel tanks with wine makers' yeast. The distillation takes place in column stills.

Cimarrón offers the following expressions for export:

- Blanco: the unaged expression.
- Reposado: aged in American oak barrels for six months.
- Añejo: aged for twelve to eighteen months.

CIMARRÓN BLANCO

Distilled from blue agave grown at an elevation of 4,620 feet in Atotonilco el Alto, Jalisco, then cooked at slow pressure and fermented with natural winemaker's yeast, Cimarrón Blanco is rich and balanced.

On the nose, it presents vegetal, earthy, and subtle spice aromas, and on the palate, it offers dry, bright agave flavors. The ABV is 40%.

CIMARRÓN REPOSADO

Cimarrón Reposado is a blend of tequila distilled from a double-column still (80 percent) and tequila distilled from pot stills (20 percent). Then it's bottled and aged for three to six months in American white oak.

Rich and aromatic, Cimarrón Reposado presents aromas of caramel and vanilla on the nose, and it offers a dry, earthy flavor on the palate, with a delicate and bright finish. The ABV is 40%.

Cimarrón Blanco

TEQUILA FUENTESECA

Fuenteseca cooks their agave hearts for about twenty-four hours in large autoclaves, then crushes them with a large screw press which squeezes the juice out of the agave. The juice ferments in large, temperature-controlled stainless-steel tanks with proprietary yeasts and is then distilled with column and pot stills.

For the aging process, Enrique uses American and European oak, American bourbon casks, Canadian rye casks, and a selection of both white and red wine casks. He also moves casks from one place to another; the maturing agave can develop at different speeds, depending on altitude, humidity levels, and wind.

Fuenteseca offers a wide range of expressions, including the following:

- Reserva 1995: This Extra Añejo tequila was distilled in double copper columns (75 percecnt) and 25 percent in copper stills in 1995. Then it was aged in 180-liter Canadian white oak barrels, previously used to mature Canadian rye whisky for six years. Then in 2001, a part of that tequila was moved into 220-liter European dark oak barrels, previously used for aging California red wine, for twelve years.

- Reserva 1998: This Extra Añejo tequila is made from 25 percent tequila distilled in copper alembic stills and 75 percent in a double copper column still in 1998. The aging occurred in American oak barrels (97 percent) and in European dark oak barrels (3 percent) for fifteen years.

- Reserva 2001: This Extra Añejo was 20 percent distilled in a double copper column and 80 percent in copper stills in 2001. Then, 90 percent was aged in American oak barrels and 10 percent in French dark oak barrels for twelve years.

- Reserva 2003: This Extra Añejo was distilled in a double copper column still (80 percent) and copper stills (20 percent) in 2003. Eighty percent was then aged in American white oak barrels and 15 percent in French dark oak barrels for nine years.

- Reserva 2005: This Extra Añejo was 100 percent distilled in copper stills in 2005, then matured in American oak barrels (80 percent) and French dark oak barrels (20 percent) for seven years.

- Cosecha 2013: This variety consists of small batches of unaged Blanco tequila, produced only when the agave harvested is of unusually high quality. Each release is unique, and each bottle is individually numbered.

Fuenteseca sustainably harvests agave and responsibly replants according to the lifespan and agave growth cycles.

FUENTESECA RESERVA EXTRA AÑEJO (2005)

An ultra-premium tequila, crafted from 100 percent blue agave and hailing from the highlands of Jalisco, Fuenteseca Reserva Extra Añejo (2005) is aged for eleven years in the very cool and dry environment of a subterranean barrel room, with the uppermost portion of the room opened to allow for soft air circulation. It is aged in a combination of American white oak and French oak barrels.

On the nose, it presents warm toffee, roasted agave, and oak aromas. It offers baking spice, dried fruit, and pepper flavors on the palate. The finish is delicate, and the ABV is 41.7%.

DON FULANO

Don Fulano was founded in 2000 by Enrique Fonseca and Sergio Mendoza, and it is produced at La Tequileña with the aim of creating a product that is artisanal and terroir driven, but also elegant and sophisticated.

Don Fulano grows 100 percent blue agave and harvests exclusively maduro (matured) and pinto agaves (advanced maturity); the agave hearts are then placed into the autoclave, where they are steam cooked at low pressure for between twenty-four and thirty-two hours. Once cooked, the agave hearts are squeezed by a screw press to obtain the juice. The fermentation occurs in open-air tanks with proprietary yeasts. Thirty percent of the fermentations include bagasse or fibers, and 70 percent are without bagasse and last for three to six days. Then, Don Fulano uses a combination of distillation techniques: a double distillation in copper alembics (to get depth and the agave character), of which between 80 and 85 percent will be part of the final blend, and a distillation in a double-column copper Coffey still (to get elegance and structure), of which between 15 and 20 percent will be included in the final blend. The tequila is then ready to be aged in European dark oak wine barrels (primarily French Limousin and Nevers oak, which previously held wines from Burgundy, Bordeaux, and the Loire Valley in France) and other Spanish and Eastern European casks. The aging takes place at different altitudes, under different climates and cellar conditions. Once matured, the tequila is blended in the vatting room for between three and six months. Then it is bottled using simple cellulose filtration.

Don Fulano's main expressions are:

- Blanco: the unaged expression, made by master distiller Enrique Fonseca and blended by Sergio Mendoza (as with all the other expressions). Fermented for seventy-two to ninety-six hours and then distilled in copper pot stills (80 percent) and in column copper coffey stills (20 percent).

- Fuerte: Blanco at 100 percent overproof.

- Reposado: aged between eight and eleven months in French Limousin oak casks.

- Añejo: matured for thirty months.

- Imperial: matured for five years in dark European oak and oloroso sherry casks.

DON FULANO AÑEJO

Don Fulano Añejo is aged for thirty months in French Limousin and Nevers oak casks that previously held wines.

On the nose, it presents aromas of vanilla counterbalanced with hints of mint. On the palate, it presents spiced flavors, such as cardamom and allspice. The finish has dark chocolate and leather notes. The ABV is 40%.

TEARS OF LLORONA

Tears of Llorona was founded by maestro tequilero Germán González Gorrochotegui in 2014. His father was Guillermo González Diaz Lombardo, creator of Chinaco, the first ultra-premium tequila imported into the United States.

Following in his father's footsteps, Germán started to work at his family's agave farm and Chinaco distillery, which he ended up managing. Eventually, he ended up founding T1 Tequila Uno, named Best Craft Tequila of 2016 by *USA Today* People's Choice.

In 2012, he shared with some friends a special batch, a family reserve artisanal expression. His friends encouraged him to release it as a limited edition. Germán decided to follow their advice, releasing the batch under the name Tears of Llorona, and started to distribute to the US market.

He said, "Tears has been on the market since 2014, with a product that began production in 2009. Each bottle has a unique combination of maturation from different barrels without losing its soul, which is the agave."

Tears of Llorona is made from 100 percent pure Weber agave azul grown in the volcanic slopes of the Mexican highlands to provide unique flavor profiles to the final product. "The agaves must be at their maximum maturity of about eight years, with the rich sugars and flavors of the land that for years has been enriched with fruit trees typical of the region," Germán said.

The agave hearts, personally inspected by Germán, are slowly roasted. The fermentation is slow and occurs with proprietary yeasts; the distillation takes place in traditional copper pot stills for twenty hours. The aging happens in three different types of oak barrels: Scotch, sherry oak, and brandy. "Like many single malt Scotches and craft bourbons, Tears of Llorona is aged for five years in three types of barrels—including Scotch, brandy, and sherry oak barrels—resulting in a layered tasting experience. It is a process that requires a careful combination of patience, care, and love."

Finally, Germán bottles the tequila at 43% ABV to balance the flavors. On the bottle, Tears of Llorona adds a logo to indicate a specific batch. As Germán said, "Each batch is unique and limited, because each bottle has its own characteristics from the terroir and the barrel aging and blending process. This, of course, only happens with an additive-free product, where we do not add any ingredients to alter the color, taste, or smell of the tequila."

Tears of Llorona does not offer Blanco or Reposado expressions, but only Extra Añejo, and its main expression is Tears of Llorona No. 3.

In terms of sustainability, Tears of Llorona is involved in a project to jump-start the reforestation and soil restoration of semiarid desert areas of Mexico. Germán added, "The agaves are classified organic and regenerative. We have also discovered that agaves help sequester significant amounts of carbon, making them the perfect plant to assist with slowing climate change. We are working with scientists to finalize allometric data and will be able to translate that into carbon credits."

TEARS OF LLORONA NO. 3

Tears of Llorona No. 3 is an Extra Añejo tequila, aged for five years in oak barrels that have previously held Scotch, sherry, and brandy, creating a complex, layered fusion that still retains clear agave notes. Best at room temperature, it is a sipping spirit to enjoy neat and possibly in a wide glass to allow the tequila to open up, as Germán suggested.

Dark in color, on the nose, Tears of Llorona No. 3 has aromas of caramel custard, dried fruit, and dark chocolate. On the palate, it offers notes of agave with baking spice, with a hint of smoke. The finish is sweet and warm. The ABV is 43%.

Q & A WITH GERMAN GONZÁLEZ GORROCHOTEGUI, MASTER DISTILLER AT TEARS OF LLORONA

What do you think about using tequila in cocktails?

Unlike most tequilas, Tears of Llorona is best enjoyed neat in a whiskey glass, a traditional cognac snifter, or a Reidel tequila glass. I recommend enjoying it alongside a T-bone steak, bold seafood dishes, chocolate cake, or even a cigar. Personally, I would not mix Tears of Llorona with anything, but I know there must be several mixologists' creations I would be willing to try.

What is the proper way to drink tequila?

I always recommend trying it neat in order to understand the flavor that tequila brings to the mix of a cocktail, but of course drinking tequila with friends is best.

How is tequila seen nowadays?

Today, tequila is seen as a luxury spirit, highly consumed by the youth of Mexico.

How can the terroir influence the production of tequila?

Agaves differ based on the types of soil and altitude where they are grown. That's why terroir is important in a super high-end tequila like Tears of Llorona. In the volcanic slopes of the Mexican highlands, where agaves grow slowly and naturally, they achieve a higher starch content. This is where I harvest the agaves for Tears of Llorona.

From my point of view, of the great variety of agaves that we have in Mexico, each one developed in a certain area due to a microclimate and human development in these areas. Flavors are developed based on the terroir, with which these products will have a unique richness with an exceptional pairing; hence the importance of preservation in the areas of origin.

What do you think were the main factors that contributed to the tequila boom?

Consumers in the United States are looking for better-quality tequilas. In my own experience, the first super-premium tequila, Chinaco, was exported by my father in 1983, so I believe he was the driving force behind this change.

Is there any change you would like to see in the industry?

The vast majority of the tequila produced today is made commercially. It is we, the small brands like Tears of Llorona, who continue to use traditional methods. What I would like to see is that the industry in general supports farmers more with education for land conservation.

How do you see tequila growing in the next few years?

I hope that growth in the market continues, because tequila, outside of Mexico and the United States, has many countries left to conquer.

MEZCAL LOS SIETE MISTERIOS

Los Siete Misterios was founded by brothers Eduardo and Julio Mestre, in collaboration with the Amador family, in Sola de Vega, Oaxaca, in 2010.

The story begins with the two brothers who used to take holiday trips to the beaches of Oaxaca, where they started their tradition of drinking mezcal, since it couldn't be found outside the area. During one of their trips, they noticed that not all the mezcals were the same, so they decided to visit every village they could find and buy mezcal to bring back home, where they started their collection. During their trips, they met the Amador family, whose mezcal they loved. Eventually, Eduardo and Julio decided to partner with the family to make the world aware of their mezcal, and that's how Los Siete Misterios was born.

Los Siete Misterios has the goal to make mezcal that reflects the customs, culture, and passion of Mexico by using traditional methods.

In 2021, Chatham Imports partnered with Los Siete Misterios, acquiring a 50 percent stake in the company.

The name of the brand comes from the seven mezcal steps that the two brothers presented to the people willing to try mezcal: the first step was Espadín, then Barril, Mexicano, Arroqueño, Coyote, Tobalá, and finally Puntas, which has a high ABV mezcal, around 75%.

Los Siete Misterios mezcal is made with 100 percent natural agave with hearts cooked in traditional underground ovens made of earth and stones and fueled by local woods for three to five days. Then, the agave hearts are milled by either a hand-carved wooden mallet or a traditional Chilean tahona horse. The fermentation occurs in large wooden open-air vats with wild yeast and pure spring water. The distillation takes place in either copper pots or clay pots, depending on the expression.

Los Siete Misterios offers the following main expressions:

- Artisanal Mezcals:

  - Doba-Yej (meaning "agave espadín" in the ancient Zapotec language): Made with agave espadín, each batch is produced by a different mezcalero either from Santiago Matatlán, San Dionisio, or Yautepec, all in the Oaxaca region.

  - Ensambles: Espadín and Cuishe, Espadín and Mexicanito, Espadín and Tepeztate, Espadín and Tobalá, Ensamble Especial (the varietals of agaves vary depending on the batch; it's a limited edition produced once a year, and blends four to five agaves). They all are distilled in copper pot stills in San Dionisio.

  - Pechuga: Distilled a third time with turkey breast, fruit, and spices, chosen by Eduardo and Julio's mother, Doña Ángeles, this varity has a unique recipe each year.

- Ancestral Olla de Barro Mezcales: Espadín, Barril, Mexicano, Coyote, Arroqueño, and Tobalá. They all are distilled in clay pot stills in Sola de Vega.

Los Siete Misterios partners with maestros mezcaleros across Mexico, helping families to create authentic, ancestral mezcal and supporting local Mexican workers. They also harvest agaves using sustainable practices.

LOS SIETE MISTERIOS ESPADÍN

Los Siete Misterios Espadín was the first product of the Olla de Barro expressions. Produced in Sola de Vega, double distilled in clay pot stills, it offers mineral notes, alongside herbal, floral, and citrus flavors. The ABV is 50.2%.

LOS SIETE MISTERIOS DOBA-YEJ
(SANTIAGO MATATLÁN)

Los Siete Misterios Doba-Yej is produced in three different parts of Oaxaca, and each of them represents a different Mexican hero. Depending on the area, the mezcal will have a different character.

Los Siete Misterios Doba-Yej from Santiago Matatlán is crystalline in color, with citrus aromas and floral, sweet caramel, and cooked agave flavors. The ABV is 44%.

Los Siete Misterios Espadín

Los Siete Misterios Doba-Yej (Santiago Matatlán)

Q & A WITH EDUARDO AND JULIO MESTRE, COFOUNDERS OF LOS SIETE MISTERIOS

Tell us more about Los Siete Misterios.

Inspired by the passion, traditions, and culture of native Mexico, Julio and I founded Los Siete Misterios in 2010 with the goal of searching for and sharing a spirit that represents the customs, culture, and passion of Mexico—mezcal. We spent years sampling mezcal from villages across Oaxaca and met local maestros mezcaleros who use traditional techniques honed over generations. In an effort to preserve this ancestral knowledge, we teamed up with maestros mezcaleros to collaborate on a contemporary approach to traditional mezcal. We are a family company: my brother Julio, our mom, and I are involved in all the areas. Los Siete Misterios may have started fourteen years ago; however, we have been drinking and enjoying mezcal for much longer.

What's your signature expression?

I would say that our Olla de Barro would be our signature product; however, the Doba-Yej is the one that sells best around the world. The Doba-Yej is a well-balanced mezcal at 44% ABV that is delicious sipped neat or in a cocktail. Doba-Yej means "maguey espadín" in the ancient Zapotec language, and each label features a Mexican war hero. They depict Doña Josefa Ortiz, Father Miguel Hidalgo, and José María Morelos.

Our signature expressions are our Olla de Barro (Clay Pot) mezcals. Olla de Barro mezcals have been in our lineup since the beginning of the brand. Clay imparts unique body, flavors, and aromas that make Olla de Barro mezcals unique examples of this beautiful spirit. Clay-pot distillation comprises less than 1 percent of all Mezcal production, in part because 40 to 60 percent of the liquid is lost during this type of distillation.

How did you choose the type of agave to use?

We didn't choose a maguey (common name for agave) type at the beginning of the brand, we just flowed with what was available at that time. After some time we needed an espadín distilled on a copper still, so we created the Doba-Yej. For the Olla de Barro and most of our products, it is more about what is available in the fields, and that means we do not produce any one specific mezcal every year.

What are your thoughts about the terroir and its influence on mezcal and the single batch?

Although the terroir does not necessarily make each batch different, the terroir of where you are producing definitely influences mezcal production. For example, agaves in valley regions lead to a more herbal mezcal, whereas agaves in mountainous regions lead to a sweeter mezcal. This is because in the flat valleys, rainwater is more easily retained in the soil, whereas in the hilly areas like Sola de Vega, there is more watershed, causing the plants to have less water and more stress. More stress causes more sugars in the plant, which leads to a sweeter distillate.

Because the terroir, among other factors, affects the production, we have three separate labels for our Doba-Yej mezcal. All our Doba-Yej mezcal is produced using the same production process, but it is made in three different parts of Oaxaca. The terroir, among other factors, may lead to a slightly different distillate, so we chose to have three slightly different labels.

The terroir wouldn't necessarily affect each batch, since the soil may not change between each harvest, but other parts of the production process may affect each batch, such as the types of wild yeast available and the season in which you are distilling.

What makes Los Siete Misterios different from others?

At Los Siete Misterios, we always begin with the highest-quality agave plants and follow artisanal and limited production methods, including: distilling with 100% natural agave sugars from ripe plants, cooking in underground ovens, milling with wooden mallets or a tahona horse, fermenting naturally, and distilling at least twice. This allows us to pursue our goal of respecting mezcal traditions and customs while supporting local Mexican workers.

We are involved in every step of the production process, from growing the agaves all the way to the bottling and filtering of the products. In each stage we use traditional techniques inherited by our maestros mezcaleros, with added proprietary steps we have found through research, to create our special signature on all our products.

Do you have any special releases or limited editions you can tell us about?

All of our releases are really special, including our limited releases. We have some which mainly are once-in-a-lifetime expressions. As we mentioned before, we have a line of Olla de Barro mezcals which comprise less than 1 percent of all mezcal production, in part because 40 to 60 percent of the liquid is lost during this type of distillation. Since we produce what's available in the fields, it is not easy to predict which type of Olla de Barro will be available.

Another limited release is our Pechuga, a celebration mezcal distilled a third time with turkey breast, fruit, and spices. These additions are chosen by our mother, Doña Ángeles, and maestra mezcalera Doña Sabina. An homage to the generations of maestros mezcaleros whose wisdom has trained and inspired us, our Pechuga serves as an expression of gratitude for our Mexican culture. With only one production a year, each with a unique recipe, this mezcal is truly special.

Are there any initiatives you are currently working on?

Besides working with more than twelve families that produce mezcal, we have our own palenque (distillery) in the heart of Villa Sola de Vega, the village that made us fall in love with this incredible spirit. We opened this palenque in 2016 with the idea to observe, study, and document the full production process, with the goal of finding opportunities for improvement. Once we identify and apply them, we invite the mezcaleros to produce one batch at our palenque so they can use and understand these improvements and apply them in their facilities if they like them.

Is there a traditional way to drink mezcal?

That would be to sip it straight.

What do you think about using mezcal in cocktails?

Why not? We believe that mezcal will always be the protagonist, and of course there are some really limited and special mezcals that we wouldn't suggest to mix, but every consumer has a different palate. I think that cocktails are the best introduction to mezcal for people who are not used to this intense spirit, and by mixing it properly you can enhance its characteristics.

What's your thought about aging mezcal?

Agave spends enough time on Earth before being harvested for making mezcal; also the production process contributes to all the flavors and aromas in the liquid, so...why should we use any type of wood to rest or age the mezcal? There's a saying that states that "mezcal is the only spirit that is born aged."

What are the misconceptions about mezcal?

I believe that right now we are beyond that point. Some would be the worm inside, or that it has to be extra smoky, but thanks to consumer education, all of those misconceptions are fading away.

Could you tell us more about any cultural significance or traditions tied to mezcal?

Maguey is something that has been in our culture since before the Spaniards conquered the Americas. The scientific name for maguey, agave, comes from the Latin word for admirable. According to different sources, when the colonizers arrived in Mexico, they marveled at all of the ways Mesoamerican people used maguey, from drinking the fermented pulque, to cooking the heart for food, to using the thorns for sewing and the tips of spears, etc....

There is also the Mexican legend of Mayahuel, a deity associated with maguey. Her grandmother was an evil goddess and killed Mayahuel while she was on Earth. A different deity, Quetzalcoátl, took her remains and planted them, and from that the maguey was born.

Mexico has around 85 percent of all the agave species in the world, which grow from Sonora all the way down to Chiapas. More than half of the states of Mexico have produced, or are producing, a maguey spirit like mezcal, bacanora, raicilla, tuxca, or comiteco.

So how are tequila and mezcal seen nowadays?

Tequila is the mainstream, most known and consumed spirit in Mexico, while mezcal is the irreverent one that is gaining more awareness and consumers sip by sip.

What do you think were the main factors that contributed to the mezcal boom?

Consumer education, and the effort of a few brands to export and promote this beautiful spirit and the culture surrounding it.

How do you see mezcal growing in the next few years?

There are a lot of opportunities with mezcal. Getting to the next level, there are still several markets where mezcal has no presence; not all bars or restaurants know mezcal, so those are areas of opportunity to introduce it into the market. In other places, we have seen a growing consumer and trade interest around the world and are excited by all the innovative ways the bar communities are using it. I believe we will be passing through the introduction phase to an expansion one.

Are you working on any initiatives to reduce the environmental impact of mezcal production?

We are working on the recycling of vinazas and bagazo. For vinazas, we are working with a doctor who has a lot of experience in the treatment of this waste, and the idea is to implement it in our palenque and then replicate it in the palenques of the families we work with.

We were also one of the first brands to create an agave nursery that documents agave growth practices. Named Rancho Concordia, it is a five-acre agave nursery with over eleven different agave species and over five thousand plants.

What about the preservation of the biodiversity of agave? Is there any initiative you have been working on?

In 2016, we created our Agave Preservation Program with our Rancho Concordia Nursery and planted five thousand agaves of eleven different species that are endemic to Villa Sola de Vega. The goal is to observe, study, and learn how agaves reproduce, so we can focus on repopulating the most exploited species and ensure sustainable harvesting practices. This way, agave consumption is both sustainable and community centered.

Since the growth of a quiote (flower stem) can impact the sugars in the agave, production plants are often harvested before the plant has a chance to flower. Preventing agaves from flowering not only stops the plant from reproducing, but also negatively impacts birds, bats, and other animals that pollinate agaves. This is why it is important for us to grow agaves to full maturity: to protect future agave populations. Growing agave from seed also helps maintain natural biodiversity within agave. Depending on each agave species' reproduction method, we collect seeds, aerial agaves, or *hijuelos* (sprouts) and plant them in open land so the agave can grow. In this land, we let most of the agaves grow quiote, so we can collect the seeds.

Is there any change you would like to see in the industry?

I would say that so far no major changes need to be made. If we go a little bit deeper, then we could revise the NOM-070 to make it more inclusive, and more small communities and producers can enter the Mezcal Origin Denomination Area. Although it is still relatively small, mezcal is a growing industry. As more corporations enter the industry, we hope that they respect the culture and tradition of mezcal and the maestros mezcaleros that make it. For example, the NOM requires that in order to be called mezcal, the product must be 100 percent maguey, and we hope that it stays this way.

MEZCAL MARCA NEGRA

Marca Negra was founded in 2010 by Pedro Quintanilla, and then in 2017 joined premium and ultra-premium spirits producer Phillips Distilling Company.

In 2017, Marca Negra won the double gold medal at the San Francisco World Spirits Competition. It is currently distributed around the world.

The brand, born with the aim of preserving ancient and traditional knowledge, works with several different palenques in various regions of Oaxaca: Jorge Mendez Ramirez in San Luis del Río, Tlacolula de Matamoros; Alberto Ortiz in Santa María la Pila, Miahuatlán; and Basilio Pacheco in La Noria, Ejutla.

Each producer uses the same traditional, handmade processes that have been used for generations. The agave used depends on the location's availability, creating unique expressions connected to the terroir of the region where they are produced, but also adjusted to the distiller's taste profile. An example is Marca Negra with an ABV of 48% or higher, because the mezcal is bottled at the alcohol level preferred by the maestros mezcaleros. Batches are usually small, and the product line changes constantly. Every bottle of Marca Negra bears the signature of its maestro mezcalero, and the black handprint on them represents the hard work of each palenque.

Marca Negra mezcals are cooked in a conical earth oven, ground with a tahona, fermented naturally in sabino (Montezuma cypress, known also as the Mexico national tree) vats, and distilled twice in copper stills.

The palenques currently produce the following expressions:

- Maestro Basilio Pacheco in La Noria, Ejutla: Espadín, Rhodacantha, and Karwinskii.

- Maestro Jorge Mendez in San Luis del Río: Espadín, Tepeztate, and Tobalá.

The limited editions are:

- Cupreata: an edition released from two different producers, maestros mezcaleros Faustino Castro and Lorenzo Gonzalez, and made with cupreata agave from Chilapa, Guerrero.

- Sierra Negra: produced by Don Baltazar Cruz Gómez in San Luis del Río, Tlacolula de Matamoros.

- Arroqueño: made by master mezcalero Alberto Ortiz in Santa María la Pila, Miahuatlán.

- Dobadàn: from *Agave rhodacantha*, made in Santa Maria la Pila by maestro mezcalero Alberto Ortiz.

MARCA NEGRA SIERRA NEGRA

Produced by Don Baltazar Cruz Gómez in San Luis del Río, Tlacolula de Matamoros, Marca Negra Sierra Negra is made with 100 percent wild sierra negra (*agave americana*). The cooked agave is milled by a stone wheel tahona and double distilled in a copper pot still.

Marca Negra Sierra Negra offers lemon sherbet and agave syrup aromas, alongside orange peel, hazelnut, and coffee bean flavors. The finish is long, and the ABV may vary between 46% and 48%.

MADRE MEZCAL

Madre Mezcal was founded in 2016 by a team of industry special-ists: adventurer and artist Anthony Farfalla, brand consultant Chris Stephenson, sustainable business entrepreneur Davide Berruto, and photographer and brand specialist Stefan Wigand, alongside the José Garcia Morales family, whom Farfalla and Wigand met during a trip to Oaxaca.

Madre Mezcal (which translates to "Mother Mezcal" and is meant to honor the land where mezcal comes from and those who are involved in its production) is made in the rolling hills of San Dionisio, Oaxaca, a family town surrounded by a variety of wild agaves, and it has been made for generations by the Morales family. They started distilling mezcal for personal use and family celebrations, and today they still plant agave, harvest it, and use traditional Zapotec methods to create Madre Mezcal. Initially sold in plastic water bottles as per tradition, Madre has gradu-ated to hand-poured glass over the past several years.

Today José Garcia Morales's family continues to provide Madre Mezcal with agaves espadín and cuishe, but they are not the only ones. Carlos Mendez Blas and his family, based in Santiago Matatlán, have produced mezcal since 1930 and are still a family-owned business, providing agave espadín. The late Natalio Vasquez's legacy is now carried on by his family, who are based in Miahuatlán and produce cuishe. Each family supplies a unique mezcal, using processes passed through generations and remain-ing committed to heritage and quality.

All of Madre Mezcal's expressions reflect the natural tastes of the agave and the land, the water, and the clean air from where it comes. At Madre Mezcal, the agave hearts are cooked over hot stones in earthen pits and crushed by a tahona. The substance is then fermented in open-air wood containers with wild yeast and finally distilled with wood fires. Using local water, natural yeast from the air, minerals within the earthen oven used

to roast the agave, and the inherent flavors of the land within the agave plant itself, Madre reflects the essence of the earth in its purest form.

As community, partnerships, and content manager Sophia Forino said, "We like to think Madre is a 'gateway spirit' that offers beautifully well-balanced flavor with a smooth finish. With less smoke than most mezcals, Madre appeals to a new cohort of mezcal drinkers, opening palates to new characteristics with its signature expressions."

Madre Mezcal's expressions are:

- Madre Ensamble: a blend of espadín and cuishe.

- Madre Espadín: made with only agave espadín, bright and earthy. By using espadín agaves from multiple geographies and terroir, chosen for distinct flavor profiles, this single varietal blend accomplishes a mouthfeel and smoothness that surpasses far more expensive and rare varietals.

- Madre Ancestral: a new release produced by third-generation maestro mezcalero Moisés Martinez Alvarez in Santa Catarina Minas from a blend of hand-crushed tobasiche and espadín, and distilled in clay pots using the ancestral method.

- Desert Water: made with artisanal mezcal and sparkling water infused with adaptogens, herbs, and fruits. This refreshing and ready-to-drink cocktail comes in four flavors: Grapefruit & Yerba Santa; Original: Mushroom, Sage & Honey; and Prickly Pear & Lemon.

They also recently released a Limited Edition Clay Pot Ensamble, their first certified Mezcal Ancestral product. Only one thousand bottles were produced, each one made from mezcal distilled in clay pots set atop an open flame.

Madre Mezcal is very dedicated to sustainability and committed to producing a quality ethical spirit. The distillery plants agave in Oaxaca and has developed social and environmental programs to support communities and those in need. They have partnered with the nonprofit organization RAICES (Refugee and Immigrant Center for Education and Legal Services) to raise funds and awareness for the immigration crisis. RAICES works to ensure that people maintain access to health and legal services, regardless of their immigration status. Madre Mezcal has also invested in local nonprofits that provide resources and education for women and underserved children in Oaxaca. Madre Mezcal also created the Institute for Mezcal Learning, a multicourse program offered through Instagram to teach about mezcal in a fun way.

MADRE MEZCAL ENSAMBLE

Made with a blend of espadín (70 percent) and cuishe (30 percent), Madre Mezcal Ensamble has less smoke than most mezcals and can be found both in 750 milliliter glass bottles and 200 milliliter flasks.

During the process of making Madre Mezcal Ensamble, the agave hearts are roasted in an earthen pot, then fermented with wild yeast and local well water, and the distillation is carried out in a copper still.

Sophia added, "While wild cuishe agaves are more difficult to harvest and make Madre Ensamble more challenging to produce, this unique agave adds dimensions of sweetness, botanicals, and mineralogy that perfectly complement the smokier espadín."

Clear in color, Madre Mezcal Ensamble has an aroma of sweet smoke and herbs on the nose; it then continues with roasted agave notes balanced by peppery and fruity notes on the palate. The finish is lingering and warm, and the ABV is 45%.

MEZCAL DE LEYENDAS

Mezcal de Leyendas (previously labeled as Mezcales de Leyenda) is an ultra-premium, certified organic distillery that produces mezcal in different regions of Mexico: Oaxaca, Durango, San Luis Potosí, Puebla, and Guerrero. The distillery was born out of La Botica, a mezcalería that opened in Mexico City in 2004. Mezcal de Leyendas has been one of the first brands to offer expressions from different regions of Mexico in order to highlight the differences in mezcal.

Every mezcal is made by local maestros mezcaleros, and each is certified organic by the USDA and the California Certified Organic Farmers (CCOF).

Over the years, Mezcal de Leyendas has built a strong relationship network with the most recognized mezcaleros and palenques, creating a limited-edition line of mezcals that highlights small production. They also decided to experiment with rare types of agaves, some of which have never been distilled before, in order to create unique products.

At Mezcal de Leyendas, the agave hearts are cooked in traditional earthen firepit ovens, and then crushed by a tahona. The fermentation occurs in open-air wooden vats, and the double distillation takes place in copper pot stills.

Besides the limited editions, the core line consists of:

- Maguey Espadín: Made by Maestro Leo Hernández.

- Maguey Verde: Produced by Maestro Juan José "Che" Hernández, a second-generation mezcalero with twenty-five years of experience. It's made with 100 percent *Agave salmiana* in San Luis Potosí at the Hacienda Santa Isabel. The agave hearts are cooked in a steam-heated steel oven and fermented in ground-level cement tanks.

- Maguey Cenizo: The maestro mezcalero is José Ventura Gallegos, and he has twenty years of experience in making artisanal mezcal. The agave used is 100 percent *Agave durangensis*, and it is made in Nombre de Dios, Durango, in the northwest Mexican Altiplano Duranguense. The agave hearts are ground with a mechanical grinder and fermented in ground-level wood vats, then distilled in a mixed alembic still made of copper and wood.

- Maguey Ancho: Made by fourth-generation mezcalero Oscar "Chícharo' Obregón, who has fifteen years of experience. This mezcal is made with 100 percent *Agave cupreata* in Mazatlán, Guerrero, in southwest Mexico, at Fábrica, where the family shares the roasting pit but each member (grandfather, father, brother, and Chícharo) uses different alembics. The agave hearts are mechanically ground and fermented in oak wood vats.

- Maguey Tobalá: Produced by first-generation mezcalero Aarón Robles, who has fifteen years of experience, this mezcal is made with 100 percent *Agave potatorum* in a palenque that can only be accessed by foot, which is situated an hour away from San Pedro Totolapa, Oaxaca. The milling process is carried out with a tahona and the fermentation occurs in oak wood vats.

- Maguey Azul: The maestro mezcalero is Guadalupe Pérez, who has twenty years of experience in the production of artisanal mezcal. Maguey Azul is made with 100 percent *Agave tequilana* in Tzitzio, Michoacán, in the western Sierra Madre Occidental (southwest Mexico) at the Don Perez Vinata. The milling is manually done with a mallet, and the fermentation happens in natural oak wood vats.

Mezcal de Leyendas aims to be fully carbon neutral by 2024. They also developed the first solar mezcal to reduce their ecological footprint. It's called Vinata Solar, and it is produced by maestro mezcalero Gerardo Ruelas, a third-generation sotol producer who also has experience with mezcal, rum, and whisky. Vinata Solar is made in Nombre de Dios, Durango, with 100 percent *Agave durangensis* and with solar energy used in every part of the process. The steam-heated oven is powered by solar panels, and the agave hearts are ground with a solar-powered mechanical grinder and distilled in a custom solar copper still.

MEZCAL DE LEYENDAS MAGUEY ESPADÍN

This mezcal is produced by Leo Hernández, a fifth-generation mezcalero with twenty years of experience in artisanal mezcal production.

Maguey Espadín is made with 100 percent *Agave angustifolia* in San Baltazar Guélavila, Oaxaca, in the Sierra Madre del Sur in southwest Mexico. The agave hearts are crushed with a stone tahona and fermented in natural oak wood vats. The distillation takes place in a copper alembic still.

On the nose, Maguey Espadín presents notes of lemongrass and fresh herbs. On the palate, it has caramelized fruit and citrus notes. The ABV is 50.1%.

MONTELOBOS MEZCAL

Montelobos was founded by Iván Saldaña and fifth-generation mezcalero Don Abel López Mateos in 2010.

Iván Saldaña was born in Guadalajara. He studied molecular plant biology at McGill University in Montreal and then completed a PhD in biochemistry and physiology at the University of Sussex, UK, studying the evolution and characteristics of agave and its ability to withstand extreme weather conditions. Years later, he cofounded Montelobos Mezcal. In 2019, Campari bought the majority stake in the company.

The distillery, Casa Montelobos, is located in Santiago Matatlán, in the state of Oaxaca, in the shadow of the namesake mountain chain (in Spanish, Wolves Mountain) in the Sierra Madre. At Casa Montelobos, Don Abel López Mateos' family uses traditional production methods, from planting, to harvesting, to distilling.

At Casa Montelobos, organic agave hearts are harvested sustainably and roasted in an enlarged firepit filled with no-resin dry hardwood and volcanic river stones. The cooked agave hearts rest between three and ten days to avoid overfermentation. The milling process is carried out by a tahona and a machete to obtain fine pieces of fiber. The fermentation occurs in open pinewood vats. Distillation takes place twice in copper stills.

Casa Montelobos is USDA and kosher certified.

Montelobos has four expressions: Espadín, Ensamble, Tobalá, and Pechuga. Espadín and Pechuga are made with espadín agave and milled with a traditional single stone tahona pulled by a mule. Tobalá and Ensamble (made with *Agave cupreata*, *Agave angustifolia*, and *Agave potatorum*) are milled with a mechanical shredder mill. All the expressions are distilled in copper stills heated with direct firewood.

Since 2011, Montelobos has been committed to sustainability practices by choosing artisanal production and supporting mezcaleros. They use 100 percent certified organic agave for Espadín and cultivated agaves to reduce the impact of removing a living plant from the ecosystem. They established a composting program for vinaza and fiber residues so they won't end up in the soil and river. They have improved Casa Montelobos to reduce waste, use recycled wood, and minimize the use of firewood to help with the deforestation problem.

MONTELOBOS ESPADÍN

This is a Blanco mezcal made with organic, sustainably grown agaves. Cooked in underground stone-pit ovens, the agave hearts are then milled using a tahona. After fermentation in open-air pinewood vats, it's double distilled in copper stills.

You can drink Montelobos Espadín neat, on the rocks, or in any cocktail of your liking.

Crystalline in color, on the nose it has freshly cut grass, damp earth, honey, and citrus notes. On the palate, there is a balance between cooked and green agave, nuts, and smoke. The finish is long and smoky. The ABV is 43.2%.

MIJENTA TEQUILA

Mijenta ("My people") was founded by former Bacardi CEO Mike Dolan, sommelier and mixologist Juan Coronado, and Ana María Romero, a maestra tequilera with over twenty-five years of experience, whom *Tequila Aficionado* magazine named the winner of the Best Maestra Tequilera in 2020.

Mijenta Tequila is produced with 100 percent blue Weber agave from regions close to Arandas, Jalisco. The agave hearts are slow cooked in traditional clay ovens. Ana María carefully chooses the yeast strains and monitors the fermentation. The double distillation takes place in small batches in copper pot stills. The aging process occurs in a mix of American white oak and European oak barrels from different regions. Finally, the tequila is bottled unfiltered.

Mijenta offers the following expressions:

- Blanco: unaged and the winner of numerous awards, including the gold medal at the USA Spirits Ratings in 2020, and the silver medal at the Los Angeles Spirits Awards in 2020.

- Reposado: aged for up to six months.

- Añejo Gran Reserva: matured for a minimum of eighteen months in four different types of barrels: American white oak, French oak, French acacia casks, and cherry barrels.

In terms of sustainability, Mijenta is very active. It uses agave waste and coffee bean bags for packaging materials and vegetable ink for printing. All glass components are recycled, and no pesticides or herbicides are allowed on the fields. Mijenta is the first tequila to receive a B Corp Certification from the nonprofit organization B Lab, which measures a firm's social impact across categories such as the environment, community, employees, and customers.

They work with several nonprofit organizations—such as Whales of Guerrero, to protect the whales living off the coast of Guerrero—and charities focused on cleaning beaches and lakefronts.

The Mijenta Foundation also helps local communities by supporting health and educational initiatives, and assists jimadores by preserving their skills and supporting their families.

MIJENTA REPOSADO

Mijenta Reposado is aged in a blend of American white oak, French oak, and French acacia casks for up to six months.

Light gold in color, it presents vanilla, bergamot, honey, and orange blossom flower aromas on the nose. It offers flavors of cooked agave, honey, vanilla, and cacao nibs on the palate. The finish is long, and the ABV is 40%.

MEZCAL UNIÓN

Mezcal Unión was founded in 2011 by a group of friends who were looking to start a mezcal brand. While visiting palenques in Oaxaca, they met an old man who explained that the future mezcaleros would not be able to do all the distilling, bottling, marketing, and sustainability practices, unless some sort of co-op or *unión* was created. That's why the group of friends decided to fund Mezcal Unión, supporting and investing in the producers and their palenques, and increasing the production volume through an artisan process and sustainable practices.

Mezcal Unión works with more than twenty producer and farmer partners, creating a network of agave farmers and distillers.

The Unión provides investment and training programs and buys the distilleries' products. Each batch is produced by an Oaxacan family.

In 2022, Diageo acquired Casa UM, owner of Mezcal Union.

Mezcal Unión is made with agaves espadín, cirial, and tobalá by different palenques that use the same production methods, starting from the same percentages of each agave for each batch. The agave hearts are cooked together in wood-fired conical stone oven pits with white oak, then ground with a horse-drawn tahona. The fermentation occurs in pinewood barrels with water. The distillation takes place in copper stills, and finally the mezcal is bottled by hand.

Mezcal Unión uses the solera aging process as well, allowing it to both work with individual families and to keep consistency in the products. The solera process, which comes from other beverage producers working with drinks such as wine and beer, consists of blending the new batches into one mother batch.

Mezcal Unión offers the following expressions:

- Mezcal Unión Uno: 100 percent artisan handmade with espadín and cirial agave in San Baltazar Guélavila, Oaxaca, and winner of the gold medal in the Spirits Selection at Concours Mondial de Bruxelles in 2019.

- Mezcal Unión Silvestre: 100 percent artisanal mezcal made with espadín and tobalá in Tlacolula de Matamoros, Oaxaca.

- Mezcal Unión El Viejo: named after the old man the founders once met, it is 100 percent artisan handmade with espadín and tobalá.

In terms of sustainability, Mezcal Unión plants espadín, tobalá, and cirial agaves. So far they have planted 750,000 agaves and 15,000 trees, such as copal and guaje (river tamarind) trees, in the mountains of Oaxaca.

MEZCAL UNIÓN SILVESTRE

Mezcal Unión Silvestre is an artisan handmade mezcal produced with five-year-old agave espadín and fourteen-year-old agave tobalá. The agave hearts are milled by a tahona and distilled in an alembic copper still.

Mezcal Unión Silvestre presents aromas of fresh herbs, flowers, and hints of fruits on the nose; it offers cooked agave, herbs, and flower flavors on the palate. The finish has cocoa and pink pepper hints. The ABV is 40%.

MEZCAL MAL BIEN

Mal Bien was founded by Ben Scott and Anthony Silas, and produced by small producers in the states of Oaxaca, Guerrero, and Michoacán.

Here are the different producers with their products.

OAXACA: VALLES CENTRALES

- Chucho and Poncho Sánchez: fourth-generation mezcaleros, they built their own palenque, Los Hijos de Juana (named after their mother) in 2019 in San Baltazar Chichicapam. For their mezcals, they use espadín, jabalí, and arroqueño. The agave hearts are cooked in a pit oven for three days with encino wood and rested for five days; then they are crushed with a wood chipper (*hebradora*) and a tahona. The fermentation occurs in ocote pine tanks for three to five days with the addition of water from the well. The double distillation takes place in copper alembic stills.

- Oscar Morales Garcia: fourth-generation mezcalero. His father, Don Lucio Morales Lopéz, produced mezcal until his death in 2021. Oscar and his family use the recipe developed by his father. Produced in San Dionisio Ocotepec, Mal Bien by Oscar Morales Garcia is made with 100 percent agave espadín cooked in a pit oven with encino oak and white pine for five to seven days. The agave hearts are then crushed with a tahona and naturally fermented in open-air pine vats for four to six days. The distillation takes place in copper pot alembic stills with a refrescador.

MIAHUATLÁN

- Felipe and Ageo Cortes: third- and fourth-generation mezcaleros in Mengolí de Morelos, they produce mezcals side by side, but separately for the cuts and final composition. The batch code ending in FC means that it's made by Felipe, and the batch code ending in AC means it's made by Ageo. They work with arroqueño, tepeztate, tobalá, jabalí, and madrecuishe. The agave hearts are cooked in a pit oven with several types of wood, such as encino and mesquite, for eight to ten days. According to the variety of agave, they will then rest for five to seven days or be milled immediately with an ox-drawn tahona. The fermentation occurs in an open-air tank with water from the well for three to eight days. The distillation takes place in copper-pot alembic stills with a refrescador.

- Victor and Emanuel Ramos: third- and fourth-generation mezcaleros in Mengoli de Morelos, they are related to the Cortes family and adopted similar practices. If the batch code ends with VFR, it means that the cut and final composition are made by Victor; if the batch code ends in ER, it's made by Emanuel. They work with several varieties of agave, such as tepextate, coyote, and tobalá. The agave hearts are cooked in pit ovens with encino and mesquite for eight to ten days, then are ground immediately or after a period of resting (depending on the agave) with an ox-drawn tahona. The fermentation occurs in open-air sabino (Montezuma cypress) tanks with well water for three to eight days. The distillation takes place in copper alembic stills with a refrescador.

EJUTLA

- Félix Ramírez Mendez: a second-generation mezcalero in the village of Yogana, he works with several varieties of agave, most commonly espadín. The agave hearts are cooked in a pit oven with several types of wood, such as encino and guaje (river tamarind), for three days, then crushed with an ox-drawn tahona after five days of resting. The fermentation occurs in open-air sabino (Montezuma cypress) tanks for three to five days, and the distillation takes place in copper alembic stills with a refrescador.

GUERRERO

- Antonio and Lorenzo Sonido: Don Antonio, the first generation of mezcaleros, started to work with wild papalote agave (*Agave cupreata*) growing on his family land when he was in his twenties, and only in 2011 built his own *fábrica* with his son Lorenzo in Pantitlán, Chilapa de Álvarez. The family works with both papalote and espadín. The agave hearts are cooked in a pit oven with encino and tepezcohuite wood for six days, then milled with a wood chipper. The fermentation occurs in open-air pine vats with spring water for nine days. The distillation takes place in copper alembic stills.

- Ciro and Javier Barranca: third- and fifth-generation mezcaleros working in Ahuacuotzingo, Chilapa de Álvarez, with agave papalote, azul, zacatoro, and espadín. The agave hearts are cooked in pit ovens with several types of wood, such as encino amarillo and tepehuaje (leadtree), for four to five days, then chopped with a hatchet and then a wood chipper. The fermentation takes place in pinewood vats with spring water for five to seven days. The distillation takes place in copper alembic stills.

- Refugio Calzada Hernández: third-generation mezcalero working in Tetitlán de la Lima, Chilapa de Álvarez, with almost only agave papalote. The agave hearts are cooked in a pit oven with different types of wood, such as encino and tepehuaje (leadtree), for six days. After one day of rest, they are chopped with a hatchet and then a wood chipper. The fermentation takes place in open-air pine vats with spring water for four days. The distillation takes place in copper alembic stills.

- Tomás and Emiliano Gutiérrez: third- and fourth-generation mezcaleros in Tepehuixco, Chilapa de Álvarez. They work with agave papalote, which is cooked in a pit oven with several types of wood, such as encino, for six to eight days. After one day of rest, it is chopped with a hatchet and then with a wood chipper. The fermentation occurs in open-air pine vats with spring water for five to six days. The distillation takes place in copper alembic stills.

- El Tigre: founded by Damian and Raquel in 2011, after meeting the mezcaleros in the Patricio García family. They use agave papalote, which is cooked in a pit oven for seven days with tepehuaje (leadtree), then ground with a wooden mallet in a wooden canoa (type of vat). The fermentation lasts for three to five days with spring water. The distillation takes place in a stainless-steel or clay pot still.

MICHOACÁN

- Isidro Rodríguez Montoya: first-generation mezcalero in Río De Parras. He works with his son with agave alto. The agave hearts are cooked in a pit oven with encino for eight days, then ground by hand in a eucalyptus canoa (type of vat). The fermentation occurs in open-air tepetate stone vats with spring water for eight to ten days. The distillation takes place in copper Filipino stills.

MAL BIEN ISIDRO RODRIGUEZ ALTO

Don Isidro is a first-generation mezcalero who worked in the communal vinata (another name for mezcal distillery) for fourteen years. In 2015, he built his own vinata where he produces exclusively with agave alto.

Crystal clear in color, Mal Bien Isidro Rodriguez Alto is bright on the nose, with aromas of tropical fruits and pepper. On the palate, it offers mineral and floral flavors. The finish is long, with fresh notes. The ABV is 46%.

MONITA TEQUILA

Monita Tequila is a new brand founded by Serita Braxton and named after her late mother.

A creator by nature, Serita Braxton is an entrepreneur, author, podcaster, and editor originally from Severn, Maryland. Based in Europe since 2016, she reawakened her love of writing in Berlin, built her business during the pandemic in Tenerife, and now works from home in Málaga, Spain. Her criminal justice degree, cocktail bar experience, and marketing mind have prepared her for navigating the spirits industry as one of the first Black female–owned tequila brands in the world.

Monita Tequila is produced in Tequila, Jalisco, by Tequila & Spirits Mexico.

Monita Tequila is made with 100 percent blue agave, and it's focused on one expression at the moment.

MONITA TEQUILA BLANCO

With its clear color and 40% ABV, Monita Tequila Blanco has a citrusy aroma on the nose and a sweet and peppery flavor on the palate.

Q & A WITH SERITA BRAXTON, FOUNDER OF MONITA TEQUILA

Here what the founder of Monita Tequila told me about how she started and what she thinks about the tequila market.

Tell us more about your new company.

Monita Tequila is named in honor of my late mother. She was someone deeply rooted in her community, who made the time to create connections with people that turned into lifelong memories. This brand was created to celebrate life like she did, by making every moment meaningful. For me, tequila is a symbol of celebration—from taco Tuesday margaritas with friends, to making my own margaritas at home for my mom and me, or taking tequila shots to jump-start a night out or celebrate a recent achievement.

The label, designed with my friend, French artist Lou Marthiens-Lartigue, pays homage to the agave plant tequila is made from and traditional Spanish tiles, and has a touch of purple—my mom's color. From the taste to the look, this tequila is a handmade product of my love for my mom and the history of the spirit that was the centerpiece of so many of my own positive memories. I offer it as a beautiful, delicious centerpiece to others' memory-making moments as well.

In what way is Monita Tequila different from other brands?

Did you know that there are tequila brands (who shall remain nameless) that reuse the same flavor profile? There's nothing wrong with sticking with what has always been done. But as a newbie in the industry, I wanted to offer a new taste that can appeal to more people, especially the skeptics who previously had a bad experience with tequila.

In Mexico, they like their tequila to burn as it goes down. My friends and I not so much. So I developed my own flavor profile with an amazing tequila technician at the distillery. The aim: you actually unscrunch your face when the tequila hits your taste buds.

Do you have any special releases or limited editions?

I launched the Blanco profile first because it's the unaged tequila, and often the first introduction to the spirit. As a new (unaged) brand, I wanted to test this flavor profile to see how drinkers enjoyed the taste (luckily the positive feedback has been unanimous so far). Now that I'm a few months into the market, I'm excited to begin developing aged profiles, canned cocktails, and a unique alternative that's currently trending up in other parts of the spirits industry. But I'll share more on that later!

Are there any new or innovative techniques you are currently experimenting with in your production?

Monita Tequila prides itself on being authentically distilled and additive-free. The development of new products will continue to prioritize that. I'm generally a fan of the original; I just want to put my personal spin on it. That's what I'll continue to do with this brand.

Are you aware of any initiatives to reduce the environmental impact of tequila production?

From what I saw in Mexico, producing tequila is simply another form of farming. There are people in the agave fields harvesting the piña of the agave plant, and that is cooked and distilled. Using traditional methods, this process appears to have a low environmental impact. But like with other types of farming, corners can be cut or environmentally harmful practices can be put into place to produce more to meet more demand. This is already happening with the additives and fillers that go into some tequilas to produce more at a lower cost. I hope that the stakeholders in the tequila industry can resist the mass market mindset that may create more environmentally harmful practices.

Can you tell us more about the cultural significance of tequila in Mexico?

It's important to honor the land and traditions where tequila comes from. When you visit the agave fields in Tequila, Jalisco, you can see how proud the locals are of the history. In order to be officially called tequila, it can only be produced in certain regions of Mexico, one of the main ones being, not surprisingly, Tequila.

The distillery I'm working with to develop my brand, Tequila & Spirits Mexico, is deeply committed to the traditional distillation process of the agave plant. All the stakeholders are on-site at the distillery, working alongside locals—mostly women from the area—to harvest, cook, process, and bottle the agave's piña that results in the delicious tequila we get to enjoy today. I definitely encourage anyone who is curious about how tequila is made to visit the land and take an official tour.

How are tequila and mezcal seen nowadays?

Mezcal is also derived from agave, but it was likely produced outside of the regions required to be considered tequila. There are so many bars around the world dedicated just to tequila and mezcal. In Accra, Ghana, there's a Mexican restaurant/tequila bar that has 150 different tequilas and mezcals on offer. You can literally build an entire bar around the two of them; I'd say their importance is here to stay.

What do you think about using tequila in cocktails?

My tequila has a unique flavor that is sweet and smooth enough to drink on its own. But the great thing about adding tequila to a cocktail is that the flavor profile blends perfectly with any cocktail recipe. It's been fun to see bartenders reimagine traditional cocktails—such as the bloody mary, which is made with vodka—by substituting tequila and introducing drinkers to new ways to enjoy the spirit.

What is the proper way to drink tequila?

When you choose a 100 percent agave tequila with nothing but the authentic taste of agave, I'd say sip it to really enjoy the flavor! I've had many people scrunch their faces up and say, "No tequila for me, it burns!" That's the stigma I'd like to break with Monita Tequila. To offer a tequila that can be enjoyed slowly and savored by everyone.

What do you think were the main factors that contributed to the tequila boom?

It would be interesting to see the official research on this, but I hate to say it: I believe that the rise in celebrity spirits brands has helped bring in more interest. Especially for people to know that there are more options than the big-name brands that have dominated the market.

There are actually thousands of tequila brands available around the world, and tequila has been in production for centuries—it's just that people were only used to seeing the same four or five bottles, with little knowledge of the industry. I'm honored to be a part of the new class of independently owned tequila brands that can introduce new audiences to this historic spirit.

How do you see tequila growing in the next few years?

I hope to see tequila production remain true to its roots. Unlike other spirits, I don't think that much needs to be added for tequila to be enjoyable to drink. But every spirits drinker likes something different! So I do see an increase in flavored tequilas, much like we saw with vodka.

Is there any change you would like to see in the industry?

I believe that the experts in Mexico who have been working in this field for generations should remain in control of any changes made to their industry. I am but a guest, grateful to develop my own brand alongside them. But I think a concern we can all take into account for the growth of tequila would be the climate. Like with any plant, they need certain conditions to grow. When those conditions change, it could lead to less viable plants to harvest or longer production times. Let's hope that doesn't happen!

Is there anything else you would like to add?

When I share the brand on social media, my Europe-based friends and followers are frustrated because they can't purchase Monita Tequila in their country (yet). Navigating the spirits industry on my own has been, at times, an overwhelming challenge, but I've learned so much along the way. Including that I need local distributors in each different country (and sometimes state). So bear with me! I've already gotten interest from Ghana, Spain, and Iceland to carry the brand, which would be the first Black female–owned tequila brand in these locations!

OLMECA ALTOS

Olmeca Altos was born among the collaborations of Henry Besant, Dre Masso, and maestro tequilero Jesús Hernández in 2009, with the aim of creating a tequila that was of high quality, accessible, and mixable in cocktails.

Masso and Besant, both world-renowned bartenders, also created the Worldwide Cocktail Club, a drinks consultancy focused on bartender training.

Jesús Hernández has been a maestro tequilero for over seventeen years and is a native of Jalisco. Olmeca Altos is crafted at the Destilería Colonial de Jalisco.

Today Olmeca Altos is owned by Pernod Ricard.

Olmeca Altos is made with 100 percent blue Weber agave, harvested from the mineral-rich volcanic soil of the highland area around Arandas. Jesús Hernández supervises every aspect of the tequila production. The agave hearts are slow cooked in traditional brick ovens for thirty-six hours; then they are shredded and pressed in the piedra tahona. The fermentation occurs with a particular yeast that Olmeca Altos isolated in the agave plant itself, creating its own strain of yeast that keeps the flavor profile consistent. The double distillation takes place in small copper pot stills. The aged tequila rests in former bourbon casks and is bottled and labeled by hand at the distillery.

Olmeca Altos offers the following main expressions:

- Plata: bottled after the distillation, without any aging.

- Reposado: aged for six to eight months.

- Añejo: aged in 200-liter bourbon barrels for a minimum of twelve months.

Olmeca Altos is very active in terms of sustainability: they compost 1,700 tons of waste, have reduced their water consumption by 16.45 percent, and recycle 97 percent of all the solid waste in the distillery, and the bottles, redesigned smaller and thinner, reduce the glass weight of the bottle by 20 percent.

Olmeca Altos also supports Sustainable Development Goals (one of the Global Goals proposed by the United Nations as part of its 2030 agenda) and is currently working with researchers to find innovative uses for agave bagasse fibers and construction materials made out of organic waste.

OLMECA ALTOS REPOSADO

The winner of several awards, such as the silver medal at the International Spirits Challenge in 2022 and Master at the Tequila & Mezcal Masters in 2022, Olmeca Altos Reposado is aged for six to eight months in white oak casks previously used to mature bourbon.

On the nose, it presents aromas of sweet citrus of orange and grapefruit, cooked agave, and vanilla. On the palate, it offers flavors of citrus notes, together with a long and well-balanced finish. The ABV is 40%.

PATRÓN

The company was founded in 1989 by billionaire John Paul DeJoria (founder of the hair care empire John Paul Mitchell Systems) and Martin Crowley, right after DeJoria asked him to bring back a bottle of good tequila from one of his trips to Mexico. Crowley returned with a hand-blown tequila bottle, and they had the idea to start a tequila company. They both flew to Mexico, where they met Francisco Alcaraz, a chemical engineer and distilling consultant who was freelancing at Siete Leguas, a family-owned distillery, which allowed him to work with the two cofounders. The first bottle of Patrón hit the market in 1989, but it was a slow and hard start. It was only in 2000 that the sales started to increase, when Patrón began to appear in ads and on TV by sponsoring motorsports.

Patrón then spread overseas; today, it has a presence in more than 150 countries. It is also considered the first ultra-premium tequila and is one of the top sellers in the world. In 2018, Patrón was sold to global spirit company Bacardi.

At Patrón, the agave hearts are hand chopped, slow cooked in the oven, and crushed by a tahona wheel and a roller mill. The fermentation lasts for three days, and the distillation takes place in small copper pot stills. Then the tequila is packaged and labeled by hand.

The tequila-making process occurs at Hacienda Patrón (opened in 2002), where only Patrón tequila is made. The distillery doesn't use any additives, sugar, or color, in order to remain authentic. They use high-quality raw ingredients and a slow distillation to deliver a complex premium tequila.

The expressions offered by Tequila Patrón are Silver, Reposado (aged in oak barrels for at least four months), Añejo (aged in a combination of French oak, Hungarian oak, and used American whiskey barrels for over twelve months), and Extra Añejo (aged in oak barrels for at least three years). Then, under the category Gran Patrón, we find: Platinum (tripled distilled, then rested in oak tanks), Piedra (aged for over four years), Burdeos (twice distilled and aged in used American and new French oak barrels, then finished in vintage bordeaux barrels). They also offer limited editions and Patron el Cielo, a silver tequila that has been distilled four times. Tequila Patrón has always been attentive to limiting the environmental impact of tequila production. That's why they developed a state-of-the-art water treatment system to recycle the water that will be used in the cooling towers and for cleaning. They also installed a natural gas pipeline to reduce CO_2 emissions.

The distillery is also funding a study with an agricultural research center in Mexico to ensure the sustainability of the Weber blue agave. They create more than 5,500 tons of fertilizer compost a year from the leftover agave fibers, which are also collected from ten other distilleries.

Since 2019, Tequila Patrón has contributed to helping the reforestation of Atotonilco el Alto in Jalisco, and it has also transplanted lime trees in the backyard of the Hacienda Patrón. They support their employees with flexible hours and after-hours education programs, and several charity organizations both at local and global levels.

TEQUILA PATRÓN SILVER

Patrón Silver Tequila is the brand's classic, lightest, and freshest expression. With a crystal clear look, it is perfect for blending with a high-quality mixer or may be easily sipped. Patrón Silver is the combination of two different productions. After being hand chopped and cooked, Weber blue agave is crushed by a two-ton volcanic stone tahona wheel and a roller mill. Then it's fermented in pine-oak tanks, triple distilled in copper stills, and handcrafted in small batches for high quality. Each bottle is signed and numbered and individually crafted by a glass artisan with recycled glass.

On the nose, Patrón Silver is rich in agave, aroma fruits, and citrus. It's a little earthy, giving a sense of the terroir of Jalisco. It displays a good texture on the mouth and is rich in agave flavors, with just a tad of ripe fruit, although peppery on the palate. The finish is long and warming, with more peppery notes. The ABV is 40%.

QUIQUIRIQUI MEZCAL

Quiquiriqui was established in 2012 by the collaboration between Melanie Symonds and the Mendez family from Matatlán, a three-generation mezcal producer with over eighty years of experience.

At the time, Melanie was a TV producer, but she fell in love with mezcal during a trip to Mexico in 2011 and decided to start a brand, by partnering with the Mendez family, after opening the UK's first mezcal bar in East London. As she said during my chat with her, "We only served mezcal, beer, and water, that's it."

The idea behind Quiquiriqui was to create high-quality traditional spirits with reasonable prices, so anyone could try mezcal.

When Melanie met the Mendez family, they were only producing their own mezcal locally. They began the partnership with Melanie to produce mezcal for Quiquiriqui, which was the first brand they ever worked on for the export market. Today, Quiquiriqui is sold worldwide.

Quiquiriqui produces 100 percent handmade mezcal. Their products are made in small batches, following the Mendez family recipes. The palenque, where Quiquiriqui is produced, has been in use for over one hundred years and is one of the five owned by the Mendez family. The agave, supplied by agave farmers and in a small amount by the family itself, is harvested by hand. The agave hearts are cooked in a fifteen-ton conical underground oven for three to five days. Once cooled down, the agave hearts are crushed with a volcanic rock tahona wheel pulled by a horse. The fermentation occurs in open-air wooden vats with spring water and wild yeasts for four days to three weeks. The distillation takes place in 350-liter alembic copper pot stills, and finally, the mezcal rests for two weeks before being bottled by hand on-site. No chemicals, colorings, preservatives, or additives are used during the production.

Every expression is made by one master distiller. Besides the special editions, Quiquiriqui offers the following expressions:

- Espadín: Joven made with 100 percent espadín agave in Santiago Matatlán, following a third-generation family recipe. That's the mezcal Melanie tested when she first met the Mendez family.

- Ensamble: made with tepeztate from Zoquitlán by Orlando Altamirano, cuishe from Sitio del Palmar by Isabel Rios, and espadín from Santiago Matatlán by the Mendez family. The mezcals are then blended at the family palenque.

- Madrecuishe: made by Isabel Rios (she took over the production after the death of her husband, maestro mezcalero Natalio Vazquez) in Sitio del Palmar.

- Tepeztate: made by Orlando Altamirano, from the town of Zoquitlán.

Quiquiriqui is involved in seed growing and sustainability programs. To fight deforestation, Melanie said, "We are taking steps by only buying wood for the oven and still that is not from critical species, and that has been felled by companies who must certify the wood they supply is from sustainable sources, is diseased, or dead."

In regard to the endangerment of agave biodiversity, she added, "All the producers we work with have a commitment to an agave replanting scheme. The family now owns 74 acres (thirty hectares) where they are able to grow their own agaves, which enables them to plant a variety of species, which helps with biodiversity and helping to maintain the

rapidly decreasing populations of other agave types such as Mexicano, madrecuishe, and tobalá."

But that's not all. Melanie continued, "We are one of only four (out of eighty) palenques in the area to build a vinazas disposal unit, which neutralizes the acidic runoff from mezcal production before it's either used as a fertilizer on the fields or returned to the river. We also work with a local company in the village who makes adobo bricks, using the bagazo [pulp] for local housing projects. The Mendez family is currently the first in the area to be working on gaining their Certification for Responsibility of Environmental Balance."

QUIQUIRIQUI ESPADÍN

Quiquiriqui Espadín is the house expression based on the original Mendez family recipe. The hearts of the agave espadín are cooked in underground pits and crushed with a tahona. Then, the agave is fermented in wooden vats and double distilled in 350-liter alembic stills.

On the nose, Quiquiriqui Espadín presents sweet agave, leather, vanilla, and pepper aromas. On the palate, it offers vegetal, earthy, woody, and black pepper flavors. The finish is slightly sweet and spicy, with dark chocolate hints. The ABV is 45%.

QUIQUIRIQUI PECHUGA DESTILADO CON CACAO

Quiquiriqui Pechuga Destilado con Cacao is made with agave espadín and double distilled. Cacao beans are added to the double distilled mezcal and left to macerate for two weeks; then, a final, third distillation takes place. The mezcal is then blended and left to rest for two weeks before bottling. On the nose, Quiquiriqui Pechuga Destilado con Cacao offers spice, pepper, and chocolate aromas. On the palate, it presents coffee, dark chocolate, and nutty flavors. The finish is sweet, with roasted cacao and peppery notes. The ABV is 48%.

Quiquiriqui Espadín

Quiquiriqui Pechuga Destilado con Cacao

Rey Campero Madrecuishe

REY CAMPERO MEZCAL

Rey Campero, meaning "King of the Countryside," is a family business passed down from generation to generation. The members of the Sanchez family carry out all tasks, from the cultivation and harvesting of the agave to the distillation and bottling of the mezcal.

The Sanchez distillery is located in Candelaria Yegolé, a small village at the southeastern end of the Tlacolula Valley and at the foot of the Sierra Sur mountain range in Oaxaca. It was founded in 1870 by the Sanchez family. Today the master distiller is Romulo Sanchez Parada, who learned how to make mezcal from his father and worked in the palenque until he was twenty. Then he moved to North Carolina and returned to Oaxaca in 2003, when he inherited the family business. He now produces mezcal under the brand names Herencia de Sanchez and Rey Campero. Both are made with the same traditional techniques, and each batch is handcrafted using wild and cultivated agaves.

In Candelaria Yegolé, more than ten species of agaves grow, and the combination of the crystal clear water, the rich materials the land provides, the soil, and the climate makes a high-quality mezcal for the market.

Rey Campero emerged on the international market in 2012 and won the 2017 Ultimate Spirits Challenge Chairman's Trophy award for their Tepextate Joven Mezcal.

After the agave hearts are cut at the Sanchez distillery, they are cooked in conical earthen pits for four to five days and then ground by a tahona. The juice is then placed in open-air pinewood vats with wild yeast for fermentation. Finally, a double distillation takes place in handmade copper stills. Each different bottling represents the name of the variety of agave that's used in the mezcal.

Some of the Rey Campero expressions are:

- Blanco Espadín: before the double distillation in copper stills, it undergoes air fermentation using wild yeasts.

- Sierra Negra: the agave used takes between 15 and 18 years to mature.

- Blanco madrecuishe: 100 percent organic and made with a completely wild variety of agave.

- Tepextate, Cuishe, Espadín: part of the field blends series born out of the idea that whichever agave is ready should be prioritized, instead of waiting for the right amount of a single varietal to mature.

- Blanco Cuishe: a crisp mezcal with earthy notes and a touch of minerality.

- Blanco Tepextate: the agave matures for 15 to 18 years before being harvested.

- Blanco Mexicano: a classic and subtle herbal character, with notes of freshly cut grass, fruit, and smoke.

Rey Campero is strongly committed to local sustainability and conserving the region's cultivated and wild magueys. In 2013, they installed a nursery, where during the first rains of 2014, they planted 8,000 seedlings of *Agave rhodacantha*, which is currently at risk of extinction due to excessive harvesting for mezcal production. In the same year, 5,000 seedlings of the same agave were grown, with plans to transplant them during the first rains of 2015. Then they expanded their nursery with a further 5,000 seedlings of *Agave rhodacantha*, 3,000 of cuishe agave, and 1,500 of tepextate agave, to ensure the preservation of the plants. The commitment is to increase the number of agaves in their nurseries by 20 percent each year.

REY CAMPERO MADRECUISHE

Rey Campero Madrecuishe is made by maestro mezcalero Romulo Sanchez Parada in Zoquitlán, Oaxaca. It's fermented with natural yeasts and double distilled in copper stills.

Clear in color, it presents earthy, floral, and grassy aromas on the nose and a balanced and mineral taste on the palate. The finish is well-balanced, and the ABV is 48.9%.

ROOSTER ROJO

Rooster Rojo was founded by master distiller Arturo Fuentes Cortes and named after one of the national symbols of the Mexican culture, considered to be the king of all roosters.

Rooster Rojo is today part of the Amber Beverage Group, a fast-growing global beverage company, and it is produced at Fábrica de Tequilas Finos, located in the city of Tequila, at the foot of Volćan de Tequila, a UNESCO-protected area in Mexico. At the same distillery, other brands are produced (such as Zapopan, Villa One, and Tonala).

Rooster Rojo has won several awards, such as a gold medal at the San Francisco World Spirits Competition in 2019 for their Añejo expression.

Rooster Rojo tequila is made with 100 percent blue Weber agave, harvested from the Los Altos de Jalisco and Tequila regions. The agave hearts are cooked in autoclaves for ten hours, then shredded by a modern shredder. The fermentation lasts for up to seventy-two hours in stainless-steel tanks with a special yeast, which is a guarded secret of Arturo Fuentes Cortes. The distillation takes place in stainless-steel pot stills. The water used for Rooster Rojo is filtered through Mexican silver (they are the first to do so). Then, the tequila is aged in controlled humidity, and each batch is blended. The bottles are inspired by the Tequila volcano.

Rooster Rojo offers the following expressions:

- Blanco: the unaged expression.

- Reposado: matured in French oak casks for at least two months.

- Añejo: aged in used American oak bourbon casks for more than twelve months.

- Añejo Smoked Pineapple: matured for at least twelve months in used bourbon barrels, infused with red Spanish cooked pineapples.

- Ahumado Tequila: the agave hearts are pit-roasted in an artisanal underground oven for 48 hours; it then rests in oak barrels for over 2 months.

Rooster Rojo also produces a mezcal made with espadín, ground with a tahona, and double distilled in a copper pot still.

ROOSTER ROJO REPOSADO

Rooster Rojo Reposado is aged for a minimum of two months in French oak barrels and can be enjoyed both by itself and in cocktails. On the nose, it presents a ripe fruit and cooked agave aroma, with slight oaky notes. On the palate, it offers vanilla, caramel, and cooked agave flavors. The finish is medium length, silky, and warm. The ABV is 38% (may vary to 40%).

REAL DE MINAS DISTILLERY

Real de Minas is a distillery located in Santa Catarina Minas, Oaxaca, and is owned by Jacob Lustig, Jose Espinoza, and eleventh-generation master distiller Germán Bonifacio Arellanes Santos. At the distillery, they produce two brands: Don Amado and Mina Real.

The Real de Minas Distillery was built by Bonifacio's father and grandfather with two clay pot stills and a roasting pit. Since Lustig and Espinoza partnered with Bonifacio, the distillery was remodeled and modernized.

At the distillery, they harvest espadín for Mina Real and different varieties of agaves for Don Amado. The agave hearts are cooked in a pit oven and then crushed with a proprietary blade-spindle shredder. The fermentation occurs in pine vats, with no chemicals and only local strains of airborne yeast. The distillation takes place in pot stills, and the bottling is done on-site. At Real de Minas, they use an ecological roasting oven that saves 25,000 pounds (11,300 kilograms) of wood per roast. All the lumber used for distillation is self-sustained.

MINA REAL

Mina Real mezcal is made with agave espadín harvested in Santa Catarina Minas at 4,800 feet. The agave hearts are steam cooked in a cantera limestone kiln oven built by Jacob Lustig, making it an ecologically sustainable mezcal since it doesn't use firewood. The cooking lasts for thirty hours, including six hours of preroasting and six hours of cooldown. The agave hearts are then milled with a shredder. The fermentation occurs in 1,400-liter pinewood vats with agave fibers and wild yeast strains, and the double distillation takes place in wood-fired 60-liter clay pot stills.

Mina Real is a Blanco expression that offers agave nectar, fig, and jackfruit aromas on the nose. It has black pepper, earthy, and citrus flavors on the palate. The finish is mineral, with cayenne notes. The ABV is 46%.

DON AMADO

Don Amado mezcal is roasted in wood-burning earthen pits over gua-múchil and mesquite wood for four days, then fermented together with the agave fibers in 1,400-liter pinewood vats. The mezcal is then double distilled in small, traditional ceramic clay pots and aged in American oak casks previously used for Pedro Domecq Mexican brandy.

Don Amado offers the following main expressions:

- Rústico: made with agave espadín harvested in Santa Catarina Minas.

- Arroqueño: made with arroqueño harvested in San Pablo Apóstol, Oaxaca.

- Largo: made with karwinskii largo agave harvested in Santa Catarina Minas, cooked alongside the agave trunks and guamúchil and mesquite wood.

- Tepeztate: made with tepeztate agave harvested in Santa Catarina Minas.

- Ensamble Tobalá and Bicuishe: a blend of agaves harvested in San Pablo Apóstol.

- Ensamble Tripón, Barril, and Bicuishe: a mix of agaves harvested in San Pablo Apóstol.

- Pechuga: made with agave espadín and a third distillation by adding seasonal fruits, nuts, and spices, such as apricots, wild criolla apples, bananas, cloves, cinnamon, raisins, almonds, and walnuts.

- Reposado: made with agave espadín harvested in Santa Catarina Minas and aged for six months.

- Añejo: made with agave espadín harvested in Santa Catarina Minas and matured for a minimum of eighteen months.

DON AMADO RÚSTICO

The flagship expression of the Real de Minas distillery, Don Amado Rústico is made with agave espadín grown in Santa Catarina Minas, and is produced by maestro mezcalero Germán Bonifacio Arellanes.

On the nose, Don Amado Rústico presents crushed walnut, roasted corn, and savory spice aromas. On the palate, it's bright with caramel, butterscotch, and fresh herb flavors. The ABV is 47%.

DON AMADO TOBALÁ & BICUISHE

Don Amado Tobalá & Bicuishe is made from a blend of tobalá and bicuishe agaves, grown in San Pablo Apóstol, Oaxaca.

On the nose, it offers summer stone fruit (such as peach and plum), soft tea rose, and toasted red chili pepper aromas. On the palate, it presents flavors of Earl Grey tea, dried orange peel, candied mango, and cinnamon. The finish is smooth, with fruity, woody, and caramel hints. The ABV is 46%.

DON AMADO REPOSADO

Don Amado Reposado is made with agave espadín, grown in Santa Catarina Minas, and distilled in clay pot stills. It's aged for six months in used Pedro Domecq Mexican brandy barrels and American white oak barrels.

Don Amado Reposado presents aromas of roasted corn, vanilla, cinnamon, and tropical fruits on the nose. It offers caramel, white pepper, vanilla, and slightly smoky flavors on the palate. The finish has slightly spicy vanilla notes. The ABV is 45%.

Don Amado Rústico

Don Amado Tobalá & Bicuishe

Don Amado Reposado

REAL MINERO

Real Minero's roots date back to Santa Catarina Minas, when Don Francisco Ángeles, known as Papá Chico, used to distill Mezcal Minero out of necessity to generate an income. His son, Lorenzo Ángeles Mendoza, started to work with him at an early age.

In 1978, Lorenzo and his friend Don Nicolás Arellanes decided to acquire the first palenque of the family, La Concepción, in Santa Catarina Minas. When they started to produce mezcal, the bottles didn't have a label, but only carried the name "Autentico Mezcal Minero." It was only in 1999 that they added a label, where no brand yet appeared. In 2004, the first label appeared bearing the first Real Minero logo. Later on, in 2009, Real Minero started to export to Germany, and then in 2015 to the US.

Today Real Minero is run by fifth-generation mezcal producers Edgar and Graciela Ángeles Carreño.

Real Minero mezcals are produced at the family palenque, according to ancestral or artisanal methods. The agave hearts are cooked in a conical ground oven, then crushed by hand with a canoa (type of vat) and mallet or a mechanical shredder. The fermentation is done with native yeast, and the double distillation occurs with the Filipino method: clay pots above a wood-burning brick oven.

Real Minero offers various expressions of mezcal, including:

- Arroqueño: a Joven mezcal made with twenty-year-old agave arroqueño.

- Barril: a Joven mezcal made with fifteen-year-old agave barril.

- Espadín: made with ten-year-old agave espadín.

- Largo/Becuela: made with fourteen-year-old agave largo and twenty-year-old agave becuela.

- Largo: made with fourteen-year-old agave largo.

- Marteño: made with agave marteño from the karwinskii species, grown in the central valley.

- Pechuga: made with agave espadín, triple distilled with fresh fruit and raw chicken breast.

- Tequilana: made with eight-year-old Agave tequilana, grown in the central valley.

- Tobalá: made with twelve-year-old agave tobalá.

Real Minero started the Lorenzo Ángeles Mendoza Project (LAM Project) to preserve agave plants, documenting the processes of pollination, flowering, and reproduction of the agaves that grow in Oaxaca in order to share all the information with other small agave producers. Working with several botanists, Real Minero has a nursery and a laboratory dedicated to the protection, study, and preservation of agave.

They have also started the creation of pollinator-friendly areas: small spaces where a diversity of flowering plants provide food and shelter for bees, bats, and birds.

REAL MINERO PECHUGA 2021

Real Minero Pechuga 2021 is made in Santa Catarina Minas with ten-year-old agave espadín, cooked in a conical earthen oven and milled with a shredder. It is then fermented with native yeast and distilled with the Filipino method. The third distillation occurs with raw chicken breast, fresh fruit, nuts, and spices.

A full-bodied mezcal, Real Minero Pechuga 2021 offers sweet, smoky, and earthy flavors. The ABV is 53.60% (but may vary).

SAUZA TEQUILA

Because of its long history, Sauza is known as the Three Generations (*Tres Generaciones*) tequila. The company was founded in 1873 by Don Cenobio Sauza when he acquired La Antigua Cruz (The Old Cross) distillery, one of the oldest distilleries in Tequila, Jalisco. Sauza renamed it La Preseverancia, and around the same time, he exported the first bottle of tequila, then named Ya Sauza, to Mexico City. A theory also says that Don Cenobio Sauza was the one to change the name vino de mezcal to tequila.

When he died in 1903, his son Don Eladio Sauza took over the business. He expanded the range of products and renovated the distillery. Don Eladio also established Guadalajara's first commercial radio station and the city's first nightclub, Club Colonial. In 1946, he also became the first global ambassador for the tequila industry, introducing Casa Sauza to the world.

He was then followed by his son Don Francisco Javier Sauza, who ensured the quality of the tequila through the finest raw materials. In 1950, he started to cook agave in small ovens, *tequila hornitos*, in order to control the cooking process and get a better-tasting tequila.

In 1976, Don Francisco Javier Sauza sold part of his shares to Casa Pedro Domecq, who bought the whole company after Sauza's death in 1990.

In 1994, Domecq was acquired by Allied Lyons, then was bought by Beam Global Spirits & Wine in 2005, which was acquired by Suntory Holdings Limited, becoming Beam Suntory, one of the largest producers of spirits in the world, in 2014.

Sauza tequilas are still made in La Perseverancia and exported to more than seventy-three countries worldwide.

At Sauza, they use the diffuser method instead of cooking and shredding the agave hearts. With the diffuser, raw agave is ground and shredded; then it passes along a conveyor, where the fibers are treated with steam and water to extract the sugar gently. The agave juice is then transformed into fermentable sugars through a six-hour hydrolysis process.

Anaerobic fermentation, carried out in stainless-steel tanks, happens through a blend of yeasts and nutrients for twenty-four to twenty-eight hours. The tanks are closed to provide a fast fermentation, and an automated cleaning process guarantees a safe product.

The first distillation takes place in steel distillation columns, while the second is done in stainless-steel stills to obtain a range of 55% to 65% alcohol.

Before being bottled, the tequila is filtered, and demineralized water is added to adjust the gradation. All of Sauza's products are non-GMO, gluten-free, and kosher certified.

Their expressions are the following:

- Sauza Hacienda: Silver and Gold, both *mixto* tequila, unaged, and double distilled.

- Sauza Conmemorativo Añejo: made with 100 percent blue agave, matured in former bourbon casks.

- Hornitos: Plata, Reposado, Añejo, and Cristalino, all made with 100 percent blue agave and double distilled. The difference is in the aging process. Reposado is distilled for at least two months, Añejo for at least twelve months, and the Cristalino is triple distilled and then carbon-filtered to remove all trace of color from the spirit.

- Tres Generaciones: Plata, Reposado, and Añejo, which are made with 100 percent blue agave and distilled three times. Reposado is aged for at least four months, and Añejo for at least twelve months.

Sauza has been recognized by the Tequila Regulatory Council and Mexico's National Quality Award for its efforts to protect the environment. They use a water treatment plant to remove more than 99 percent of pollutants from wastewater. The residual solids from the water treatment plant are combined with leftover agave fibers to provide a natural, nutrient-rich fertilizer. They use recycled glass and wooden bottle closures from sustainable forests; if they are made of plastic, they can be recycled. Cardboard and paper labels come from sustainable sources, and Sauza asks their vendors to use transportation that has passed emission testing.

SAUZA HACIENDA SILVER TEQUILA

Sauza Hacienda Silver is a highly versatile tequila. It's a mixto tequila that works best in mixed drinks. It is 51 percent agave, with the remainder coming from pure cane sugar.

At Sauza, the agave is brought from plantations directly to the factory, where it is shredded. After a diffuser extracts the sugar, the agave is cooked via a hydrolysis process that takes up to six hours. After being distilled, the Silver tequila is sent to the dilution area, where demineralized water is used to dilute the alcohol content.

With a crystal clear color and hints of silver, this tequila has apple and jasmine notes on the nose, with a hint of herbs. The tasting notes include fresh blue agave and green apple. The Silver tequila has a medium-bodied, bitter citrus finish. The ABV is 38% (and may vary up to 40%).

TEQUILA SIETE LEGUAS

Siete Leguas was founded by Don Ignacio Gonzalez Vargas in 1952, in the small highland town of Atotonilco el Alto, Jalisco. Siete Leguas is named after the horse of Pancho Villa (a Mexican revolutionary who fought against the Mexican bourgeoise), who was able to travel "seven leagues" in one day.

Siete Leguas originally produced Patrón tequila, but in 2002 John Paul DeJoria and Martin Crowley, Patrón's owners, opened their own distillery. Today Siete Leguas is run by Juan Fernando Gonzalez, Don Ignacio Gonzalez Vargas's grandson, keeping the family traditions.

Siete Leguas consists of two distilleries sitting side by side, about 150 yards (140 meters) apart: Fábrica el Centenario, the original distillery opened in 1952, and Fábrica La Vencedora, considered the modern facility, opened in 1984.

Siete Leguas makes tequila with the artisanal method. They grow most of the blue agave in their fields (a few of the piñas are bought on the spot when needed, and some of them are harvested from lands that they don't own). When they harvest the agaves, they also save a small part of the green leaf, which is an ingredient in the production of their tequila.

At Fábrica El Centenario, they have small stone ovens to cook the agave hearts; then they use a roller mill and three tahona wheels, pulled by three pairs of mules that only work every two days, one hour and thirty minutes per day. As Juan Fernando explained during my visit to the distillery, "We cut the piñas in half; we take away the stalk, because otherwise you will get sour and bitter notes. We only cook the heart of the agave. We don't work with pressure; it's a slow cooking process to make sure that all the sugar is extracted. The hearts are cooked for three days, then rest for eighteen hours. To squeeze the fibers and extract the juice, we use a one-of-a-kind tahona, because we are the only tequila company

with a closed tahona. Normally in other companies, they have a tahona with drainage to separate the fibers from the juice. But here the only way to transport the juice to the tanks is to let the fibers reabsorb the juice again, and then we would fill the baskets and pour the fibers and juice in the tans. So the fibers and the juice are fermented together. We use all the fibers. That would give you more of the agave flavor, and the consistency; you get more texture. Also, you will be able to have more complex notes, such as butter, banana, and more lactic notes that you wouldn't get normally with the fermentation of the juice only. With the roller mill we only use the juice, but with the tahona we use the fibers and then we do the blend. That's because when we produce with the roller mill, we get a subtle, herbal, floral tequila, but with the tahona, we get a more spicy, buttery tequila. So we blend them. When you want a complex tequila, you need to cover four aroma groups: floral, fruity, spices, and herbal. When you cover all four, you have a well-balanced and rich tequila. We have the roller mill to cover the herbal and floral, and the tahona to cover fruits and spices. When we blend them, we have a very rich and complex tequila that you won't get tired of."

They ferment the *mosto*, agave fibers, and natural yeast in wooden tanks. They distill in copper pot stills; one of these is the original still from 1952, while the others date from the 1970s. They use the fibers in the first distillation, but not for the second distillation. The copper stills and fermentation tanks are all custom-made by artisans from Jalisco.

Before being bottled, the tequila goes through a simple cellulose pad filtration.

Siete Leguas' main expressions are:

- Siete Leguas Blanco: the unaged expression.

- Siete Leguas Reposado: rested for eight months.

- Siete Leguas Añejo: matured for twenty-four months.

- Siete Leguas de Antaño: aged for five years and classed as Extra Añejo.

- Siete Leguas Single Barrel: matured for between eight and twelve months.

SIETE LEGUAS BLANCO

Siete Leguas Blanco is the unaged expression, made with 100 percent blue agave.

Crystal clear with hints of silver, Siete Leguas Blanco is a full-bodied and rich tequila that presents aromas of cooked and raw agave, herbs (such as grass, spearmint, and mint), orange blossom, roses, and citrus (such as grapefruit and lime) on the nose. Warm and silky, it offers cooked agave, herbal, and citrus flavors on the palate. The finish is long, with fruity and sweet hints. The ABV is 40%.

SIETE LEGUAS DÉCADAS BLANCO

Siete Leguas Décadas Blanco is a special edition that celebrates Siete Leguas' seventieth anniversary.

It's made with agave criollo, which grows in the wild. The agave hearts, which are smaller but richer, are cooked in small stone ovens for three days; then they are ground by a tahona mill. They're then fermented in open-air tanks with wild yeasts and double distilled in small copper pots with agave fibers.

Clear in color, Siete Leguas Décadas Blanco presents aromas of cooked agave and citrus on the nose. On the palate, it offers flavors of cooked agave, citrus, and pepper. The finish is lingering, and the ABV is 42%.

Siete Leguas Blanco

Siete Leguas Décadas Blanco

TEQUILA PARTIDA

Tequila Partida was founded by J. Gary Shansby, chairman of the board and CEO of Shaklee Corporation, with the aim of creating a premium tequila. In 2005, he partnered with Sofia Partida, whose uncle is Enrique Partida, a third-generation agave farmer with 5,000 acres of agave crop in Amatitán, southeast of the city of Tequila and northwest of Guadalajara. The master distiller is José Valdez. In 2022, Tequila Partida, winner of several awards, was purchased by Dutch spirits producer Lucas Bols.

Tequila Partida is made from only blue agave grown in the Tequila Valley. The agave hearts are slowly roasted in a stainless-steel autoclave for twenty-four hours at low temperatures, then crushed by a roller mill. The fermentation happens in open-air 20,000-liter stainless-steel fermentation vats for a minimum of two days. The distillation takes place in small stainless-steel stills equipped with copper coils at very low temperatures and in a five-hour cycle. Tequila Partida rests only in Jack Daniel's barrels. Coming from Tennessee, they are washed with water and then used to age the tequila, retaining as much of the Jack Daniel's sweetness as possible.

Tequila Partida offers the following lines:

- La Familia: Blanco, Reposado (aged for at least six months), Añejo (aged for eighteen months), Elegante (aged for a minimum of forty months), and Añejo Cristalino (aged for eighteen months in used bourbon barrels and then charcoal filtered).

- Roble Fino: meaning "fine oak," this range was inspired by José Valdez's visit to Scotland in 2018. The range consists of Roble Fino Reposado (aged for a minimum of six months in former bourbon barrels and for another two months in single-malt, sherry-seasoned casks); Roble Fino Reposado Cristalino (finished in former single-malt, sherry-seasoned casks and then charcoal filtered), and Roble Fino Añejo (aged for eighteen months in former bourbon barrels and for an additional five months in former single-malt, sherry-seasoned casks).

TEQUILA PARTIDA BLANCO

Tequila Partida Blanco is the unaged expression of the brand. Bright silver in color, it offers aromas of pepper and tobacco, followed by dried fruits and citrus on the nose. On the palate, it presents flavors of vanilla, tropical fruits, cooked agave, and volcanic minerals. The finish is light and lingering. The ABV is 40%.

Q & A WITH JOSÉ VALDEZ, MAESTRO TEQUILERO AT TEQUILA PARTIDA

What do you think are the most important things to know about your company and your products?

The most important things to know about Tequila Partida are:

- It is a tequila brand that takes very seriously the quality and consistency of every production batch since 2005, when we started.

- The tequila uses only fully matured agaves from the Tequila Valley; it is produced, aged, and bottled in the same distillery located in the town of Tequila, which is the heart of the Tequila Valley.

- The water used in the production process (milling or extraction of cooked sugar), fermentation, and dilution comes from a well located inside the distillery with a depth of 150 meters. This spring and mineral water is naturally filtered through the volcanic soil for many years.

- Tequila Partida is an additive-free-certified brand in its whole portfolio. It is part of our DNA to make 100 percent natural tequilas.

- Tequila Partida products are the result of a "go beyond" philosophy, which means [we] invest more quality in every aspect of the agave selection (highest sugar content, fully mature, fresh, close harvesting, highest weight), production process time (low and slow), barrels (fresh bourbon barrels from the source), and longer aging time; we also change the barrels after three to four years of use and taste every batch to ensure consistency.

- Our base product is the Tequila Blanco, so we put a lot of effort, time, money, and passion into making an excellent Tequila Blanco in every production that will either be to bottle as Blanco or to be aged and used to create the rest of our products: Reposado, Añejo, Añejo Cristalino, Extra Añejo, and the double aging line called Roble Fino, with Reposado, Reposado Cristalino, and Añejo.

How do you choose the type of agave you use?

The most important aspect in agave is the maturation, which is directly related to the sugar content and normally the age of the plant.

We visit every agave field before the production to make a visual inspection. We select random agaves that are harvested in that moment, and we take them to our laboratory at the distillery to measure the sugar and weight while we review the official CRT documents that include the age and quantity of plants.

Is there anything that makes your production different from others?

Yes, the rigors and meticulous quality standards in the selection of agave, which has to have at least 24 percent sugar (ART total reducers sugar), at least 30 kilograms in weight, not longer than 2 centimeters, and to ensure freshness we cook the agave no later than 24 hours after the harvesting happens.

Also, the fact that we don't use additives (any caramel color, natural or artificial essences and sweeteners) which are allowed to be used.

We go beyond the minimum in quality standards that the law requires, such as the aging time, the quality of the barrels (we use them only for three years), and using less methanol and bad alcohols than the maximum allowed, and we cut more heads and tails in the distillation (see page 35).

Also, the water used in both our production process and dilution process comes from a 150-meter-deep well that extracts spring and natural filtered water rich in minerals.

Moreover, we harvest the agave in the same region where the distillery is located, in the heart of the Tequila Valley in the town of Tequila. It is produced, aged, and bottled in the same distillery.

How can the terroir influence the production of tequila?

The terroir influences every cultivation of agave that will produce tequila. We can tell that because we are an additive-free brand, meaning that ours is a 100 percent natural production, and every batch is unique and different. We follow the same production method; however, we make minimal adjustments, depending on the average percentage of sugar of every batch that is processed.

Do you have any special releases or limited editions you can tell us about?

We do have the Roble Fino line, which is a special and limited production. Partida Roble Fino is the single malt of tequila, combining the world's highest-rated tequila and the most sought-after sherry oak casks. When I visited Scotland for the first time, I immediately felt the connection to the homeland of the world's finest single malts. I envisioned an amazingly rich product that combines Edrington's best in cask management and the world's highest-rated tequila. From this vision came Roble Fino.

Roble Fino Reposado. Roble Fino Reposado begins with Partida's highly acclaimed Reposado, which is aged for a minimum of six months in bourbon barrels to develop a brilliant, full body with notes of caramel, vanilla, and charred oak. This harmonious and well-balanced Reposado then continues its aging for an additional two months in single malt, sherry-seasoned casks from the most sought-after Scotch whisky. The result is an intense and complex spirit that is bottled at 43% ABV for optimal flavor and body.

Roble Fino Reposado Cristalino. Roble Fino Reposado Cristalino is naturally filtered to remove all color, while retaining its defined body and the complex flavors and aromas achieved through the double aging process. It is bottled at 40% ABV.

Roble Fino Añejo begins with Partida's highly acclaimed Añejo, which is aged for an extensive eighteen months in bourbon barrels to develop a full-bodied tequila with hints of spice, maple, and chocolate. This intensely flavored and spiced tequila then continues its finishing for an additional five months in single malt, sherry-seasoned casks from the most sought-after Scotch whisky. To appreciate the complexity and depth in flavor, the tequila is finished at 45% ABV, bringing together the two worlds in perfect harmony.

Are there any new or innovative techniques or ingredients you are currently experimenting with in your production?

For Cristalinos, we are using activated carbon. Also, the double aging process using American and European oak with different products used before.

Is there a cultural significance associated with the production of tequila in Mexico?

Tequila is part of the culture, history, and traditions of Mexico, even before the constitution of this country in 1810. The Mexican government has found distilleries more than 500 years old among the Mexican Indians (Aztecs, Mayans, Mexicas, Olmecs, etc.). Tequila is a reference of Mexican products around the world. Tequila is more than a beverage and a town in Jalisco. It is an iconic reference to being Mexican. I always said that I was baptized with tequila.

Agave has always had great importance in Mexican culture, alongside tequila and mezcal. So how are they seen nowadays?

Mezcal is growing in a bigger percentage than tequila; however, mezcal still represents a small portion of what tequila is.

I believe tequila is easier to taste; it is not as complex and strong as mezcal that combines more than twenty varieties of agave (espadín, tobalá, karwinskii, cupreata, etc., including blends) and different states of Mexico, while tequila uses only one agave (blue tequilana Weber) in only one complete state of Jalisco and a few towns around it, in states such as Guanajuato, Nayarit, Michoacán, and Tamaulipas (not close to Jalisco).

Agave spirits will continue growing, such as mezcal, destilados de agave, raicilla, bacanora, etc.

What do you think about using tequila in cocktails?

I believe it is the most versatile spirit beverage in the world. It goes excellent with citrus and creates margaritas and palomas using Blanco. But also it can be used for traditional cocktails of vodka and gin, because it is a white spirit. Moreover, aged tequilas (Reposado, Añejo, Extra Añejo, or double aged, such as Roble Fino) can create cocktails that normally are made with rum, cognac, whiskey, or bourbon.

Basically, tequila can create any cocktail if you choose the right category of tequila with the right ingredients that pair.

What is the proper way to drink tequila?

Either sipping neat or in cocktails. Neat can be either with a chaser such as water, sparkling water, beers (pairing the type of beer with the type of tequila; for instance, IPA with a Reposado or lager with a Blanco), or something else, such as sangrita (orange, tomato juice, spices, and spicy chili).

In Mexico, for decades we have been drinking tequila and soda, either cola (charro negro) or grapefruit soda (paloma). Nowadays it is more common to use 90 percent sparkling water and just 10 percent of cola or grapefruit. I believe we are a healthier generation that prefers quality over quantity (premiumization).

Also, tequila can pair with any type of food, whether it is an appetizer, such as caprese salad or white fish ceviche with Blanco, or tuna or beef carpaccio with Reposado; or a main course, such as mole or pork tacos with Añejo; or Extra Añejo with a dessert such as crepes or chocolate cake.

What do you think were the main factors that contributed to the tequila boom?

I believe consumers worldwide are discovering the goodness of real and fine 100 percent ultra-premium tequilas. It is a huge difference, today's offering of tequila brands from that of twenty years ago.

The tequila goodness is the versatility of enjoying either neat for sipping or for cocktails or with soda.

The tequila *categorías*—Blanco, Reposado, Añejo, Extra Añejo, and Joven—each one tastes completely different. Also, if we consider the region (highlands and Tequila Valley) and the production method (ancestral, artisanal, and industrial), that is why there are 2,000 different tequila brands produced in 170 distilleries, most of them in Jalisco.

Tequila is an agave spirit, just like mezcal, raicilla, bacanora, etc. The raw material is an agave that takes five to nine years to reach maturity, and the sugar inside this plant (inulin) has great properties that are actually good for human consumption. I believe the energy that the plant takes from the sun and the earth in this period of time is captured in every drop of tequila. I would say tequila is healthier than other spirits in the world.

When tequila demands grew, that led to industrializing the process of making it. Is there any change you would like to see in the industry?

Yes. The industrialization of tequila is growing, using the most efficient technology (diffuser and distillation columns), which is necessary for the nicer organoleptic tequilas. Tequila Partida has had a very consistent artisanal production process since 2005.

Tequila gained an important place in the market. How do you see it growing in the next few years?

It will continue growing. Recently tequila became the second-largest spirit category in the US in value, just behind vodka, but the experts predict it will become the number one later this year (in 2023). We have the commitment to keep quality and consistency, even if we continue growing as we have done every year since 2005.

Are there any initiatives or efforts being taken to reduce the environmental impact of tequila production?

We have invested in the correct disposal of the residuals of the tequila process, making compost with the cooked and squeezed agave fiber and the distilled fermented mosto.

We don't use additives during the production process, including chemicals in the fermentation. Also, we don't use agaves that have been cultivated with pesticides.

We minimize the use of water-using technology in the extraction and distillation process. We have the policy of only using agaves from the Tequila Valley, the region where our distillery is located. We only use premium agaves that reach maturity, which means they cost more and take more time, but it is the natural way; we don't look for agaves that are fast cultivated with a lot of chemicals and fertilizers that generate big agaves in a short period of time but affect the soil.

THE LOST EXPLORER MEZCAL

The Lost Explorer was founded by David de Rothschild in 2015, outside Southern California, as a lifestyle brand selling a range of wellness products, clothing, and a limited small-batch mezcal. It was inspired by what de Rothschild saw during his travels.

Only later, in 2020, did de Rothschild decide to cofound The Lost Explorer Mezcal with Thor Björgólfsson and maestro mezcalero Don Fortino Ramos and his family. In particular, Don Fortino's daughter, Xitlali, has worked closely with him in order to become the family's second-generation maestra mezcalera.

Maestro mezcalero Don Fortino Ramos has been working with agave and mezcal for the past forty years. The Lost Explorer is produced in Valles Centrales, in Oaxaca, through the artisanal process: they cook agave for three days in conical earthen ovens with local wood only. After letting the cooked agave cool for two to three days, The Lost Explorer uses a shredder for the milling process (instead of a donkey-towed tahona), ferments the agave in open-air oak barrels with wild yeast and spring water, and double distills in copper alembic stills in small batches.

They offer three different expressions, Espadín, Tobalá, and Salmiana; each of them is represented on the bottle by a different animal, illustrated by Daniel Barba.

- Espadín: 100 percent espadín agave.

- Tobalá: an earthy expression made with agave harvested in San Pablo Huixtepec, Oaxaca.

- Salmiana: an herbaceous expression made with agave harvested in San Pablo Huixtepec.

To promote biodiversity and sustainability, The Lost Explorer is involved in different projects:

- They plant three new wild agaves for every one hand harvested, use reclaimed wood, and capture rainwater (working with Isla Urbana, an NGO that contributes to water sustainability in Mexico), all actions that are implemented in their in-house Lost Laboratory. There, they also germinate seeds of genetically diverse agave on distillery land.

- They use glass bottles, made in Mexico from over 50 percent recycled crystal scraps, hand labeled, sealed with natural biodegradable cork, and finished with a kiss of natural beeswax.

- They launched their first brand marketing campaign, "Celebrate the Earth," to drive attention toward education and in-house sustainability and biodiversity practices, such as transforming agave waste into fertilizer and *copitas*, or mezcal tasting bowls.

- They have installed solar panels in agave fields to create renewable energy.

- They work alongside several nonprofit organizations, such as SiKanda and Mujeres AVE, to help women-led businesses.

Q & A WITH TIFFANY JAY, SENIOR GLOBAL BRAND AMBASSADOR FOR THE LOST EXPLORER

Could you tell us a bit about the brand?

The Lost Explorer Mezcal is a handcrafted spirit made from 100 percent agave, cultivated in the sun-soaked Valles Centrales, Oaxaca, in Mexico. In partnership with expert maestro mezcalero Don Fortino Ramos, The Lost Explorer Mezcal is a toast to empowering sustainable Mexican enterprise, while protecting the ancient artisanal craft, heritage, and biodiversity of Mexico. Harvested in harmony with the elements and in tune with the rhythm of nature, the Lost Explorer Mezcal range consists of three uniquely profiled varietals, Espadín, Tobalá, and Salmiana, that celebrate the Earth and seek to inspire people to live curiously and explore the diversity and wonder of the sacred agave plant.

The Lost Explorer Mezcal is produced in partnership with Don Fortino Ramos and his daughter, Xitlali, who are shareholders in the business.

The Ramos family has a long-standing connection to mezcal. Don Fortino Ramos is an internationally recognized and award-winning maestro mezcalero, who is responsible for the production and creation of each varietal within The Lost Explorer Mezcal range. Maestro Fortino has been perfecting his craft for well over four decades. A handcrafted, artisanal mezcal, The Lost Explorer Mezcal is produced at Don Fortino's family palenque (distillery) in San Pablo Huixtepec, Oaxaca, which sits alongside Fortino's family home, where he and his family have lived for many years.

Is there anything that makes your production different from others?

From seed to sip, the process of making The Lost Explorer Mezcal is carefully thought through. Every bottle of mezcal serves as a toast to empowering sustainable Mexican enterprise, while also protecting the ancient artisanal craft, heritage, and biodiversity of Mexico.

The three varietals are made from 100 percent agave plants that have reached their full maturity and are either cultivated or left to grow wild, harvested by hand in harmony with the elements and in tune with the rhythm of nature. They are double distilled and bottled entirely in Oaxaca, and are presented in beautiful glass bottles designed and produced in Mexico from over 50 percent recycled crystal scraps.

You are very attentive to the environment and the sustainability side of production. Could you tell us more?

Supply chain: Our production partners are selected based on their environmental ethos and quality, and in support of Mexican enterprise. Our bespoke bottles are made from over 50 percent recycled crystal scraps, and have been designed in partnership with a carbon-neutral Mexican glass producer based in Mexico City. Each of our bottles is hand labeled and sealed with biodegradable natural beeswax, sourced from the Guadalajara-based studio ALB Lacre y Caligrafía, which has impressive practices such as operating in a 100 percent solar-powered plant and using natural beeswax that has been sustainably harvested.

Biodiversity initiatives: The Lost Explorer Mezcal team replants at least three new agaves for every one harvested, to maintain sustainable production of mezcal in Mexico. Land has been purchased close to the distillery for maestro mezcalero Fortino Ramos to further develop and scale the replanting program, along with growing seedlings of genetically diverse agave.

Agave waste: The by-products of mezcal production—agave waste—are a big topic in the industry. Many producers avoid talking about it, but it is a reality; in some cases, vinazas (liquid residuals) are thrown into rivers, contaminating the ecosystem, or bagassos (fibers) are just left in the land, exhausting the soils. In addition to repurposing our agave waste into fertilizer, one of the initiatives we currently have underway at The Lost Laboratory is the upcycling of our agave waste into traditional *copitas* (cups) for people to enjoy tasting and sipping our mezcal from. This endeavor has been months in the making, overseen by our mezcalera-in-training, Xitlali Ramos. We also use the remainder of the agave waste to create adobe bricks.

In pursuit of preserving and promoting the diversity of agave varieties, we have also established The Lost Laboratory, a research-and-development entity where we will continue to actively explore ways to push industry standards, through ongoing experimentation and studies in support of environmental improvements in the making of sustainable, artisanal mezcal. While being respectful of the great depths of wisdom and tradition from the past, we are also looking to the future and seeking ways to build further sustainability through constant experimentation.

The Lost Laboratory at our brand home is way more than just a physical space—it is a concept that represents an ethos of living curiously through constant questioning and experimentation. As The Lost Explorer Mezcal grows and evolves, there will undoubtedly be questions, challenges, failures, successes, and breakthroughs that can be applied to the production of The Lost Explorer Mezcal, and hopefully to the wider mezcal industry too.

The Lost Laboratory is currently germinating seeds of genetically diverse agave on distillery land and experimenting with replanting initiatives in our conservation fields, to help expand and scale our replanting program.

Is there any change you would like to see in the industry?

Mezcal is much bigger than just a spirits category. It also encompasses significant cultural heritage, and in its essence is based and built around community. The global demand for mezcal puts at risk the existence of plants and species endemic to Mexico, the ecological relationships they maintain, and the economic systems the local communities rely upon to live on.

The larger drinks companies that are now coming in and acquiring land and production rights from small producers need to understand the moral obligations that they have in supporting these communities, moving forward. As demand increases, there are so many small family-run producers, who have been making agave spirits for many years, that are losing land that has been in their families for generations. It's important that these big acquisitions are replaced with partnerships rather than outright ownership; otherwise, the marginalization of smaller family-led producers will continue, and generations of traditional and unique mezcal-making techniques and flavor profiles will inevitably disappear.

GAS L.P. VAPOR →

THE LOST EXPLORER ESPADÍN

This expression utilizes an eight-year-old espadín agave harvested in San Pablo Huixtepee, The Lost Explorer Espadín can be sipped neat or in cocktails. It presents on the nose the aroma of fresh herbs, with hints of wood from the firepit. On the palate, it has chopped agave, mesquite, sweet red apple, and ripe fruit flavors. The finish is smooth and fruity. The ABV is 42%.

THE LOST EXPLORER TOBALÁ

Made with 100 percent agave from ten-year-old tobalá, which grows in arid, high-altitude canyons, this mezcal presents aromas of dry tobacco, wood, and cocoa on the nose. On the palate, it offers flavors of vanilla, leather, and clay. The finish is smooth and earthy, with hints of citrus and fresh grass. The ABV is 42%.

THE LOST EXPLORER SALMIANA

This mezcal is made with 100 percent twelve-year-old *Agave salmiana*, and it's the most herbaceous expression of The Lost Explorer. It presents aromas of green chili, grapefruit peel, and fresh agave on the nose. On the palate, it offers flavors of fresh citrus and dried herbs. The finish is spicy, earthy, and mineral. The ABV is 42%.

TEQUILA TROMBA

Tequila Tromba was founded in 2007 by Australians Nick Reid and James Sherry and Canadian Eric Bass, in partnership with master distiller Marco Cedano (who worked for Don Julio for seventeen years) and his son Rodrigo. Tromba gets its name from the "rainstorms" of the Jalisco highlands.

Tequila Tromba was previously produced at Casa Tequilera de Arandas, but it recently moved to Tequila el Viejito, located just west of Arandas in the south highlands of Los Altos in Jalisco, Mexico. Blue agave is hand harvested after seven years, and, once roasted in brick ovens, the agave hearts are ground with a roller mill. The fermentation occurs with wild yeast and a proprietary yeast strain produced by maestro tequilero Marco Cedano to give Tromba a distinct flavor. The distillation takes place in copper pot stills.

Tromba offers the following main expressions:

- Blanco: bottled straight after the distillation.

- Reposado: aged for up to twelve months in American whiskey barrels.

- Añejo: matured for at least twenty months and up to twenty-four in white American whiskey barrels.

- Tromba XA: Extra Añejo aged over thirty-six months in American white oak barrels.

Tromba created the Endangered Agave Program (EAP) to restore endangered species of agave and to establish a sustainable source of seeds. With every one hundred bottles they sell, Tequila Tromba plants a wild endangered agave. None of those planted agave will be harvested, but instead will be allowed to naturally mature, flower, and seed.

TEQUILA TROMBA BLANCO

Crystal clear in color, Tequila Tromba Blanco presents an aroma of sweet citrus and agave on the nose. It offers flavors of freshly cut green herbs, pineapple, caramelized agave, lime, honey, and mint on the palate. The finish is clean, and the ABV is 36% (may vary).

TEQUILA OCHO

Tequila Ocho was founded in 2008 by Carlos Camarena and Tomas Estes, aiming to prove that the concept of terroir exists in tequila as well.

Global brand ambassador for Tequila Ocho Jesse Estes explained, "Tequila Ocho, being the world's first single-field tequila, is proof that terroir exists in tequila. With the production process staying the same from batch to batch, what changes is the location of the agaves used. Each field will have its own unique terroir characteristics: soil composition, altitude, microclimate, drainage and subsoil, and orientation toward the sun, among many other factors. While each harvest of Tequila Ocho is recognizable as having the same 'DNA,' each production is also always notably different from the others. Some releases may be more floral, others more fruity, earthy, or vegetal, etc., due to the specific terroir in any given field."

Carlos Camarena is a fifth-generation farmer, a third-generation tequilero, and now the master distiller of Tequila Ocho. His great-grandfather was credited with bringing blue agave to the highlands of Jalisco.

Tomas Estes was a bar and restaurant owner for over forty-five years and also worked to promote tequila, agave spirits, and Mexican culture in Europe and across the world. That's why he was named the official Tequila Ambassador to Europe by the Mexican National Tequila Chamber.
In the beginning, Tequila Ocho was produced at La Alteña Distillery,

where other brands are made. In 2021, the production was moved to the Los Alambiques distillery, which was built from the ground up for Tequila Ocho so it could have everything needed to keep growing.

The reason behind the name comes from different factors: Tequila Ocho is made from the eighth sample created by Camarena for Tomas Estes, and it was founded in 2008. Agave takes eight years to ripen, and eight kilograms are needed to make one liter of tequila. It takes eight days for the agave to reach the distillery, where it will become Blanco tequila. Ocho Reposado is aged for eight weeks and eight days. Carlos Camarena has eight brothers and sisters, and the Camarena family is currently in the eighth decade of tequila production.

Tequila Ocho won the Distiller of the Year award from the San Francisco World Spirits Competition in 2005, a gold star from the World Marketing Organization in 2009, and the Chairman's Trophy at the 2020 Ultimate Spirits Challenge. Tequila Ocho is now sold in over thirty countries and is one of the most popular premium tequilas in the world.

Jesse said, "Tequila Ocho is the world's first single-field tequila, meaning that each bottle of Ocho designates the specific field and year of harvest. Ocho's primary goal is to create the most agave-forward tequila, creating a rich and complex tequila that highlights the flavor of the raw material." Jesse also explained the Tequila Ocho production method: "First of all, even though we harvest from only one field at a time, we do not harvest the whole field; we only harvest the ripest plants, which are handpicked by our team of experienced jimadores. So, we start our process with extremely ripe agave plants. Our fields are all family owned; we never source from the open market, meaning that we know that no chemical pesticides or herbicides are ever used on our plants or in the soil. Next, the agave hearts (*piñas*) are steam cooked in traditional stone brick ovens (*hornos de mampostería*) for a total of seventy-two hours. We then crush the cooked agaves using a *molino*, or roller mill, in order to extract the sweet juices, which will then go to fermentation. We use open-air oyamel pine vats to ferment in, using natural airborne yeast. Because the *mosto* is wild fermented, the process varies in duration, typically taking around four to five days. The first distillation takes place in a medium-sized stainless-steel pot still with copper components, and the second (and final) distillation takes place in a small, fully copper pot still. In order to preserve the essence of agave, our core range of aged expressions (Reposado, Añejo, and Extra Añejo) is aged minimally in matured American white oak barrels."

Tequila Ocho expressions include Blanco (unaged), Reposado (rested for two months and eight days in former American whiskey barrels made of oak), Añejo (aged for one year in oak barrels), and Extra Añejo (aged for three years in oak barrels that previously held American whiskey). In 2022, they released Tequila Ocho Reposado Barrel Select Widow Jane, aged for eight weeks and eight days in barrels sourced from the Widow Jane distillery in Brooklyn, New York. As Jesse said, "This year we will be relaunching the latest release of our Barrel Select range. Barrel Select involves experimenting with barrel aging our tequilas in different types of casks and employing different methods. The special edition from 2022 is more robust than our normal Reposado and bottled at 45.5% ABV. It was so popular last year that we will be rereleasing a very limited quantity this year."

Despite the fact that Tequila Ocho is loyal to the traditional production method, they still like to innovate, according to Jesse: "We were also (to my knowledge) the first tequila to age (and finish) in former rum casks. Last year, we released Tequila Ocho Puntas, which is an overproof Blanco tequila made from taking a very thin cut of the second distillation, starting toward the end of the heads and ending at the beginning of the hearts."

In regard to sustainability, Jesse said, "In terms of growing our agaves, no chemical herbicides, pesticides, or fertilizers are used in Ocho's fields. All the agaves used for Ocho's production are owned by the Camarena family, which means they have complete control over how the plants and soil are treated. The weeds are cut with machinery or by hand, and the fertilization is organic (compost and manure). Crops are rotated in order to ensure that the soil remains healthy (and does not get depleted of nutrients)—generally this involves eight to ten years of one full growth cycle of agave, some time for the field to lay fallow, and then one to two crop rotations of other plants, like corn and beans, to allow the field to fully recover before a new agave field is established. At our distillery, we incorporate many different aspects of ecological sustainability efforts into our practice. All organic residues from production (leftover agave fibers and vinazas) are used to elaborate compost, which will in turn go back to our agave fields as fertilizer. Additionally, all the packaging materials that are not used in the final product (cardboard, defective bottles, paper, wooden crates, etc.) are sent to recycling companies. We are very proud to have won the Sustainable Spirit Award from Tales of the Cocktail in 2017."

Even if Tequila Ocho is no longer produced at La Alteña Distillery, it is still part of the Bat Friendly Project: "As a tequila producer, we are only allowed, by law, to use one variety of agave—the blue agave. With that said, because of the way that blue agave has been propagated over the last century or so, it has now been deemed a monoculture; the genetic diversity across the whole category is so small that there is concern that one pest or disease could potentially wipe out the entire variety. Because of this, we form part of the Bat Friendly Project, in which we allow a small percentage of our quiotes to flower, providing food for bats (being nocturnal animals, and the agaves' flowers also open up at night) but also enlisting the bats' help, so to speak, in helping us pollinate agaves over large areas. In this way, we hope to reintroduce diversity, over time, in the blue agave species, using natural means."

Q & A WITH JESSE ESTES, GLOBAL BRAND AMBASSADOR FOR TEQUILA OCHO

Agave has always had great importance in Mexican culture, alongside tequila and mezcal. So how are they seen nowadays?

Agave has indeed played an import role historically in Mesoamerica and in what is now Mexico. So much so that the pre-Hispanic civilizations there had a goddess of agave, Mayahuel. Agave was used as food (when cooked) or to make pulque (a fermented beverage believed to be the oldest alcoholic drink of the Americas). The leaves and fibers could be used for thatching roofs, making paper and tapestry, and even paving roads. Today, I believe agave still plays an important role, primarily in the production of tequila and mezcal. I believe these spirits represent Mexican culture and identity, and are international exports that generate a great deal of pride.

What's the cultural significance associated with the production of tequila in Mexico?

Tequila is Mexico. The spirit itself is tied inextricably to the land from which it comes. Legally, tequila can only be produced in specific regions within Mexico, with almost all tequila coming from one state: Jalisco. Tequila is a source of great national pride in Mexico, as it should be.

What's your opinion about tequila-based cocktails?

I love using tequila as the base in cocktails. In fact, I've always said, "Whatever gin/vodka/whiskey/rum can do, tequila and mezcal can do better!"

What is the proper way to drink tequila?

I recommend drinking tequila neat, at room temperature, in a fluted tasting glass. This will highlight the organoleptic characteristics of the tequila, bringing out a maximum amount of flavor and aroma. However, tequila is best consumed however a person enjoys it most. I have seen people drinking it on the rocks, as a highball with soda water, and, of course, in cocktails.

What do you think were the main factors that contributed to the tequila boom?

I think the education that people like my father, Tomas Estes, have been doing over the past several decades has finally reached a tipping point of sorts. Bartenders, agave aficionados, and brand owners have all been extolling the virtues of drinking tequila, and it is now paying off. Enough people now understand and enjoy tequila, and are able to discern between different levels of quality. Regardless of my own opinion on this topic, I would be remiss not to mention celebrity brands. The sheer number of celebrity-owned or -endorsed tequila brands launched in the last few years is staggering, and of course this is drawing a lot of attention to the category.

How do you see tequila growing in the next few years?

I think tequila will continue to grow at a rapid rate. One of the main factors impeding its growth will be on the supply side, as I believe the demand for tequila today, globally, is enormous. So I believe the question is how well producers can keep up with this demand.

Is there any change you would like to see in the industry?

I would like to see a new category of tequila added to the two existing categories, tequila and tequila 100 percent agave. Under current regulations, even 100 percent agave tequilas are allowed to use additives. I think the introduction of a third category denoting additive-free tequila (which Ocho is) would add transparency for the final consumer. I believe many people see the words "100 percent agave" and infer that there is nothing else added (I would do the same if I did not have further knowledge of regulations and common practices in the industry). Typical additives include things like sugar, caramel, glycerin, and oak extract.

TEQUILA OCHO BLANCO CERRO DEL GALLO 2022

Tequila Ocho is the first to indicate on the bottle both the year of production and the field or rancho where the blue agave is sourced. This means that each batch, coming from different areas, will have distinctive characteristics.

In this case, Tequila Ocho Blanco was produced from 100 percent blue Weber agave harvested at the Cerro del Gallo estate and harvested in 2022.

Tequila Ocho Blanco Cerro del Gallo 2022 offers aromas of crisp agave and fresh herbs, with a crisp minerality on the nose. It presents flavors of fresh-cut grass and cooked agave. The finish is long, and the ABV is 40%.

TIEMPO TEQUILA

Tiempo Tequila was founded by James Hughston, working with a fifth-generation family of tequileros, including master distiller Augustin Sanchez Rodriguez.

Born in the North of the UK, James was not immune to the experience of cheap shots and expensive headaches, having limited access to quality tequila growing up. Traveling in Mexico over ten years ago, James started the journey of learning about the craft and culture of tequila, becoming passionate about the people and what was a very misunderstood but incredible spirit. It was this experience that led to wanting to share it with everyone through the world of Tiempo.

"Tiempo is a small, young, and independent brand, formed at a time (2015) when there was an opportunity for people in the UK to experience this enigma of a spirit (tequila) in new and interesting ways, in a world where it was becoming ever more popular, thanks to its synonymous relationship with the beautifully charismatic country that is Mexico. Both in a literal and spiritual sense, the spirit of Mexico," James said.

Tiempo Tequila harvests 100 percent blue agave from Los Altos, where the soil is rich and mineral, resulting in a sweeter taste of agave, and in Tequila Valley, where the volcanic soil provides an earthy, vegetal-tasting agave.

"We use both highland and lowland agave from Jalisco from our distillery's own estate or reputable farmers, who are contracted to ensure they received a fair price for the agave during price fluctuations. The agave is always mature at around five to seven years and a minimum of twenty-three Brix for an effective fermentation at around sixty hours," James said.

The agave hearts are slow cooked for forty-eight hours in a combination of traditional brick ovens and autoclaves; then they are crushed by a roller mill. During the fermentation, which lasts for sixty hours, only natural yeast and volcanic spring water are added. The distillation takes place in pot stills.

Tiempo Tequila currently offers one expression, which is Puro Reposado Cristalino.

In regard to future projects, James said, "2023 is a huge year for Tiempo, and we are making moves to radically evolve what we are doing. The timeline is yet to be fully determined as I write this, but part of this journey will see us work with some of the most forward-thinking minds in the industry. Off the back of this, we will be doing several special releases, so watch this space."

On the sustainability matter, James said, "There is lots going on in the industry to tackle the environmental impact, and as a small brand we have a responsibility to be thoughtful leaders in some respect, as it is very difficult for the big players to implement huge change in a short amount of time. One area we are looking at is water sourcing, which is a scarce resource in Mexico already, because there is a huge demand when producing tequila—approximately fifteen liters of water makes one liter of tequila. In the highlands of Jalisco, where most tequila is made, the groundwater has been exploited to a degree the government has declared it a closed zone, which is not the case in the Valley of Tequila, despite the availability being less than the demand. This means that it is not possible to concede for new regulations in the highlands due to the decline of the resource, making it challenging to maintain availability.

"The other side to the sourcing of water is the waste during distillation, which is highly contaminated and, if not disposed of correctly, can poison the environment. This will require effective recycling processes, and [that's] something we're looking to work on with our distillery.

"From a different perspective, we have designed our bottles to be upcycled into candles, and profits from sales are given to causes that look to preserve the ecosystem surrounding the production of tequila. This will enable us to help charities such as the Bat Friendly Project, with their goals to directly tackle issues that have come about as a direct result of tequila and mezcal production. This aims to use bat-friendly practices in the farming of agave by allowing 5 percent of the agave population to flower, ensuring there is nectar for bats to feed on and in turn promote pollination of agave. Amazing."

TIEMPO PURO REPOSADO

Tiempo Puro Reposado is aged for eight months in American oak whiskey casks, and then it goes through a light charcoal filter to remove the tannins, while maintaining a light color.

A special edition was released as Batch #001, for which a box and an A4 poster were created by Latin American illustrator Alan Berry Rhys.

On the nose, it presents aromas of sweet vanilla, caramel, and oak. On the palate, it offers flavors of citrus, caramel, and pepper. The ABV is 40%.

Here is what founder James Hughston said about Tiempo Puro Reposado: "Our first, and (currently) only, expression is very much aimed at the curious and uninitiated to drink good tequila in several ways: sip, mix, and shake. The profile is a Reposado (aged for five to eight months), with a specific type of filtering to remove dry or heavy oak and leave a sweeter and softer agave experience. The key is not to overfilter; otherwise you lose the agave and bring alcohol to the forefront. All this while being pure, with no additives or chemicals used during the process, and produced from only three ingredients: 100 percent mature blue Weber agave (five to eight years), volcanic spring water, and natural yeast."

Q & A WITH JAMES HUGHSTON, FOUNDER OF TIEMPO TEQUILA

What do you think are the most important things to know about your company?

We had spent a lot of time in Mexico prior to the inception of Tiempo and felt an overwhelming affinity for everything that it stood for and the experiences you have. Even the warm, dusty sensation you feel on your face when stepping out into the Jalisco heat has a story to tell. It quickly became apparent that everyone needs to know, experience, and taste Mexico, so enter Tiempo. Tiempo is a vessel to connect, indulge, and educate consumers on the world of tequila and Mexico in the most authentic and integral manner, and why we work with a fifth-generation family distillery, have a zero-additive policy, and use a process that engenders the highest-quality spirit—no diffusers.

Surrealism is at the heart of our brand ethos, which is a centric force for perceptions to see tequila in a different way; an evolution (or revolution) from the lime, salt, and slammer days, if you will. The passage of time is important in this concept, with how things change or are seen differently over time; hence Tiempo ("Time" in Spanish). It's also a nod to the length of time it takes to make quality tequila and the labor involved. However, the fundamental is Mexico, the culture, the people, and the art of making a spirit that is as deep in history as it is flavor. We are not a fashion accessory and always shine a light on all the incredible people who make Tiempo possible, the "real celebrities" as we like to say. We are grateful always.

We have seen many who have been on the fence with tequila completely changed by Tiempo, which is exactly what we aimed to do. It's a beautiful world, that of agave, and if we can help people on their journey, then it's of great value to all that we stand for.

Is there anything that makes your production different from others?

We spent several years perfecting a new (but old) technique of filtering for our current expression—we will use it only on this expression, and it is now widely used, but, in our view, incorrectly. It was a technique lifted from the rum industry, which uses it to make the rum clear after aging.

It is important to note that all tequila is filtered in some way; this is to remove any impurities which could be damaging to the taste or consumer; there are just different techniques to do it. We use activated charcoal (from wood), which is a natural source of carbon. Many aficionados will scowl at this technique, which by law makes a "Cristalino" tequila, and to be honest, we did (and still do) when it is overused. The trick is to have the correct size charcoal molecules and the correct amount of time in contact with the liquid; otherwise you will overfilter and lose agave flavors and all the tannins from the oak, and your tequila will just smell and taste like alcohol—so if you ever see a crystal clear "Cristalino," try to avoid it, as it'll be overfiltered and likely have additives in it to make up for the flavor loss. We were told we had to put Cristalino on the label by law, despite performing such little filtering.

The result is a well-rounded, lighter tequila, which perfectly met the objective to create a profile that was versatile but would welcome the uninitiated to sipping tequila. It is aimed at the wider market who prefers a softer and sweeter agave profile. We feel this is important for consumers to have that stepping stone into the world of agave.

What do you think about using tequila in cocktails?

Who doesn't love a margarita?! It's the world's most popular cocktail, which is just crazy, and amazing, given tequila is relatively new to the global market compared to other spirits.

I love tequila in cocktails; in fact, I rarely drink any other spirit in a cocktail. For its purity (depending on the brand), natural taste, and variety, I challenge anyone to name a cocktail that tequila doesn't work well in. It's such a versatile spirit and one of a few spirits that have a natural taste—for most spirits, aging, botanicals, or additives create the flavor. One of our favorites over at Tiempo is the "old timer," a simple blend of Lapsang souchong tea, agave syrup, and a dash of bitters; it's a take on an old fashioned but smoky, and the sweeter profile side of Tiempo shines with the agave and oak. Delicious.

What is the proper way to drink tequila?

Now this is a question that could be debated for a long time, likely over a few tequilas!

Tequila is a beautifully versatile spirit that is commonly misunderstood. Tequila has been drunk in all forms for a long time, and there are still new and interesting ways being created. We want people to drink tequila however they wish; all we do is provide a great product and guide on ways to get the best out of the spirit and flavor.

For me personally, I love to sip, neat, at room temperature. This is the most natural way to experience tequila (mezcal) in its purest form; there is no hiding. Once you become accustomed to sipping and indulging in the flavors, you can really tell everything about the tequila: what process is used, where the agave is from, and if there are any additives or unnatural flavors.

But it takes time to become accustomed to sipping; thus, it's not for everyone (immediately). We have tried to be conscious of this and with our first expression have created a tequila that is of the highest quality to sip, with a profile that is welcomed by newcomers but also versatile to mix and shake (or all three).

Can you talk about any traditions or cultural significance associated with the production of tequila in Mexico?

I love this question. As a forenote, it's important to remember that "all tequila is mezcal, but not all mezcal is tequila." Here I will refer to mezcal as the overarching term for tequila and mezcal collectively.

As I mentioned earlier, mezcal, both in a literal and spiritual sense, is the spirit of Mexico. Mezcal's creation and evolution are steeped in history and have been ever present during its rise to fame today.

Mezcal is a symbol of Mexico and its culture; there is a distinct synergy with how you drink and experience it which is entwined with everything that is Mexico, from its people and their beliefs, to the country and its history, to the flora and fauna that prosper there. It is not seen as a pretentious spirit, perhaps as whiskey is, and this is because it evolved out of a rather lewd drinking culture in the sixteenth century, where pulque (agave beer) reigned. Bernal Díaz del Castillo, a sixteenth-century con-quistador, said the Indians "engorged themselves through the rectum, using canes. They would stuff their bowels with the wine they make as we would take medicine. Such lewdness has never been heard before."

The invasion by the Spanish conquistadors impacted Mesoamerica in two ways: first, through the creation of the Mexican people/nation—the mestizo—who were a mix of Indian and Spanish blood, and second, as a by-product of pulque, which we now know as mezcal, due to the con-quistadors bringing the art of distillation from Spain, where brandy was commonly made.

This then created vino de mezcal, after the plant, which was known as mezcal, maguey, or, as most know it today, agave. Despite numerous prohibitions, mezcal wine grew in popularity, in particular the vino from the region now known as Tequila Valley. This was because the blue Weber was prevalent there, which had a high sugar content and pro-duced high-quality vino. By the end of the eighteenth century, fields of agave were being cultivated, and it became the birthplace of Mexico's national drink, vino de mezcal de Tequila (tequila). By 1887, tequila was well established; however, it was seen as a lower-class drink till 1990, despite being the "spirit of the fighters" during the Mexican Revolution. The turning point was post–World War II, when the margarita paved the way for tequila to truly become what it is today.

You can see how mezcal has so much cultural significance to Mexico and how it is possible that only now it has risen to fame. Mezcal is cele-brated globally now and is totally synonymous with its originating country.

How can the terroir influence the production of tequila? And does it affect the flavor of a singular batch?

Terroir is exceptionally important in the production of tequila: "You are what you eat."

First, the quality of terroir directly determines the quality of your agave—the soil, the cleanliness of the air, exposure to cold/heat, rainfall, etc.—these are all factors that, when balanced, will produce a beautifully ripe agave with a high sugar content, perfect for fermenting. We use agave that is matured for five to seven years (we're seeing more five years, now that the climate is heating up) at around twenty-three Brix (a sugar content indicator). This means we get a good fermentation without the need to add chemicals.

Second, the flavor will be affected, depending on the region, altitude, and soil. We are not the purveyors (currently) of terroir in the "single estate" sense. We take from both highlands and lowlands for a more complex mix of sweet and vegetal, respectively. Each batch will taste and look similar (with minor variations of taste and appearance, because we don't use additives to make them the same), aiming for consistency opposed to a profile based on a specific terroir. A brand that we love who is the expert in this is Ocho.

In the past few years, we have witnessed a tequila boom. What do you think were the main factors that contributed to that?

The first and main factor is premiumization. In the past twenty years, brands have seen incredible success by doing a good job showing the world a more premium take on tequila. This, in turn, has created a platform for heritage brands and boutique brands, like Tiempo, to be seen. Here it is important to note that education is a key driver in enabling the consumer to decipher what "premium" means, and it is not price. The prevalence of 100 percent agave tequilas, which has become the primary indicator for most (sometimes mistakenly) to be a mark of quality, has complemented a market that has evolved to be more health conscious and willing to spend more on "quality" spirits; the perfect storm.

To support the above, we have seen tequila become a fashion accessory to many celebrities. While in some respects, that has been detrimental to the quality and authenticity of tequila, it has raised the profile tremendously. While we (unfortunately) live in a celebrity culture where society is heavily influenced by such, consumers are drinking more than ever, and for us this is a great opportunity to highlight the real tequila and the real celebrities...celebrities don't make tequila, the talented workforce of a distillery does. It's important to remember that.

Third, Mexico's culture, charm, and charisma are trending globally, from global travel to Mexico to the presence of "tequila and tacos" restaurants across the world. For us, this is just incredible, because Mexico really deserves its time in the limelight. We hope it continues for many years to come.

How do you see tequila growing in the next few years?

Early forecasts see tequila set to grow at around 60 to 70 percent globally in the coming years, which is huge! We see that tequila will evolve to suit consumer habits: being presented in more flavorful forms, RTDs (ready to drink), and anything else that innovation brings.

This is amazing for Mexico, and we hope brands are conscious about the impact this will have on production and the environment surrounding it. We are certainly committed to respecting authenticity, to preserve the true nature of tequila and the sustainability of it.

Is there any change you would like to see in the industry?

Numero uno: transparency.

While we only launched in 2021, we spent many years prior (since 2015) developing our product and brand. In this time, we have learned a huge amount about everything that is tequila: its production, its spirit, and its culture. These learnings continue to mold what we are doing, who we are, and what we stand for in a positive and beautiful way that respects our values, tequila, the consumer, and Mexico as a whole.

Being able to see behind the scenes, we see brands lying and misguiding consumers, spouting buzzwords like "small batch," "sustainable," and "100 percent agave" to entice customers, with little or no intention of ever being true to their word.

The industrialization of mezcal, tequila in particular, has meant for the mass-produced brands that it is impossible to yield such quantities to meet demand without the use of machinery, such as the diffuser. While there is nothing wrong with this, we think it is important for consumers to know how the tequila has been made and what that means. Acid washing unripe agave in a diffuser will not make a great-quality tequila and will create harmful by-products, which consumers should know about. A tequila can still be 100 percent agave but made using industrialized techniques, and thus the consumer should be aware. The same goes for the use of additives. This is why we detail our process on our labels, so it is clear to the consumer.

VAGO

Vago was founded by Judah Emanuel Kuper and his friend Dylan Sloan. Their story begins when, in 1994, they went to visit Oaxaca and tried mezcal for the first time. Kuper fell in love with it, and later on, he opened a bar with his friend on the beach of an island in Puerto Escondido. There, he met his wife, Valentina, whose father, Aquilino García López, had produced mezcal for generations. Kuper started to buy mezcal from him to sell at his bar, while learning more and more about mezcal. Eventually, with his friend Dylan, Kuper decided to found Vago, and in 2013 they managed to export to Texas.

Most of the mezcal they produce comes from the Aquilino García Distillery, but other expressions are made in more remote villages from different master mezcaleros.

In 2017, Vago started to use different color labels for the different mezcaleros they work with. In 2018, they began a partnership with Samson & Surrey, which was later acquired by Heaven Hill Distillery.

Vago mezcal is made with 100 percent natural agricultural methods that have been passed down through the generations. On the label, all the information can be found, from the village where it comes from, to the type of agave used, to the details of the process (and more, according to the regulations). Vago mezcal is made by four different mezcaleros, each of whom has his own production method:

- Aquilino García López: His palenque is in Candelaria Yegolé, a three-hour drive from Oaxaca City. His family has been making mezcal for at least five generations, and now his sons are keeping the traditions alive. They grow agave espadín and Mexicano, and wild harvest agave tobasiche and tepeztate. Before working with Vago, they had never produced mezcal commercially, and now they exclusively work with Vago. At the palenque, they grind the cooked agave with a traditional stone tahona; then they ferment it in pine vats where only water is added to the natural airborne yeasts. After one week (depending on the ambient temperature), the García family distills the agave mash before all the sugar has fermented (which is sooner compared to what other mezcaleros do). The distillation takes place in a 250-liter copper still. Then the mezcal goes through a triple-sediment filtration through tubular cellulose filters and is then bottled by hand in Oaxaca City. The color of the label for Aquilino García mezcal is tan.

The expressions they offer are: Vago Elote (Hijos de Aquilino García), Vago Mexicano (Hijos de Aquilino García), and Pechuga de Mateo y Cuauhtémoc García (Los Hijos de Aquilino).

- Salomón Rey Rodriguez (Tío Rey): His palenque is situated in Gulerá, Sola de Vega (a 2.5-hour drive from Oaxaca) and is best known for the most diversity of agave in Oaxaca. Salomón Rey cultivates at least fifteen varieties of agave, such as espadín, coyote, arroqueño, mexicano, tobalá, sierra negra, madrecuishe, and barril. Like the García family, Salomón Rey had never before commercially produced mezcal, and he exclusively works for Vago. He uses two different ovens and cooks each batch for two or three days. Then the agave hearts are ground with wooden mallets (mazos) and chopped with a machete, then placed on a wooden platform where the mash is pounded with the mallets. The fermentation happens in pine cylindrical vats (he also has one made from the trunk of a pine tree), and the distillation takes place in clay pots (called *olla de barro*). As with the García family, Salomón Rey's mezcal goes through a triple-sediment filtration through tubular cellulose filters and is then bottled in Oaxaca City with a red label.

He produces: Vago Espadín en Barro (Tío Rey) and Esamble en Barro (Tío Rey).

- Emigdio Jarquín Ramirez: He produces mezcal in El Nache district of Miahuatlán de Porfirio Díaz (2.5 hours from Oaxaca City), where several varietals of agave grow: espadín, mexicano verde, tobalá, tepeztate, arroqueño, pulquero, madrecuishe (or madrecuixe), and cuishe. The Ramirez family uses a conical pit dug into the earth, roasts the agave for five to seven days, and lets it cool in the sun for one to two weeks. The agave hearts are milled by a cement tahona pulled by a mule to crush them. For the fermentation, they use ocote wood vats, and for the distillation a 300-liter copper still. In the case of the madrecuishe agave, Emigdio Jarquín adds a refrescador to the still (which has a stainless-steel cylinder surrounding it) to allow a double distillation in one pass. Then the mezcal undergoes a triple-sediment filtration through a tubular cellulose filter and is then bottled in Oaxaca City with a blue label.

  Their expressions are: Vago Espadín (Emigdio Jarquín), Vago Madrecuishe (Emigdio Jarquín), Vago Ensamble (Emigdio Jarquín), and Pechuga de Emigdio Jarquín.

- Joel Barriga Aragón: He is a third-generation distiller who works with his son at their ranch in Tapanalá, Oaxaca. They mainly work with espadín, roast the agave hearts with different local hardwoods, and grind them with 3.5-ton masonry and a stone tahona. The fermentation happens in sabino (Montezuma cypress) wood vats, and the distillation takes place in 300-liter copper pot stills. The label color is gold.

  He produces: Vago Espadín (Joel Barriga) and Pechuga de Joel Barriga.

Vago is committed to the preservation of the agave: they plant three agaves for each that has been harvested. They use sustainable agricultural methods to grow forty types of agave plants. They also let at least 5 percent of the agave sprout a *quiote* (flower stalk), so bats and hummingbirds can cross-pollinate plants. They recycle the leftover agave fiber to make naturally dyed paper for their labels.

VAGO MEXICANO

Vago Mexicano is made by Hijos de Aquilino García in Candelaria Yegolé. Created following the method of the artisanal production, Vago Mexicano is a well-balanced mezcal that offers fruity aromas on the nose, honeycomb and cinnamon flavors on the palate, and a mineral, dry finish. The ABV is 50.8% (and may vary).

VILLA LOBOS

Villa Lobos was born from the partnership between Carlos Camarena and Dale Sklar in 2010.

The Sklar family started to distill vodka and slivovitz plum brandy in the 1850s in Widze (back then, the town was part of Imperial Russia, and now it belongs to Belarus). Due to the pogroms, the Sklar family moved to London, where they opened a wine and spirit store, which was later destroyed in the London Blitz during World War II. The family then moved to Leicester in the UK, where they carried on the wine and spirit business. Only after World War II did they establish a liquor import company, called Sklar of London. Renamed Capital Wine Agencies, the company began a partnership with a seventeenth-century wine shipper, Joseph Travers and Sons Limited, under the name Capital Wine & Travers Limited, which imported and distributed world-famous brands. The company secured the distribution rights for all wines and spirits from the Soviet Union into the UK and the supply rights of all Scotch whisky and London gin to the USSR.

Eventually, Dale Sklar joined the family business as sales and marketing director. In 1969, he went to Mexico, where he decided to open his own company, Wine & Spirit International, intending to sell French and Italian wines. But in 1988, approached by a UK trader, he started to work with the Camarena family, importing both Tapatío and El Tesoro tequilas. It was only in 2010 that, following the steps of the partnership between Camarena and Denton, Dale and Carlos started to work together with the brand Villa Lobos (inspired by a lady, Lupita Villalobos, Dale met during his first time in Mexico).

Villa Lobos' process of making tequila involves a traditional brick oven where the agave hearts are cooked for thirty-six hours, followed by another twenty-four hours of cooling down. Then they are crushed in a mill and fermented in traditional large old pine tanks with only local natural yeasts. The double distillation takes place in a stainless-steel pot still and then in a smaller copper pot still.

Villa Lobos offers the following expressions:

- Blanco.
- Reposado: rests for eleven months.
- Añejo: aged for twenty-four months in American oak barrels.
- Extra Añejo: aged for four years.
- Distillation Strength Blanco: rested for a minimum of six months in stainless-steel tanks and distilled at 55% ABV.
- Los Hombres: a limited edition that rests for ten years in American oak barrels.

VILLA LOBOS BLANCO

Villa Lobos Blanco is not bottled straight after the distillation. It is left to age for six months in stainless-steel tanks. Clear in color, it has citrus and spicy white pepper notes on the nose and caramelized pineapple and pine nut notes on the palate. The finish is smooth and warm, silky and elegant. The ABV is 40%.

VILLA LOBOS REPOSADO

Villa Lobos Reposado is aged for eleven months in single-use American oak barrels.

It has a honeydew and soft amber color, and offers citrus and clove aromas on the nose. It presents sweet fruit and honey flavors on the palate, with a hint of spicy and mellow agave. The finish is long, with notes of spice, cinnamon, and caramel. The ABV is 40%.

COCKTAILS

2 AM IN OAXACA

I recommend using Bruxo X because of its citrus flavors and delicate floral notes that add brightness to the 2 AM in Oaxaca.

1½ oz. (45 ml) mezcal

½ oz. (15 ml) Whey Syrup (see page 470)

⅓ oz. (10 ml) Ube-Infused Cointreau (see page 471)

⅓ oz. (10 ml) freshly squeezed lemon juice

1 barspoon (5 ml) Chili Tincture (see page 472)

3⅓ oz. (100 ml) soda water

1 Chia Seed Cracker (see page 473)

1. Fill a mixing glass or a metal shaker with ice.
2. Pour the mezcal, Whey Syrup, Ube-Infused Cointreau, lemon juice, and Chili Tincture into the chilled vessel and stir rapidly with a bar spoon for 17 to 20 seconds.
3. Strain into a chilled highball glass over ice.
4. Top with the soda water and garnish with the Chia Seed Cracker.

WHEY SYRUP

An easy-to-make preparation that can be very handy when you have some leftover milk. It can be combined with caramel to make it even richer.

YIELD: 500 g

500 g whole milk

2 g citric acid solution 10 percent

1 kg (2.2 pounds) granulated sugar

1. Pour the milk into a pot and bring it to boil.
2. Once the milk is rising, add the citric acid solution 10 percent and mix until dissolved.
3. Take the pot off the heat and let it cool down.
4. Once cool, strain through a coffee filter until clarified.
5. Add the sugar and mix until dissolved.
6. Bottle and store in the fridge for up to 2 weeks.

If you don't have citric acid, you can use 2 oz. (60 ml) lemon juice.

UBE-INFUSED COINTREAU

Ube is a purple yam, and you can find the powder online. It will add body, vegetable and nut notes, and color to your drinks. Make sure it's well blended; otherwise you will get sediments out of the infusion.

YIELD: 200 g

10 g ube powder

200 g Cointreau

1. Combine the ube powder and Cointreau in a Thermomix and blend at speed 8 for 8 minutes.
2. Strain through a coffee filter.
3. Bottle and store in the fridge for up to 1 month.

CHILI TINCTURE

This style of tincture is very common. Just be careful with the dose of the chili, because it can turn out very spicy, since some chilies are spicier than others.

YIELD: 100 g

1 ancho whole dry chili

100 g vodka

1. Combine the ancho whole dry chili and vodka in a vacuum bag or jar at room temperature for 12 hours.
2. Strain through a coffee filter.
3. Bottle and store at room temperature for up to 3 months.

CHIA SEED CRACKERS

A healthy and light cracker that you can use as a garnish on cocktails or have with your food. Water becomes the binder to the seeds, so they stay together.

YIELD: 6–8 crackers

200 g water

30 g granulated sugar

50 g chia seeds

1. Combine the water and sugar in a container and mix until the sugar is dissolved.

2. Soak the chia seeds in the water mixture, mix, and let it infuse for 24 hours, until it thickens.

3. Spread the mixture on a parchment paper sheet and place in a dehydrator for 12 hours.

4. Break into small pieces and store in a container with a lid in a dry place for up to a week.

MIDNIGHT SERENADE

Calle 23 Blanco, with its smoked tobacco notes and fruitiness, is the best tequila for the Midnight Serenade.

¾ oz. (25 ml) tequila

½ oz. (15 ml) mezcal

⅓ oz. (10 ml) Campari

½ oz. (15 ml) freshly squeezed lime juice

½ oz. (15 ml) Mixed Herbs Syrup (see page 476)

1 mint sprig

1 Pineapple Crisp (see page 477)

1. Combine the tequila, mezcal, Campari, lime juice, and Mixed Herbs Syrup in a small metal shaker.

2. Fill with ice cubes to the top and close the shaker. Shake hard for 10 seconds until the shaker is frozen.

3. Double strain into a chilled tiki mug and top with crushed ice.

4. Garnish with the mint sprig and Pineapple Crisp.

MIXED HERBS SYRUP

If you use herbs for cooking, keep the stems and use them for the syrup. In this way, you will make a sustainable syrup without wasting anything. The flavor will be slightly lighter.

YIELD: 500 g

5 fresh sage leaves

3 fresh rosemary sprigs

5 fresh dill sprigs

3 fresh bay leaves

2 coriander sprigs

500 g water

granulated sugar

1. Blend the herbs and water together in a blender.
2. Let it rest in the fridge for 2 hours.
3. Strain the liquid through a cheesecloth first, and then a coffee filter.
4. Weigh the liquid, combine with an equal weight of sugar in a bowl, and mix until the sugar is dissolved.
5. Bottle and store in the fridge for a week.

PINEAPPLE CRISP

This crisp is a smart way to use the waste from a pineapple. It can also be served as a garnish for a dessert, or as a treat.

YIELD: 18 crisps (may vary, depending on how big you break them)

200 g pineapple pulp

250 g sugar

1. Juice a fresh pineapple and strain through a fine-mesh sieve.
2. Use the pulp left in the sieve to make the crisp.
3. Combine the pulp with the sugar and spread very thin on a tray covered with parchment paper.
4. Put the tray in the oven for 1½ hours at 320°F (160°C) or until it becomes crispy.
5. Remove from the oven and let cool.
6. Break into small pieces and store in a container with a lid in a dry place for up to 2 weeks.

AQUA DE VIDA

Go for Tequila Ocho Blanco, because its minerality and herbal notes, combined with crème de menthe white and ODVI Armagnac, will add freshness to the Aqua de Vida.

11/6 oz. (35 ml) tequila

¾ oz. (25 ml) Armagnac

⅔ oz. (20 ml) crème de menthe white

2 dashes Angostura bitters

1 mint leaf

1. Fill a mixing glass or a metal shaker with ice.
2. Pour the tequila, Armagnac, crème de menthe white, and Angostura bitters into the chilled vessel and stir rapidly with a bar spoon for 17 to 20 seconds.
3. Strain into a chilled Nick & Nora glass.
4. Garnish with the mint leaf.

BE ROOTS

In the Be Roots, I combined the fruity aromas and sweet agave flavors of Don Julio Blanco with sloe gin to amplify the fruity notes and add some tartness to the drink. Then, I added three different ingredients, each of them with a purpose. The Carrot Cordial adds sweetness and body to the drink, the Beetroot Soda brings earthiness and fizziness, and the ginger bitters give spiced notes. The Be Roots is the drink that led me to the finals of the World Class GB 2023 Competition. I hope you enjoy it as much as I did!

1⅙ oz. (35 ml) tequila

½ oz. (15 ml) sloe gin

¾ oz. (25 ml) Carrot Cordial (see page 482)

3 drops ginger bitters

1⅔ oz. (50 ml) Beetroot Soda (see page 484)

1 Carrot Crisp (see page 485) and 1 carrot leaf

1. Fill a mixing glass or a metal shaker with ice.
2. Pour the tequila, sloe gin, Carrot Cordial, and ginger bitters into the chilled vessel and stir rapidly with a bar spoon for 17 to 20 seconds.
3. Strain into a ceramic cup over a block of ice.
4. Top with the Beetroot Soda and garnish with the Carrot Crisp and carrot leaf on top.

CARROT CORDIAL

YIELD: 750 g

1 kg carrots

250 g honey

30 g green peppercorns

5 g Maldon salt

1.5 parts Nettle Tea Kombucha (see page 483)

1. Combine the carrots, honey, green peppercorns, and Maldon salt in a vacuum bag and gently warm it in a water bath for 24 hours.

2. Remove and let the mixture cool down. Weigh out the total of the carrot mix, and add 1.5 parts Nettle Tea Kombucha.

3. Place in a Thermomix and blend for 5 minutes at speed 6.

4. Let cool and strain through a cheesecloth first, and then a coffee filter.

5. Bottle and store in the fridge for up to a week.

NETTLE TEA KOMBUCHA

YIELD: 1 liter

1 liter hot water

17 g dry nettle leaves

150 g sugar

1 kombucha SCOBY or starter

1. Combine the hot water with the nettle leaves and let infuse for 20 minutes.

2. Strain through a coffee filter and add the sugar. Mix until the sugar dissolves and let cool down.

3. Place the nettle tea in a Cambro (plastic container) under the SCOBY and leave to ferment for 5 days.

4. After 5 days, strain through a coffee filter and pasteurize at 70°C (158°F) for 1 hour in a sous vide.

5. Strain into a bottle and store in the fridge for up to 3 weeks.

BEETROOT SODA

YIELD: 1.5 liters

200 g beetroot stems

1.5 liters filtered water

20 g coconut oil

1. Place the beetroot stems and filtered water in a vacuum bag, seal it, and place in the freezer for 24 hours.

2. Remove from the freezer and blend in a Thermomix for 5 minutes at speed 8.

3. Strain through a coffee filter. Then, melt the coconut oil in the microwave and mix it with the beetroot water.

4. Place the bag in the freezer for 24 hours.

5. Remove the bag, let it defrost, and, when melted, strain through a cheesecloth first, and then a coffee filter.

6. Pour into a Drinkmate or a soda maker and carbonate the mixture.

7. Bottle and place in the fridge for up to 5 days.

CARROT CRISP

YIELD: 8–10 crisps

Carrot pulp (leftover from Carrot Cordial)

Granulated sugar (see below)

1. When straining the Carrot Cordial through a coffee filter, the pulp of the Carrot Cordial that remains in the strainer needs to be blended with granulated sugar (weigh out the waste and add an equal amount of sugar).

2. Then spread on a parchment paper sheet and place in the dehydrator for 24 hours.

3. Break the crisps apart in 8–10 pieces and place in a container with parchment paper to keep them separate.

4. Close the container with a lid and store in a dry place for up to 1 week.

BEYOND THE DREAMERS

Go for Storywood Speyside 7 Reposado, because, having been aged in Scotch Speyside whisky barrels, it gains vanilla, honey, and caramel notes that make this tequila more pronounced on the sweet side.

1⅔ oz. (50 ml) tequila

¾ oz. (25 ml) freshly squeezed lime juice

½ oz. (15 ml) Clear Apple Juice (see page 491)

½ oz. (15 ml) Dill and Basil Oleo (see page 490)

2 dashes Angostura bitters

Soda water, to top

1 apple slice

1. Combine the tequila, lime juice, Clear Apple Juice, Dill and Basil Oleo, and Angostura bitters in a small metal shaker.

2. Fill with ice cubes to the top and close the shaker. Shake hard for 10 seconds until the shaker is frozen.

3. Double strain into a chilled highball glass and fill with crushed ice.

4. Top with soda water and garnish with the apple slice.

DILL AND BASIL OLEO

This oleo is not just a dream ingredient, but it's also very versatile. Try it as the sweet part in your daiquiri or gimlet.

YIELD: 200 g

7 lime zests (all pits removed)

100 g granulated sugar

3 fresh dill sprigs

6 fresh basil leaves

2.5 g salt

50 g water

1. Combine the lime zests and sugar in a vacuum bag, push out all of the air, and leave it at room temperature overnight.
2. Remove the lime zest from the syrup and blend the syrup with the fresh dill, fresh basil, salt, and water in a blender.
3. Pour the oleo mixture into a jar.
4. Stir thoroughly, strain, and bottle.
5. Store in the fridge for up to 2 weeks.

CLEAR APPLE JUICE

This is a very easy and fast preparation, but if you don't have time, you can buy it in any food store. You can make this juice with any kind of apple you like; in this instance, we're using red. Use it in cocktails or drink it by itself.

YIELD: depends on the size of the apples

10 red apples

1 g ascorbic acid

1. Juice the fresh apples and strain through a coffee filter to get a clear result.
2. Stir the ascorbic acid into the juice and store it in the refrigerator for up to 1 week.

BITTER PAYA

I recommend using Mina Real, because the gentle smoke, floral sweetness, and peppery finish will make this twist on a Negroni very complex.

1⅓ oz. (40 ml) mezcal

1 oz. (30 ml) Papaya and Mango Vermouth (see page 494)

⅔ oz. (20 ml) Campari

1 Mango Disk (see page 495)

1. Fill a mixing glass or a metal shaker with ice.
2. Pour the mezcal, Papaya and Mango Vermouth, and Campari into the chilled vessel and stir rapidly with a bar spoon for 17 to 20 seconds.
3. Strain into a chilled rocks glass over a block of ice.
4. Garnish with the Mango Disk.

PAPAYA AND MANGO VERMOUTH

This homemade fortified wine is very versatile. Use it in a dry martini or in gin-based cocktails. You can also add 0.5 g of gentian liqueur to give a more complex flavor to the Papaya and Mango Vermouth.

YIELD: 450 g

110 g papaya flesh

20 g mango flesh

350 g dry sauvignon blanc

0.25 g wormwood

1 g dried lemon

2.5 g brown sugar, plus more as needed

1 g salt

20 percent vodka (see instructions)

1. Cut the papayas into quarters and scoop out the seeds.
2. Cut the papaya flesh away from the skin.
3. Cut the mango into small pieces and remove the peel.
4. Combine the papaya flesh and the mango flesh, and blitz for 2 minutes at speed 3.5.
5. Place the papaya-and-mango mixture, sauvignon blanc, wormwood, dried lemon, brown sugar, and salt in a vacuum bag.
6. Place the vacuum bag in the refrigerator and chill for 12 hours.
7. Strain through a cheesecloth first, and then a coffee filter into a container.
8. Weigh out the liquid and add 20 percent of its weight in brown sugar and 20 percent in vodka.

9. Stir until the brown sugar is dissolved and bottle.

10. Store in the fridge for up to 2 weeks.

MANGO DISKS

1. Wash a mango and cut it with a mandoline slicer into thin slices (about 2 cm). With a cake stamp or cookie cutter, cut out a round from a slice and use it as garnish.

CAMPANELLO

Go for Don Amado Rústico because of its fresh and herbal notes and savory, spicy flavor, which go very well with this aperitivo-style cocktail.

1 1/6 oz. (35 ml) mezcal

½ oz. (15 ml) amontillado sherry

½ oz. (15 ml) Aperol

⅓ oz. (10 ml) Campari

½ oz. (15 ml) sweet vermouth

1 eucalyptus leaf

1. Fill a mixing glass or a metal shaker with ice.

2. Pour all ingredients except for the eucalyptus leaf into the chilled vessel and stir rapidly with a bar spoon for 17 to 20 seconds.

3. Strain into a chilled coupe.

4. Garnish with the eucalyptus leaf.

CATS HAVE NO LORD

I recommend using Pensador Espadín for its delicate and gentle floral and herbal notes, which make the Cats Have No Lord an herbal, bittersweet cocktail.

1 oz. (30 ml) mezcal

⅔ oz. (20 ml) Calvados

⅓ oz. (10 ml) Bénédictine

½ oz. (15 ml) Cocchi Americano

2 dashes Angostura bitters

1 lemon twist

1. Fill a mixing glass or a metal shaker with ice.
2. Pour the mezcal, Calvados, Bénédictine, Cocchi Americano, and Angostura bitters into the chilled vessel and stir rapidly with a bar spoon for 17 to 20 seconds.
3. Strain into a chilled coupe.
4. Garnish with the lemon twist.

COCO WAVES

The reason this cocktail needs to rest in a coconut shell is because the aging process develops fruity notes that will slow the sweetness of the drink, making it more tropical, more complex, and fruitier. The longer you age it, the fruitier it will be. I personally recommend letting it rest for 3 months. Choose a tequila such as Pueblo Viejo Blanco from Casa San Matías, because it will highlight the fruity and earthy notes of the drink.

1 coconut

1⅓ oz. (40 ml) tequila

⅓ oz. (10 ml) sorrel

⅓ oz. (10 ml) Campari

⅔ oz. (20 ml) sweet vermouth

⅔ oz. (20 ml) filtered water

2 dashes Angostura bitters

2 dashes orange bitters

1. Drill a small hole in the coconut to remove the coconut water.

2. With the help of a funnel, pour the tequila, sorrel, Campari, sweet vermouth, filtered water, Angostura bitters, and orange bitters through the hole.

3. Seal the hole with a lid. (Use anything you have at home that will cover the hole; it can be a lid, a wine cap, or a wine cork.)

4. Place the coconut in the fridge for a minimum of a month and up to 1 year.

5. Once ready, remove the lid and pour the drink into a chilled rocks glass over a block of ice.

DAISY GOT LOST

I suggest using Casa Don Ramón Mezcal Joven for its fruity, herbal notes, which in this sour cocktail highlight the smoky toasted agave notes.

1½ oz. (45 ml) mezcal

1 barspoon (5 ml) Bénédictine

½ oz. (15 ml) orgeat syrup

½ oz. (15 ml) freshly squeezed lime juice

½ oz. (15 ml) freshly squeezed lemon juice

⅔ oz. (20 ml) egg white

2 dashes orange bitters

Passion Fruit Husk Powder (see page 505)

1. Combine the mezcal, Bénédictine, orgeat syrup, lime juice, lemon juice, egg white, and orange bitters in a small metal shaker.

2. Fill with ice cubes to the top and close the shaker. Shake hard for 10 seconds until the shaker is frozen.

3. Double strain into a large chilled coupette glass.

4. Garnish with Passion Fruit Husk Powder.

DANCING WITH A PECHUDO

Make sure the ginger beer is stored in the fridge before you use it. Also, place the mezcal and dry curaçao in the freezer for 1 hour before preparing the drink; the colder they are, the more flavor you will get out of the Dancing with a Pechudo.

1⅔ oz. (50 ml) mezcal

½ oz. (15 ml) dry curaçao

⅓ oz. (10 ml) freshly squeezed lime juice

3 dashes Angostura bitters

3⅓ oz. (100 ml) ginger beer

2 mint sprigs

1. Pour the mezcal, dry curaçao, lime juice, and Angostura bitters into a chilled highball glass filled with ice.

2. Gently stir until chilled.

3. Top with the ginger beer and garnish with the mint sprigs.

EL SUSURRO

Sipello is an aperitif made with gooseberries. You can use it instead of Campari in a classic Negroni and instead of Aperol in a classic Aperol spritz. If you are a lover of aperitivi, Sipello should definitely be in your collection. But in case you can't find it, you can use Aperol: similar notes, but in the Italian way!

Go for Casa Don Ramón Punta Diamante Reposado; its notes of citrus and cooked agave will be the perfect pairing to this drink.

1 oz. (30 ml) tequila

⅔ oz. (20 ml) Sipello liqueur

½ oz. (15 ml) agave syrup

⅔ oz. (20 ml) freshly squeezed grapefruit juice

⅓ oz. (10 ml) freshly squeezed lime juice

1 lime coin

1. Combine the tequila, Sipello, agave syrup, grapefruit juice, and lime juice in a small metal shaker.

2. Fill with ice cubes to the top and close the shaker. Shake hard for 10 seconds until the shaker is frozen.

3. Double strain into a chilled Nick & Nora glass.

4. Garnish with the lime coin.

HOLIDAY DREAMERS

Go for Don Amado Rústico, because the fruitiness of this mezcal adds extra layers to this rich drink, which is then wrapped in clay finish notes.

1⅓ oz. (40 ml) mezcal

½ oz. (15 ml) banana liquor

¾ oz. (25 ml) freshly squeezed lime juice

⅔ oz. (20 ml) pineapple juice

1 oz. (30 ml) coconut water

½ oz. (15 ml) Simple Syrup 2:1 (see page 512)

1 pineapple wheel

1. Combine the mezcal, banana liquor, lime juice, pineapple juice, coconut water, and Simple Syrup 2:1 in a small metal shaker.

2. Fill with ice cubes to the top and close the shaker. Shake hard for 10 seconds until the shaker is frozen.

3. Double strain into a chilled highball glass and fill the glass with crushed ice.

4. Garnish with the pineapple wheel.

SIMPLE SYRUP 2:1

You can either buy this syrup or follow this easy recipe to always have fresh simple syrup at home. All cocktail recipes in this book are made with Simple Syrup 2:1, which is two parts sugar and one part water.

YIELD: 200 g

200 g water

400 g granulated sugar

1. In a jar, combine the water and sugar and stir until the sugar is dissolved.
2. Strain into a bottle and store in the fridge for up to 3 months.

FLYING GOAT

A twist on a classic margarita, with richer notes due to the presence of the goat cheese. A creamy and bright cocktail that will blow your mind.

1⅓ oz. (40 ml) Goat Cheese–Infused Tequila (see page 514)

⅔ oz. (20 ml) Cointreau

⅔ oz. (20 ml) Citrus Stock (see page 515)

2 dashes 10 Percent Saline Solution (see page 514)

1 Pear Disk (recipe below)

1. Combine the Goat Cheese–Infused Tequila, Cointreau, Citrus Stock, and 10 Percent Saline Solution in a small metal shaker.

2. Fill with ice cubes to the top and close the shaker. Shake hard for 10 seconds until the shaker is frozen.

3. Double strain into a chilled Nick & Nora glass.

4. Garnish with the Pear Disk.

How to Make a Pear Disk: Take one pear (I use Conference), cut it with a mandoline vegetable slicer into slices, and, with a cake stamp or cookie cutter, cut out the shapes you like. If you need to prepare them in advance for your guests, soak them with lemon juice and cold water so they don't oxidize and turn dark.

GOAT CHEESE–INFUSED TEQUILA

An easy infusion you can use in many drinks. Try it in a classic paloma or a bloody maria to give it an extra texture. I used Garrotxa cheese, but you can choose the one you like the most. Of course, the flavor will change, depending on the cheese.

YIELD: 700 g

100 g salted goat cheese

700 g tequila

1. Combine the salted goat cheese and tequila in a jar, stir well, cover, and then refrigerate for 48 hours; the liquid will separate and become clarified.

2. Strain twice through a coffee filter.

3. Bottle and store in the fridge for up to 2 weeks.

10 PERCENT SALINE SOLUTION

YIELD: 200 g

200 g cold-filtered water

20 g Maldon sea salt flakes

1. Combine the water with the Maldon sea salt flakes in a jar; stir until the salt is dissolved.

2. Bottle, and it is ready to use. Store in the fridge for up to 3 weeks.

CITRUS STOCK

YIELD: 400 g

1 orange

1 grapefruit

1 lemon

2 limes

400 g water

1. Peel all the fruits and set them aside.
2. Place the pulp of the fruits in a pot and boil for 30 minutes.
3. Strain through a cheesecloth first, and then through a coffee filter.
4. Bottle and store in the fridge for up to a week, or pour into an ice cube tray and freeze.

Do not throw the peels of the fruit away. You can either use them to make beautiful garnishes for your cocktails or you can use them to make candied citrus peels.

GRAPE APERITIVO

Go for Pasote Blanco tequila, because it will add tropical and citrus notes with a hint of pineapple that, combined with the Cocchi Americano, will make this Grape Aperitivo rich and balanced.

1⅓ oz. (40 ml) tequila

⅔ oz. (20 ml) Cocchi Americano

2/5 oz. (12.5 ml) White Grape Syrup (recipe below)

3⅓ oz. (100 ml) tonic water

2 green olives

1. Pour the tequila, Cocchi Americano, and White Grape Syrup into a chilled highball glass filled with ice.

2. Gently stir until chilled.

3. Top with the tonic water and garnish with the green olives on a skewer.

WHITE GRAPE SYRUP

YIELD: 500 g

500 g water

200 g white grapes

250 g granulated sugar

1. Combine the water, white grapes, and sugar in a saucepan.

2. Place over medium heat and cook until the sugar is dissolved.

3. Once cooled, strain through a cheesecloth and bottle.

4. Store in the fridge for up to 2 weeks.

GREEN MOONLIGHT

Go for Monita Tequila Blanco, because it brings to the Green Moonlight that peppery and smoky kick that will be perfectly combined with the Midori's sweet melon flavor.

1 oz. (30 ml) tequila

1 oz. (30 ml) Midori melon liqueur

1 oz. (30 ml) freshly squeezed lemon juice

1. Combine the tequila, Midori, and lemon juice in a small metal shaker.

2. Fill with ice cubes to the top and close the shaker. Shake hard for 10 seconds until the shaker is frozen.

3. Double strain into a chilled Nick & Nora glass.

GREEN PIÑA SOUR

11/6 oz. (35 ml) tequila

⅔ oz. (20 ml) Pineapple Leaf Water (see page 522)

½ oz. (15 ml) Basil Syrup (see page 523)

¾ oz. (25 ml) freshly squeezed lemon juice

¾ oz. (25 ml) egg white

2 drops ginger bitters

1 lemon wheel

4 micro basils (small sprigs of basil)

1. Combine the tequila, Pineapple Leaf Water, Basil Syrup, lemon juice, egg white, and ginger bitters in a small metal shaker.

2. Fill with ice cubes to the top and close the shaker. Shake hard for 10 seconds until the shaker is frozen.

3. Double strain into a chilled single rocks glass over a block of ice.

4. Garnish with the lemon wheel and micro basils.

PINEAPPLE LEAF WATER

This green water saves the leaves of the pineapple, instead of throwing them away. A unique combination of vegetal and earthy notes that will bring extra complexity to your drinks.

YIELD: 600 g

300 g pineapple leaves

600 g water

2 g sodium bicarbonate (baking soda)

1. Wash the pineapple leaves and blend them with the water and sodium bicarbonate in a blender for 10 minutes at full speed until you get a smooth texture.
2. Strain through a cloth and bottle.
3. Store in the fridge for up to 5 days.

BASIL SYRUP

Basil Syrup is a delicious herbal, sweet ingredient that can be fun to play with. You can use it in cocktails, but also to garnish your dishes. It can give an extra kick and at the same time be a beautiful garnish on the plate.

YIELD: 300 g

300 g water

2 g matcha powder

20 fresh basil leaves

300 g granulated sugar

1. Bring the water to a boil over high heat.
2. Remove from heat and combine the boiling water with the matcha powder.
3. Let the tea cool down.
4. Stir in the sugar until it is dissolved.
5. Cool and strain into a bottle.
6. Store in the fridge for up to 2 weeks.

HIERBA SANTA

I recommend using Siete Leguas Blanco for its sweetness from the agave, its fruitiness, and its complex flavor. Siete Leguas Blanco in the Hierba Santa brings bright and fresh notes.

Raspberry lemon kombucha can be found online. There are just a few brands producing it. Choose the one that you like the most.

1 oz. (30 ml) tequila

⅓ oz. (10 ml) fino sherry

½ oz. (15 ml) Sipello liqueur

½ oz. (15 ml) Watermelon Cordial (see page 526)

¼ oz. (7.5 ml) Yerba Mate Tincture (see page 527)

2⅔ oz. (80 ml) raspberry lemon kombucha

1 piece (4 cm x 4 cm) dry nori seaweed

1. Fill a mixing glass or a metal shaker with ice.
2. Pour the tequila (such as Siete Leguas Blanco), fino sherry, Sipello, Watermelon Cordial, and Yerba Mate Tincture into the chilled vessel and stir rapidly with a bar spoon for 17 to 20 seconds.
3. Strain into a chilled highball glass over ice.
4. Top with the raspberry lemon kombucha and garnish with the piece of dry nori seaweed.

WATERMELON CORDIAL

To juice the watermelon, cut it into small cubes and squeeze them through a slow juicer until you get the amount you need.

YIELD: 300 g

300 g watermelon juice, store-bought or homemade

300 g granulated sugar

1. In a saucepan over medium heat, combine the watermelon juice and sugar.
2. Cook until the sugar is dissolved, stirring occasionally.
3. Remove from heat and let it cool down.
4. Strain into a bottle and store in the fridge for up to 1 week.

YERBA MATE TINCTURE

Yerba mate is an herb that has been used in South America for a long time, and normally it's drunk like tea. It's quite strong and herbal, as well as being good for digestion.

YIELD: 100 g

3 g yerba mate

100 g tequila

1. Combine the yerba mate and tequila in a jar and let it sit at room temperature for 12 hours.

2. Strain through a coffee filter and bottle.

3. Store at room temperature for up to 3 months.

IL SIERO

Go for Tiempo Puro Reposado Cristalino, because the caramel and pepper flavors will pair well with the Fig-Infused Sweet Vermouth and the fresh, fruity flavor of the ODVI Armagnac.

1⅓ oz. (40 ml) tequila

⅓ oz. (10 ml) Armagnac, such as ODVI Armagnac

1 oz. (30 ml) Fig-Infused Sweet Vermouth (see page 530)

3 dashes Angostura bitters

½ fig

1. Fill a mixing glass or a metal shaker with ice.
2. Pour the tequila, Armagnac, Fig-Infused Sweet Vermouth, and Angostura bitters into the chilled vessel and stir rapidly with a bar spoon for 17 to 20 seconds.
3. Strain into a chilled rocks glass over a block of ice.
4. Garnish with the half fig.

FIG-INFUSED SWEET VERMOUTH

An herbal and pungent fig sweet vermouth. I suggest using Cocchi Dopo Teatro Vermouth Amaro for the vermouth in this recipe, because it adds complexity and depth.

YIELD: 500 g

20 g fig leaves

500 g sweet vermouth

1. In a blender, place the fig leaves and vermouth and blend them for 10 minutes at speed 6.
2. Place the blended leaves and sweet vermouth in a vacuum bag or in a jar in the fridge for 24 hours.
3. With a coffee filter, strain the liquid into a bottle and store in the fridge for up to 3 months.

LOVE, LOVE, MISS YOU

Fresh and crisp, this cocktail has a bitter and slightly sweet flavor coming from the Campari and Aperol. The Clear Green Apple Juice adds fruitiness and a tart finish, while the Cocchi Americano brings subtle herbal and floral notes to balance the bitterness and sweetness of the other ingredients. For the Clear Green Apple Juice, follow the recipe on page 491, but use Granny Smith apples.

1⅓ oz. (40 ml) mezcal

⅓ oz. (10 ml) Cocchi Americano

½ oz. (15 ml) Campari

⅓ oz. (10 ml) Aperol

1 oz. (30 ml) Clear Green Apple Juice

2 dashes orange bitters

1 orange coin

1. Pour the mezcal, Cocchi Americano, Campari, Aperol, Clear Green Apple Juice, and orange bitters into a mixing glass or a metal shaker.

2. Fill the vessel with ice and stir rapidly with a bar spoon for 17 to 20 seconds.

3. Strain into a chilled coupette glass.

4. Squeeze the orange coin into the drink and discard the orange.

Q & A WITH JAY KHAN, FOUNDER OF COA

Tell us a bit about yourself.

I'm born and raised in Hong Kong. I've been bartending since 2005. My first encounter with mezcal was in 2010, while working at a bar in Hong Kong (Lily & Bloom). We didn't have mezcal in Hong Kong back then; the bottle of mezcal was brought over by an American bartender. The mezcal I tasted left me curious and intrigued. The flavors were overwhelming (in a good way).

How do you choose which mezcals and tequilas to feature on your menu?

I make sure the menu is well-balanced and diversified. I need to have a mezcal for everyone. Although I'm a big fan of traditional higher ABV mezcal, I make sure I have some softer lower ABV mezcal as a segue for beginners. Our mezcal menu at COA is categorized by the agave species, with plenty of descriptions for guests to delve into if they are interested.

How do you educate your customers about mezcal?

Most of the education is on the job; however, we also do biweekly mezcal tastings for charity, called Mezcal Mission. One hundred percent of the proceeds go to charity. It is an initiative I started with Andrew Davis, a good friend of mine who loves agave spirits. It's been about three years and still going strong.

What are some popular cocktails made with mezcal that you serve at your bar?

Currently it is a drink called Bloody Beef Maria with mezcal, beef stock, tomato water cordial, Sichuan pepper, and morita chili. And also La Paloma de Oaxaca, which is obviously a take on the classic paloma with an Oaxacan influence.

What are some of the most memorable or interesting experiences you've had while running the bar?

I'm sure there are so many, and each night is a special night. One of the most memorable experiences for us was to see COA fully packed for the first time. It was a dream come true.

Another big one for us was to be awarded best bar in Asia in 2021 and 2022. When we first decided to open an agave bar, we had to struggle quite a lot to make sure we could sustain the business. So it meant even more for us.

Have you had any difficulties in creating COA in Hong Kong?

So many. We opened in late 2017. For the first eighteen months, we were barely breaking even each month. It was around 2019 when we started doing better. With the help of industry friends and through word of mouth, we did better progressively. Most of the difficulty was due to the concept of selling agave spirits. As Hong Kong was not quite ready.

What do you think about using mezcal in cocktails?

I'm going to sound biased, but anything with mezcal tastes slightly better!
Mezcal can be used as a base spirit or even as a seasoning for cocktails in smaller portions. Mezcal adds a lot of depth and complexity to drinks, if used properly.

What are your thoughts about aging mezcal?

Personally I like mezcals in their purest form. But again, I don't mind having one or two mezcals in the bar that are aged, for someone who likes aged spirits and is not familiar with mezcal. Something they can relate to and a segue for them to get interested.

What are some common misconceptions about mezcal that you encounter in your work?

Most of the locals here in Hong Kong have not heard of mezcal, to be honest. Which I think is better than someone having a little knowledge which often is a misconception. But once in a while there will be someone thinking mezcal is made with cactus or that all mezcals contain worms. Just the classic stuff.

What trends are you currently seeing in the mezcal industry?

Destilado de agave is definitely becoming more popular, and for good reason.

What challenges does the mezcal industry currently face?

I'm sure there are many to point out, but one that I think needs some awareness would be the liquid waste that is being generated due to the increased demand. According to Mexico's Regulatory Council for Mezcal Quality, more than 8 million liters of mezcal were certified in 2021, generating about 136,000 metric tons of solid waste and 80 million liters of liquid waste.

How do you think the increasing popularity of mezcal will impact the bar industry in the long term?

With more guests opting for mezcal, it will definitely encourage bartenders to delve even deeper into the category of agave spirits. And with time, we will see more than just one or two bottles of mezcal behind bars.

How do you think the global demand for mezcal has changed over the past few years, and what do you see as the future of the industry?

Due to its popularity, I see more celebrities and big commercial companies getting involved with mezcal.

How do you think the industry is addressing the issue of sustainability? Are there any specific initiatives or practices you think are particularly effective in ensuring that mezcal production is environmentally and socially responsible?

There are many brands of mezcal that are doing different things, but in Hong Kong and Asia, ecoSPIRITS is doing some great things. Among many other categories of spirits, they have also recently launched La Travesía Destilado de Agave. Their main objective is eliminating nearly all packaging waste from their house pour supply chain, and dramatically reducing the carbon footprint.

MAÍZ OLD FASHIONED

Go for Quiquiriqui Espadín because of the smoky and woody flavors, which work perfectly in this old fashioned–style cocktail. For the garnish, cut a corn into a 3-cm wheel and toast with a blowtorch or a flame.

2 oz. (60 ml) mezcal

1 barspoon (5 ml) Corn Oleo (recipe below)

4 dashes Angostura bitters

2 dashes orange bitters

1 Torched Corn Wheel

1. Fill a mixing glass or a metal shaker with ice.

2. Pour the mezcal, Corn Oleo, Angostura bitters, and orange bitters into the chilled vessel and stir rapidly with a bar spoon for 17 to 20 seconds.

3. Strain into a chilled rocks glass over a block of ice.

4. Garnish with the Torched Corn Wheel.

CORN OLEO

YIELD: 600 g

500 g corn

500 g granulated sugar

1. Combine the corn and sugar in a vacuum bag or a jar and let them sit for 48 hours at room temperature.

2. Strain through a cheesecloth and bottle.

3. Store in the fridge for up to 6 days.

MAÍZ COLADA

This drink is a twist on a piña colada, the holiday cocktail for many. Have you ever tried it with mezcal? If not, this is the ultimate mezcal piña colada.

1⅓ oz. (40 ml) mezcal

⅓ oz. (10 ml) Amaretto Disaronno

⅔ oz. (20 ml) Coco Lopez

½ oz. (15 ml) Coconut and Corn Milk (see page 539)

1 oz. (30 ml) Tepache (see page 539)

½ oz. (15 ml) freshly squeezed lime juice

⅓ oz. (10 ml) double cream

2 dashes 10 Percent Saline Solution (see page 514)

champagne

1 pineapple wedge

1. Combine the mezcal, Amaretto Disaronno, Coco Lopez, Coconut and Corn Milk, Tepache, lime juice, double cream, and 10 Percent Saline Solution in a blender with half a scoop of crushed ice.

2. Blend for 15 to 30 seconds.

3. Pour into a chilled highball glass over a block of ice.

4. Top with champagne and garnish with the pineapple wedge.

COCONUT AND CORN MILK

YIELD: 300 g

300 g coconut milk

150 g corn

1. Place the coconut milk and corn in a blender or Thermomix for 5 minutes at speed 7.

2. Strain through a cheesecloth and bottle.

3. Store in the fridge for up to 5 days.

TEPACHE

YIELD: 1 liter

1 pineapple

200 g unrefined sugar

1. Cut the pineapple into small pieces, remove the skin (you can use it for Pineapple Oleo; see page 613), and place the flesh in a jar with the unrefined sugar.

2. Cover with water and give it a stir.

3. Seal the jar and let it rest for 3 days in a dry place.

4. Remove the foam from the top with a spoon.

5. Strain the liquid through a cheesecloth and place in a new jar.

6. Let it rest for 24 hours and strain through a coffee filter.

7. Bottle and store in the fridge for up to 3 weeks.

MANO DE OBRA

Go for Quiquiriqui Pechuga Destilado con Cacao. It can be seen as a hazardous move, since Pechuga is usually drunk neat and on special occasions. But Quiquiriqui Pechuga Destilado con Cacao is the best pairing for the Mano de Obra; dark chocolate and tobacco notes represent the bitter and sweet days of the jimadores. Nixta Licor de Elote is a Mexican corn liqueur with vanilla, corn, and caramel notes. It's amazing for your coffee.

1⅓ oz. (40 ml) mezcal

⅔ oz. (20 ml) coffee liqueur

⅓ oz. (10 ml) Nixta Licor de Elote

2 oz. (60 ml) hot water

1 marshmallow

1. Combine the mezcal, coffee liqueur, Nixta Licor de Elote, and hot water in a mug or cup.

2. Give it a quick stir and serve it hot.

3. Garnish with the marshmallow.

MURMUR OF BEES

1⅔ oz. (50 ml) Beeswax-Infused Tequila (see page 543)

⅔ oz. (20 ml) Fig Honey (see page 543)

⅔ oz. (20 ml) freshly squeezed lemon juice

1 fig leaf coin

1. Combine the Beeswax-Infused Tequila, Fig Honey, and lemon juice in a small metal shaker tin.

2. Fill with ice cubes to the top and close the shaker. Shake hard for 10 seconds until the shaker is frozen.

3. Double strain into a chilled Nick & Nora glass.

4. Garnish with the fig leaf coin.

BEESWAX-INFUSED TEQUILA

YIELD: 500 g

500 g tequila

50 g beeswax

1. Combine the tequila and beeswax in a vacuum bag and place in a sous vide for 3 hours at 165°F (75°C).
2. Place the bag in the freezer for 24 hours.
3. Strain through a coffee filter and bottle.
4. Store at room temperature for up to 3 months.

FIG HONEY

YIELD: 500 g

400 g honey

200 g hot water

20 g fig leaves

1. Combine the honey, hot water, and fig leaves in a blender and blend until you get a smooth texture.
2. Strain through a cheesecloth and bottle.
3. Store at room temperature for up to 3 months.

MY LITTLE ZEN

I recommend Don Amado Reposado because it's a rich, full-bodied, and medium smoke mezcal, perfect for the My Little Zen because the caramel notes will add texture to the drink.

2 oz. (60 ml) mezcal

1 oz. (30 ml) Pedro Ximénez sherry

2 dashes orange bitters

coconut powder

1 amaranth micro herb

1. Fill a mixing glass or a metal shaker with ice.
2. Pour the mezcal, Pedro Ximénez sherry, and orange bitters into the chilled vessel and stir rapidly with a bar spoon for 17 to 20 seconds.
3. Strain into a chilled rocks glass over a block of ice.
4. Garnish the top of the ice cube with coconut powder and the amaranth micro herb.

PAPER TOWN

Cimarrón is the tequila to go for if you are making the Paper Town, thanks to its bright and rich agave notes and fresh vegetable and spice flavor.

3 raspberries

1⅓ oz. (40 ml) tequila

⅔ oz. (20 ml) sorrel

¾ oz. (25 ml) freshly squeezed lime juice

⅓ oz. (10 ml) Peppered Grenadine (see page 548)

2⅓ oz. (70 ml) soda water

1 Milk Shard (see page 549)

1. Combine the raspberries, tequila, sorrel, lime juice, and Peppered Grenadine in a small metal shaker.

2. Fill with ice cubes to the top and close the shaker. Shake hard for 10 seconds until the shaker is frozen.

3. Double strain into a chilled highball glass over a block of ice.

4. Top with the soda water and garnish with the Milk Shard.

PEPPERED GRENADINE

A spiced grenadine, simple and easy to make. A combination of sweet and spicy notes that you can try in a classic margarita (adding 5 ml), it will add brightness and spiciness.

YIELD: 300 g

300 g grenadine

5 g black peppercorns

5 g pink peppercorns

1. Combine the grenadine, black peppercorns, and pink peppercorns in a vacuum bag and place in a water bath for 2 hours at 165°F (75°C).

2. Strain through a fine-mesh sieve and bottle.

3. Store in the fridge for up to 3 months.

MILK SHARD

A sweet and milky cracker that will be delicious paired with spicy drinks. It will cut the heat, if you are not used to a bit of spice in your cocktails.

YIELD: 6–8 shards

40 g whole milk

35 g granulated sugar

25 g glucose syrup

1. Cover a dehydrator tray with plastic wrap and make sure to pull it tight.
2. Combine the whole milk, sugar, and glucose syrup in a Thermomix and blitz for 2 minutes at speed 3 at 165°F (75°C).
3. Repeat for another 8 minutes at speed 6 at 165°F (75°C).
4. Pour the mixture onto the cling-filmed dehydrator tray.
5. Spread the mixture by moving the tray in a circular motion.
6. Place the tray in the dehydrator and set the timer for 12 hours.
7. Once complete, remove the tray and place the dehydrated milk shard in a container with a lid.
8. Store at room temperature for up to 3 weeks.

SUSI SAZERAC

Go for Los Amantes Joven, because its citrus and delicate smokiness will complement the plum flavors.

1⅓ oz. (40 ml) mezcal

⅔ oz. (20 ml) Plum Tea Tincture (see page 552)

1 barspoon (5 ml) Plum Syrup 2:1 (see page 553)

2 dashes absinthe

4 dashes Peychaud's bitters

1 plum wheel

1 maraschino cherry

1. Fill a mixing glass or a metal shaker with ice.
2. Pour the mezcal, Plum Tea Tincture, Plum Syrup 2:1, absinthe, and Peychaud's bitters into the chilled vessel and stir rapidly with a bar spoon for 17 to 20 seconds.
3. Strain into a chilled single rocks glass.
4. Garnish with the plum wheel and maraschino cherry on a skewer.

PLUM TEA TINCTURE

If you have a plum tree in your garden, just dehydrate the leaves and use them instead of the tea.

YIELD: 100 g

3 g plum tea

100 g overproof whisky

1. Combine the plum tea and overproof whisky in a vacuum bag or a jar.
2. Seal it and leave at room temperature for 12 hours.
3. Strain through a coffee filter and bottle.
4. Store in a cool, dry place for up to 3 months.

PLUM SYRUP 2:1

A fruity syrup that you can use in many classic cocktails, from a Tom Collins style to an old fashioned.

YIELD: 300 g

200 g fresh plums

300 g granulated sugar

300 g water

1. Wash the plums, cut them into small pieces, and place them in a saucepan with the sugar and water. Cook over medium heat for 10 minutes or until the sugar is dissolved and the plums are soft.

2. Strain through a cheesecloth and bottle.

3. Store in the fridge for up to 3 weeks.

RED CLIFF

A boozy, sparkling drink with mineral and pomegranate notes that give the cocktail freshness and brightness. It's a good cocktail for those who have just started to drink mezcal.

2 strawberries

1⅓ oz. (40 ml) mezcal

⅓ oz. (10 ml) fino sherry

¾ oz. (25 ml) freshly squeezed lime juice

½ oz. (15 ml) grenadine

champagne

1 grapefruit coin

Blue Paint (recipe below)

1. Combine the strawberries, mezcal, fino sherry, lime juice, and grenadine in a small metal shaker.
2. Fill with ice cubes to the top and close the shaker. Shake hard for 10 seconds until the shaker is frozen.
3. Double strain into a chilled flute glass.
4. Top with champagne, squeeze the grapefruit coin on the top, and then discard the grapefruit.
5. Garnish the glass with a stripe of Blue Paint up the side.

How to Make Blue Paint: I decorate the glass with a blue stripe, a nice touch you can add to your glasses to give them a new style. Brew 4 g butterfly pea flower tea for 20 minutes, strain through a coffee filter, and slowly pour it in 200 g glucose with 3 g vanilla essence and 50 g water until you reach a smooth mixture with good texture and brightness.

RÊVE

Go for Banhez Ensamble: the fruity notes of pineapple and banana will make you dream for more.

1 oz. (30 ml) mezcal

⅔ oz. (20 ml) Armagnac

1 barspoon (5 ml) maraschino liqueur

1 oz. (30 ml) Punt e Mes

2 dashes Peychaud's bitters

1 orange coin

1 strip orange zest

1. Fill a mixing glass or a metal shaker with ice.
2. Pour the mezcal, Armagnac, maraschino liqueur, Punt e Mes, and Peychaud's bitters into the chilled vessel and stir rapidly with a bar spoon for 17 to 20 seconds.
3. Strain into a chilled Nick & Nora glass.
4. Squeeze the orange coin over the top, then discard the orange coin.
5. Garnish with the orange zest.

ROSSO APERITIVO

A twist on a classic Americano. This highball is made for a perfect and refreshing aperitivo time with friends and family.

1 oz. (30 ml) mezcal

¾ oz. (25 ml) Campari

1 oz. (30 ml) Banana Bread–Infused Sweet Vermouth (see page 560)

Pomegranate Soda (see page 561)

3 green olives

1. Pour the mezcal, Campari, and Banana Bread–Infused Sweet Vermouth into a chilled highball glass.

2. Top with Pomegranate Soda and fill the glass with ice.

3. Garnish with the green olives.

BANANA BREAD-INFUSED SWEET VERMOUTH

If you have leftover banana bread, you can use it for this easy infusion. It will give a nice flavor to the sweet vermouth.

YIELD: 500 g

100 g banana bread

500 g sweet vermouth

1. Cut the banana bread into small pieces and toast them in the oven for 10 minutes at 280°F (140°C).

2. Place the vermouth and toasted banana bread in a bowl and cover with plastic wrap.

3. Place in the fridge for 8 hours.

4. Strain through a cheesecloth first, and then through a coffee filter.

5. Bottle and store in the fridge for up to 2 weeks.

POMEGRANATE SODA

This is a fruity soda you can use in cocktails but also as a refreshing summer drink. Just add as much sugar as you like, and enjoy. You can either use fresh pomegranate juice or, if you prefer, buy it in-store. If you want to make it fresh, just wash and cut a pomegranate to remove the seeds. Puree the seeds in a blender until they become liquid. Filter with a chinois strainer and make sure you force the juice for more yield. Bottle and place in the fridge for up to 5 days.

YIELD: 500 g

500 g pomegranate juice

soda siphon and 1 soda charger

1. Store the pomegranate juice in the fridge for a minimum of 5 hours.
2. Pour the juice into and charge the soda siphon with the soda charger.
3. Give it a shake, and it's ready to use.
4. Store in the fridge for up to a week.

SMOKED DRAGON

I suggest using Amarás Mezcal Verde because of the classic smoky notes of the cooked agave, a quite sweet and nutty dry fruit flavor. It's a well-balanced mezcal that works well with the Smoked Dragon.

1 oz. (30 ml) mezcal

1 oz. (30 ml) Campari

3 ⅓ oz. (100 ml) Hojicha Sparkling Tea (recipe below)

1 dragon fruit ball

1. Pour the mezcal, Campari, and Hojicha Sparkling Tea into a chilled highball glass filled with ice.

2. Garnish with the dragon fruit ball.

HOJICHA SPARKLING TEA

YIELD: 1 liter

12 g Hojicha tea

1 liter hot water

150 g granulated sugar

soda siphon and 1 soda charger

1. Brew the Hojicha tea in the hot water for 5 minutes.

2. Strain through a cheesecloth into a bottle.

3. Combine it with the sugar and stir until dissolved.

4. Place the liquid in the fridge for 2 hours.

5. Pour into the soda siphon and charge it with the soda charger.

6. Store in the fridge for up to a week.

SUMMER LOST

Madre Mezcal is a great match for this drink; the vegetable notes will round out the drink and balance the flavor perfectly.

1⅓ oz. (40 ml) mezcal

½ oz. (15 ml) Tomato Agave Syrup (see page 566)

¾ oz. (25 ml) freshly squeezed lemon juice

2 to 3 basil leaves

2 oz. (60 ml) prosecco

1 basil leaf

1. Combine the mezcal, Tomato Agave Syrup, lemon juice, and 2 to 3 basil leaves in a small metal shaker.

2. Fill with ice cubes to the top and close the shaker. Shake hard for 10 seconds until the shaker is frozen.

3. Double strain into a chilled rocks glass over a block of ice.

4. Top with the prosecco and garnish with the basil leaf.

TOMATO AGAVE SYRUP

A very easy way to bring more complexity to your agave syrup. You can use this to make a twist on a mezcal margarita. It will be delicious, but do not add more than 5 ml of the syrup; otherwise the drink will become overly sweet.

YIELD: 280 g

200 g agave

100 g Tomato Water (see page 567)

1. Mix the agave and Tomato Water in a vacuum bag.
2. Sous vide for 1 hour at 160°F (70°C).
3. Allow to cool and bottle.
4. Store in the fridge for up to a week.

TOMATO WATER

You can use this mix in a classic bloody mary or in the Summer Lost. A heads-up: you can freeze it in an ice cube tray and use it whenever you need it.

YIELD: 140 g

6 medium-sized tomatoes, such as beefsteak tomatoes

1. Cut the tomatoes and blend in a blender until smooth in texture.
2. Filter through a cheesecloth first, and then through a coffee filter, until you get clear red water.
3. Bottle and store in the fridge for up to 3 days.

TACOS DROP IN THE JUNGLE

A twist on a classic jungle bird cocktail with a strong corn flavor that you can drink with your Mexican food.

1⅙ oz. (35 ml) mezcal

⅔ oz. (20 ml) Masa Flour–Washed Tequila (see page 570)

⅓ oz. (10 ml) Campari

½ oz. (15 ml) Corn Syrup (see page 571)

¾ oz. (25 ml) freshly squeezed lime juice

⅓ oz. (10 ml) pineapple juice

1 barspoon (5 ml) Chipotle Tincture (see page 571)

1 dehydrated pineapple slice

1. Combine the mezcal, Masa Flour–Washed Tequila, Campari, Corn Syrup, lime juice, pineapple juice, and Chipotle Tincture in a small metal shaker.

2. Fill with ice cubes to the top and close the shaker. Shake hard for 10 seconds until the shaker is frozen.

3. Double strain into a chilled double rocks glass over a block of ice.

4. Garnish with the dehydrated pineapple slice.

MASA FLOUR-WASHED TEQUILA

Masa is the flour used to make taco shells. Infuse it into your tequila to add texture and toasted notes.

YIELD: 500 g

30 g masa flour

500 g tequila

1. Lightly toast the masa flour in a saucepan until it turns a light brown color.

2. Combine it with the tequila in a jar. Mix vigorously.

3. Let it infuse for 15 minutes at room temperature.

4. Strain through a cheesecloth first, and then through a coffee filter.

5. Bottle and store at room temperature for up to 3 months.

CORN SYRUP

YIELD: 300 g

200 g corn

400 g granulated sugar

200 g water

1. Place the corn in a blender and blend until it gets smooth.
2. Combine it with the sugar and water in a saucepan over medium heat.
3. Stir until the sugar is dissolved and let it cook for another 10 minutes.
4. Strain through a coffee filter and bottle.
5. Store in the fridge for up to a week.

CHIPOTLE TINCTURE

A heads-up: be careful with the infusion. The longer you leave it, the spicier it will get! You can make this kind of tincture with any variety of chili you like.

YIELD: 100 g

1 chipotle chili

100 g overproof rum

1. Combine the chipotle and overproof rum in a jar.
2. Seal it and let it infuse at room temperature for 8 hours.
3. Strain through a coffee filter and bottle.
4. Store at room temperature for up to 3 months.

TEQUILA MELON SOUR

Go for Pueblo Viejo Blanco from Casa San Matías, because its notes of cooked agave, caramel, and sweet fruits are the perfect pairing for this sour cocktail.

1⅔ oz. (50 ml) tequila

¾ oz. (25 ml) freshly squeezed lime juice

½ oz. (15 ml) Melon Oleo (recipe below)

2 dashes grapefruit bitters

1 grapefruit coin

1. Combine the tequila, lime juice, Melon Oleo, and grapefruit bitters in a small metal shaker tin.

2. Fill with ice cubes to the top and close the shaker. Shake hard for 10 seconds until the shaker is frozen.

3. Double strain into a chilled coupette glass.

4. Garnish with the grapefruit coin.

MELON OLEO

YIELD: 500 g

400 g cantaloupe

400 g granulated sugar

1. Cut the cantaloupe into small cubes (do not remove the peel), place in a vacuum bag with the sugar, push out the air, and let it rest for 48 hours at room temperature.

2. Strain through a cheesecloth and bottle.

3. Store in the fridge for up to 3 weeks.

THE APPLE BANDIT

11/6 oz. (35 ml) tequila

½ oz. (15 ml) applejack

¾ oz. (25 ml) freshly squeezed lemon juice

½ oz. (15 ml) Citrus Honey (recipe below)

1 apple coin with cinnamon powder

1. Combine the tequila, applejack, lemon juice, and Citrus Honey in a small metal shaker.

2. Fill with ice cubes to the top and close the shaker. Shake hard for 10 seconds until the shaker is frozen.

3. Double strain into a chilled rocks glass over a block of ice.

4. Garnish with the apple coin covered with cinnamon powder.

CITRUS HONEY

YIELD: 450 g

400 g honey

100 g water

4 medium lemon peels

5 medium lime peels

1. Place the honey, water, lemon peels, and lime peels in a vacuum bag.

2. Microwave for 2 minutes on high. Let it rest for 2 minutes. Repeat 3 times.

3. Let it cool down and strain through a chinois strainer to remove the citrus peels.

4. Bottle and store in the fridge for up to 3 weeks.

THE GOLDEN STAIRS

If you don't have pisco, you can go full mezcal (60 ml), and you will have a mezcal sour with notes of fruitiness.

1 oz. (30 ml) mezcal

⅔ oz. (20 ml) pisco

½ oz. (15 ml) Passion Fruit Agave Syrup (recipe below)

¾ oz. (25 ml) freshly squeezed lime juice

⅔ oz. (20 ml) egg white

1 bunch amaranth micro herbs

1 passion fruit husk

1. Combine the mezcal, pisco, Passion Fruit Agave Syrup, lime juice, and egg white in a small metal shaker.

2. Fill with ice cubes to the top and close the shaker. Shake hard for 10 seconds until the shaker is frozen.

3. Double strain into a frozen coupette glass.

4. Garnish with the amaranth micro herb in the passion fruit husk.

PASSION FRUIT AGAVE SYRUP

YIELD: 300 g

5 passion fruits

300 g agave syrup

100 g hot water

1. Cut the passion fruits in half and remove the flesh.

2. Place the flesh, agave syrup, and hot water in a blender and blend until it's all combined.

3. Strain through a cheesecloth and bottle.

4. Store in the fridge for up to a week.

THE GREAT FIRE

I suggest using Tequila Partida Blanco because it adds tropical notes, but also citrus and mineral flavors, to highlight a cocktail that's spicy and herbal.

1 oz. (30 ml) tequila

⅓ oz. (10 ml) Cynar liqueur

⅓ oz. (10 ml) Ancho Reyes

⅓ oz. (10 ml) pineapple juice

⅔ oz. (20 ml) freshly squeezed lemon juice

⅓ oz. (10 ml) Simple Syrup 2:1 (see page 512)

⅔ oz. (20 ml) egg white

1. Combine all ingredients in a small metal shaker.

2. Fill with ice cubes to the top and close the shaker. Shake hard for 10 seconds until the shaker is frozen.

3. Double strain into a chilled rocks glass over a block of ice.

THE MANHATTAN BRIDGE

1 oz. (30 ml) mezcal

⅔ oz. (20 ml) whiskey

½ oz. (15 ml) sweet vermouth

1 barspoon (5 ml) maraschino liqueur

2 dashes Angostura bitters

2 maraschino cherries

1. Fill a mixing glass or a metal shaker with ice.
2. Pour the mezcal, whiskey, sweet vermouth, maraschino liqueur, and Angostura bitters into the chilled vessel and stir rapidly with a bar spoon for 17 to 20 seconds.
3. Strain into a chilled Nick & Nora glass.
4. Garnish with the maraschino cherries.

THE MANGOES

Go for Quiquiriqui Espadín to bring peppery and spicy flavors; combined with the mango, it's a back-and-forth of sweet and spicy fusion.

1⅔ oz. (50 ml.) mezcal

⅓ oz. (10 ml.) Mango Mead (see page 584)

⅔ oz. (20 ml.) freshly squeezed lemon juice

⅓ oz. (10 ml.) Ginger Syrup (see page 585)

1 mango wedge

2 edible flowers

1. Combine the mezcal, Mango Mead, lemon juice, and Ginger Syrup in a small metal shaker.
2. Fill with ice cubes to the top and close the shaker. Shake hard for 10 seconds until the shaker is frozen.
3. Double strain into a chilled highball glass and fill it with crushed ice.
4. Garnish with the mango wedge and edible flowers.

MANGO MEAD

YIELD: 300 g

400 g honey

1.5 liters hot water

2 g wine yeast

200 g fresh mangoes, peeled

1. Combine the honey and hot water in a Cambro (plastic container).

2. Take 100 ml of the honey water and combine it with the wine yeast in another Cambro. This will activate the yeast.

3. Once activated (meaning the yeast is melted in the water), combine with the rest of the honey water and ferment for 5 days. Place a kitchen cloth on top of the container and store in a dry place.

4. Once the mixture is fermented, wash the mangoes, peel them, cut them into small cubes, and blend them with the mead (the fermented honey water) in a blender.

5. After blending, allow to infuse for 24 hours.

6. Strain through a cheesecloth and store in the fridge for up to 3 weeks.

The mead fermentation is very easy. Just make sure you taste it every day, since the temperature may vary. Leave it in a cupboard, away from any heat source.

GINGER SYRUP

To make the Ginger Syrup, you need to start by making ginger juice:

YIELD: 150 g

200 g gingerroot

1. Wash and dry the gingerroot, then peel it.
2. Cut the roots into small chunks and place in a blender.
3. Blend for 2 minutes or until you get a pasty pulp.
4. Strain the liquid through a muslin cloth into a jar or bottle and cover.
5. Store in the fridge for up to 2 weeks.

Then, proceed with making the Ginger Syrup:

YIELD: 200 g

200 g ginger juice
200 g granulated sugar

1. Combine the ginger juice and sugar in a saucepan over medium-high heat, stirring until the sugar is dissolved.
2. Strain into a bottle, cover, and store in the fridge for up to a week.

THE ROCK HEART

RinQuinQuin is a French aperitif made from white grapes and peaches and sweetened with sugarcane syrup. You can use it in an Aperol spritz instead of Aperol or try it in a Negroni to add more sweetness, if you don't fancy the bitter notes of the classic cocktail.

1 oz. (30 ml) tequila

⅔ oz. (20 ml) Campari

⅓ oz. (10 ml) Punt e Mes

½ oz. (15 ml) RinQuinQuin liqueur

2 dashes Peychaud's bitters

1 micro basil leaf

1. Pour the tequila, Campari, Punt e Mes, RinQuinQuin, and Peychaud's bitters into a mixing glass or a metal shaker.

2. Fill the vessel with ice and stir rapidly with a bar spoon for 17 to 20 seconds.

3. Strain into a chilled Nick & Nora glass.

4. Garnish with the micro basil leaf.

THE CARAMEL WAY

Go for Mezcal Amarás Espadín, because this cocktail needs a full-bodied mezcal to highlight the flavor of the caramel and bitters.

1⅔ oz. (50 ml) mezcal

1 barspoon (5 ml) Salted Caramel Syrup (see page 590)

2 dashes orange bitters

4 dashes Angostura bitters

1 orange coin

1 red-veined sorrel leaf

1. Pour the mezcal, Salted Caramel Syrup, orange bitters, and Angostura bitters into a mixing glass or a metal shaker.
2. Fill the vessel with ice and stir rapidly with a bar spoon for 17 to 20 seconds.
3. Strain into a chilled rocks glass over a block of ice.
4. Squeeze the orange coin on the top and discard the orange.
5. Garnish with the red-veined sorrel leaf.

SALTED CARAMEL SYRUP

This caramel syrup recipe is not so simple. Because of the high heat and watchful eye required to make it, it's definitely a more advanced syrup recipe. But don't let that stop you from trying it! If you are in a rush, you can always buy it at the store.

YIELD: 250 g

300 g water

300 g granulated sugar

3 g Maldon salt

1. Combine the water and sugar in a medium saucepan over medium heat. Stir until the sugar is dissolved.

2. Turn the heat to medium-high. Cover and boil for about 3 minutes. Remove the lid and stir constantly until the mixture is a light amber color.

3. Remove from heat immediately.

4. Add the Maldon salt and bring to room temperature.

5. Store in an airtight container in the fridge for up to a month.

Though they sound similar, caramel syrup is quite different from caramel sauce. The latter is usually made with heavy cream and butter. The consistency is thick.

Caramel syrup is a thinner liquid, which makes it ideal for stirring into drinks. It's much runnier than caramel sauce. It still tastes like caramel and has that same caramel color. Plus, it's dairy-free!

THE UNDOING PROJECT

I recommend using Tapatío Blanco, since the other ingredients in the cocktail mirror the flavor of the tequila: the Discarded vermouth and Angostura bitters lift up the spice notes, while the lime juice highlights the citrusy flavor.

1 oz. (30 ml) tequila

¾ oz. (25 ml) Discarded Sweet Cascara Vermouth

¾ oz. (25 ml) freshly squeezed lime juice

⅓ oz. (10 ml) Simple Syrup 2:1 (see page 512)

1 dash Angostura bitters

2⅓ oz. (70 ml) soda water

1 cucumber slice

½ strawberry

1. Pour the tequila, vermouth, lime juice, Simple Syrup 2:1, and Angostura bitters into a chilled highball glass.

2. Top with the soda water and add a column of ice.

3. Garnish with the cucumber slice and half a strawberry on a skewer.

TOMATONIC

Go for Bozal Ensamble in this 2-ingredient cocktail, since the herbal notes of the mezcal really shine with the flavor of the Tomato Tonic.

2 oz. (60 ml) mezcal

3⅓ oz. (100 ml) Tomato Tonic (see page 595)

1 cucumber ribbon

1. Pour the mezcal into a chilled highball glass.

2. Top with the Tomato Tonic over a block of ice.

3. Garnish with the cucumber ribbon on a skewer.

TOMATO TONIC

For a better result, you can place the Tomato Tonic in a soda siphon to make it even fizzier. If you want to make more of the tonic, just remember that the ratio of the syrup and soda water needs to be 1:4. So for every 100 grams of syrup, you need to combine it with 400 grams of soda water.

YIELD: 400 g

600 g Tomato Water (see page 567)

13 g cinchona bark

1 lemon peel

1 grapefruit peel

200 g granulated sugar

1.4 g citric acid powder

400 g soda water

1. Combine the Tomato Water, cinchona bark, lemon peel, grapefruit peel, and sugar in a saucepan over medium-high heat for 10 minutes, and for another 10 minutes at low heat.
2. Let it rest for 20 minutes.
3. Strain through a cheesecloth first, and then through a coffee filter.
4. Bottle and place in the fridge for 3 hours.
5. Combine with the citric acid powder and mix until the powder is dissolved.
6. Weigh 100 g of the syrup and combine it with the soda water.

SPICED PEACHY SWIZZLE

I recommend to use ArteNOM Selección NOM 1414, as the spices and fruity notes work amazingly with the Peach Curaçao and Homemade Falernum. Absolutely delicious!

1⅓ oz. (40 ml) mezcal

⅔ oz. (20 ml) Peach Curaçao (see page 598)

½ oz. (15 ml) Homemade Falernum (see page 599)

⅔ oz. (20 ml) freshly squeezed lemon juice

2 dashes chocolate bitters

1 peach slice

1 mint sprig

1. Fill a metal shaker with the mezcal, Peach Curaçao, Homemade Falernum, lemon juice, and chocolate bitters, plus half a scoop of crushed ice.

2. Shake for 8 seconds and pour the cocktail into a chilled sling glass.

3. Place a straw in the glass and top with crushed ice.

4. Garnish with the peach slice and mint sprig.

PEACH CURAÇAO

YIELD: 200 g

200 g dark rum

20 g dehydrated peaches

Peels of 3 medium oranges

1. Combine the dark rum, dehydrated peaches, and orange peels in a vacuum bag and push out the air.

2. Sous vide for 3 hours at 160°F (70°C).

3. Remove from the water bath and let it cool down, preferably in ice-cold water, for 30 minutes.

4. Strain through a coffee filter and bottle.

5. Store in a cool, dry place for up to 3 weeks.

HOMEMADE FALERNUM

Homemade Falernum is very versatile. Try it in a classic Hemingway breakfast or a Royal Bermuda Yacht Club daiquiri.

YIELD: 400 g

400 g white rum

3 g dehydrated peaches (shredded)

4 g grated ginger

Peels of 3 medium oranges

2 g cloves

200 g muscovado sugar

2 g star anise

Zest of 3 medium limes

2 cinnamon sticks

1. Combine all ingredients in a vacuum bag.
2. Sous vide for 2 hours at 130°F (55°C).
3. Remove from the water bath and let it cool down, preferably in ice-cold water, for 30 minutes.
4. Strain through a coffee filter and bottle.
5. Store in the fridge for up to 3 weeks.

UNTOLD STORY

Masa is the main base for tortillas, and this is an amazing opportunity to highlight its flavor. Using Bruxo X not only will pull out the minerality of the fino sherry, but it also will add gentle notes such as chamomile, citrus, and a hint of smoke.

1⅓ oz. (40 ml) mezcal

⅓ oz. (10 ml) fino sherry

¼ oz. (7.5 ml) Epazote Tincture (see page 602)

⅓ oz. (10 ml) Masa Cordial (see page 603)

1 dash absinthe

1 grapefruit wedge

1. Fill a mixing glass or a metal shaker with ice.

2. Pour the mezcal, fino sherry, Epazote Tincture, Masa Cordial, and absinthe into the chilled vessel and stir rapidly with a bar spoon for 17 to 20 seconds.

3. Strain into a chilled rocks glass over a block of ice.

4. Garnish with the grapefruit wedge.

EPAZOTE TINCTURE

Epazote is an herb that has been used in Mexican culture for years. Do not leave it to rest for more than 30 minutes, or it will be too bitter and will overpower the flavor of your drink.

YIELD: 100 g

12 g dried epazote

100 g tequila

1. Combine the dried epazote and tequila in a jar.
2. Let it sit for 30 minutes at room temperature.
3. Filter through a coffee filter and bottle.
4. Store at room temperature for up to 3 months.

MASA CORDIAL

A rich syrup with corn flavor. Use 5 ml in a classic old fashioned to add richness, sweetness, and body to the drink.

YIELD: 500 g

12.5 g masa flour

500 g water

500 g granulated sugar

1. Toast the masa flour in a small pan over medium heat. Stir occasionally.
2. Mix with the water in a container.
3. Strain through a coffee filter and add the sugar to the strained liquid.
4. Bottle and store in the fridge for up to 3 weeks.

WALNUT OLD TIMER

I suggest using The Lost Explorer Espadín. As the main ingredient, it will provide smoke and earthy notes to the drink, with flavors of roasted agave and a slightly spicy kick.

Place the mezcal in the fridge at least 3 hours before preparing the cocktail to get the best result.

2 oz. (60 ml) mezcal

1 barspoon (5 ml) Walnut Syrup (recipe below)

2 dashes walnut bitters

2 dashes orange bitters

1 walnut, shelled

1. Fill a mixing glass or a metal shaker with ice.

2. Pour the mezcal, Walnut Syrup, walnut bitters, and orange bitters into the chilled vessel and stir rapidly with a bar spoon for 17 to 20 seconds.

3. Strain into a chilled rocks glass over a block of ice.

4. Garnish with the walnut.

WALNUT SYRUP

YIELD: 500 g

500 g water

100 g shelled walnuts

500 g granulated sugar

1. Place the water and walnuts in a Thermomix and blend at speed 6 for 3 minutes.

2. Add the sugar to the Thermomix and blend for 8 minutes at speed 8, until the sugar is completely dissolved.

3. Strain through a cheesecloth and store in the fridge for up to 3 weeks.

WHY SO BLUE?

Go with Tequila Partida Blanco, as its sweet and tropical notes are the right pairing for this refreshing granita-style cocktail.

1 oz. (30 ml) tequila

⅔ oz. (20 ml) blue curaçao

⅔ oz. (20 ml) Citrus Zest Tincture (see page 608)

⅔ oz. (20 ml) Spiced Apple Cordial (see page 609)

1 orange slice

1. Combine the tequila, blue curaçao, Citrus Zest Tincture, and Spiced Apple Cordial in a blender with one scoop of crushed ice.
2. Blend until you get a smooth texture.
3. Pour into a chilled short highball glass.
4. Garnish with the orange slice and serve with a straw.

CITRUS ZEST TINCTURE

The heavy citrus notes that flavor this tincture will be very present, both on the nose and palate. You can use it to make a delicious classic margarita.

YIELD: 400 g

400 g tequila

Zest of 2 medium limes

Zest of 3 medium oranges

Zest of 2 medium lemons

1. Combine the tequila, lime zests, orange zests, and lemon zests in a vacuum bag or a jar.

2. Let the mixture infuse in the fridge for 24 hours.

3. Strain through a cheesecloth and bottle.

4. Store in the fridge for up to 3 months.

SPICED APPLE CORDIAL

A combination of herbal notes and fruitiness makes an amazing syrup that you can use in an apple martini or even in a mojito or virgin mojito.

YIELD: 450 g

400 g Clear Apple Juice (see page 491)

2 pears (washed and sliced)

3 rosemary sprigs

400 g granulated sugar

Pinch of salt

1. Combine the Clear Apple Juice, pear slices, rosemary sprigs, sugar, and salt in a saucepan and cook for 15 minutes, until the sugar is dissolved.

2. Strain through a cheesecloth and bottle.

3. Store in the fridge for up to 2 weeks.

MEZCAL PARADISE

1⅓ oz. (40 ml) mezcal

½ oz. (15 ml) Cocchi Americano

1 barspoon (5 ml) pear liqueur

½ barspoon (2.5 ml) bergamot liqueur

⅓ oz. (10 ml) Pineapple Oleo (see page 613)

5 dashes 10 Percent Citric Acid Solution (see page 613)

1 pear flower

1. Fill a mixing glass or a metal shaker with ice.

2. Pour the mezcal, Cocchi Americano, pear liquor, bergamot liquor, Pineapple Oleo, and 10 Percent Citric Acid Solution nto the chilled vessel and stir rapidly with a bar spoon for 17 to 20 seconds.

3. Strain into a chilled Nick & Nora glass.

4. Garnish with the pear flower.

PINEAPPLE OLEO

YIELD: depends on the pineapple

300 g pineapple peel

300 g granulated sugar

1. Cut the pineapple and place the peel in a vacuum bag with the sugar.
2. Allow to infuse for 48 hours at room temperature, until the sugar is dissolved.
3. Strain through a cheesecloth and bottle.
4. Store in the fridge for up to 2 weeks.

10 PERCENT CITRIC ACID SOLUTION

YIELD: 100 g

100 g filtered water

10 g citric acid powder

1. Combine the filtered water and citric acid powder in a jar and stir until the powder is dissolved.
2. Bottle the mixture, and it is ready to use. Cover and store in the fridge for up to a month.

A MIDSUMMER CURE

1⅔ oz. (50 ml) Hibiscus-Infused Tequila (see page 615)

⅔ oz. (20 ml) freshly squeezed lime juice

⅓ oz. (10 ml) Galangal Syrup (see page 616)

⅓ oz. (10 ml) Honey Water (see page 617)

2 dashes Angostura bitters

Mezcal spray (see below)

1. Combine the Hibiscus-Infused Tequila, lime juice, Galangal Syrup, Honey Water, and Angostura bitters in a small metal shaker.

2. Fill with ice cubes to the top and close the shaker. Shake hard for 10 seconds until the shaker is frozen.

3. Double strain into a chilled rocks glass over a block of ice.

4. Garnish with mezcal spray.

Pour a little bit of mezcal in a spray bottle and spritz the top of the cocktail twice, so you will get a straightforward smoky aroma on the nose. It will provide an additional layer of aroma and enhance the overall drinking experience.

HIBISCUS-INFUSED TEQUILA

YIELD: 400 g

10 g dry hibiscus flowers

400 g tequila

1. Combine the dry hibiscus flowers and tequila in a vacuum bag and seal it.
2. Place in a water bath for 1 hour at 165°F (75°C).
3. Remove and strain through a cheesecloth.
4. Bottle and store at room temperature for up to 3 months.

GALANGAL SYRUP

To make the Galangal Syrup, you need to start by preparing the juice:

YIELD: 150 g

300 g galangal root

1. Wash and dry the root, then peel.
2. Cut the root into small chunks and place in a blender.
3. Blend for 2 minutes or until you get a pasty pulp.
4. Strain the liquid through a muslin cloth into a jar or bottle and cover it.
5. Store in the fridge for up to 2 weeks.

Then, proceed with making the Galangal Syrup:

YIELD: 200 g

200 g galangal juice
200 g granulated sugar

1. Combine the galangal juice and sugar in a saucepan over medium-high heat, stirring until the sugar is dissolved.
2. Strain into a bottle, cover, and store in the fridge for up to a week.

HONEY WATER

300 g honey

100 ml boiling water

1. In a jar, combine the honey and hot water.
2. Stir until smooth and well mixed.
3. Strain through a muslin cloth and bottle.
4. Store in the fridge for up to a month.

ULTIMO PUNCH

5 oz. (150 ml) Lemongrass-Infused Tequila (see page 619)

2⅔ oz. (80 ml) Calvados

5 oz. (150 ml) Spicy Raspberry Liqueur (see page 619)

2⅔ oz. (80 ml) freshly squeezed lime juice

2 cups (500 ml) brewed Darjeeling tea

½ cup (80 g) cane sugar

1 cup (250 ml) whole milk

Soda siphon and 1 soda charger

1 raspberry

1. Combine the Lemongrass-Infused Tequila, Calvados, Spicy Raspberry Liqueur, lime juice, brewed Darjeeling tea, and cane sugar in a jar.

2. Stir until the sugar is dissolved.

3. In a medium saucepan, bring the whole milk to a boil, reduce the heat to low, and let it cook for 10 minutes.

4. Add the milk to the jar with the other liquids and cover with plastic wrap.

5. Place the jar in the fridge overnight.

6. Strain through a coffee filter and repeat the straining, using the same filter, until it's perfectly clear.

7. Once you have the split punch, refrigerate for 3 hours.

8. Pour the punch into the soda siphon and charge it with the soda charger.

9. Place in the fridge for an hour and serve in a chilled lowball glass with a block of ice.

10. Garnish with the raspberry, placing it on top of the ice.

How to Make Darjeeling Tea: Bring 2 cups water to a boil, remove from heat, and add 20 g Darjeeling tea. Let it brew for 10 minutes, strain through a coffee filter, and let it cool before using it in the cocktail.

LEMONGRASS-INFUSED TEQUILA

YIELD: 350 g

25 g lemongrass

350 g tequila

1. Cut the lemongrass into sections and bash it with the base of a small pot.
2. Place it with the tequila in a vacuum bag and sous vide for 3 hours at 130°F (55°C).
3. Strain through a cheesecloth and bottle.
4. Store at room temperature for up to 3 months.

SPICY RASPBERRY LIQUEUR

YIELD: 300 g

10 g raspberries

300 g Ancho Reyes

1. Combine the raspberries and Ancho Reyes in a blender and blend until you get a smooth texture.
2. Strain through a cheesecloth and bottle.
3. Store in the fridge for up to 2 weeks.

ABOUT THE AUTHOR

EMANUELE MENSAH is the co-founder of Liquid Nation, a drink creative agency, and an experienced bartender. He has worked in some of the best bars in the world, like Eau de Vie in Sydney, and Lyaness and The Connaught Bar in London. He is the winner of numerous bartending competitions, such as Uncle Nearest UK Challenge Competition 2022, and a finalist at the World Class GB 2023, hosted by Diageo. He lives in London with his partner and daughter, and loves traveling, photography, and, of course, creating cocktails. He is also the author of *Mezcal and Tequila Cocktails*, and *Rosé Cocktails*.

CREDITS

Page 21 by Stephan Hinni on Unsplash; Page 25 by Ajai Arif on Unsplash; Pages 32, 34, 36–37, 49, 50, 54, 55, 67, 69, 77, 80, 81, 85, 88–89, 96, 107, 117, 119, 122, 132, 133, 135, 136, 139, 163, 164, 169, 171 (barrels), 173, 174, 176, 178, 179, 180–181, 187, 202, 212, 222, 223, 232, 237, 249, 255, 258, 259, 260, 261, 262–263, 266, 279, 281, 285, 291, 294, 296–297, 298, 300, 301, 304, 309, 346, 349, 352, 361, 368, 370, 375, 385, 387, 390, 391, 392, 400–401, 403, 404–405, 406, 408, 409, 420, 423, 424, 425, 430, 431, 432, 436, 445, 468, 475, 479, 481, 488, 493, 496, 499, 500, 503, 506, 509, 510, 517, 518, 521, 524, 529, 536, 541, 550, 555, 556, 559, 562, 565, 568, 573, 574, 577, 578, 581, 587, 588, 593, 596, 601, 604, and 607 courtesy of the author; Pages 46–47 by Mary West on Unsplash; Page 53 used under official license from Adobe Stock; Pages 60–61 by Alice Kotlyarenko on Unsplash; Page 62 courtesy of Phil Bayly; Page 75 courtesy of Agua Mágica; Page 95 courtesy of Dali Nelio; Page 98 courtesy of Alex Jandernoa; Page 108 courtesy of Julie Spicy; Page 115 by Cesar Cabrera on Unsplash; Page 118 by Fred Crandon on Unsplash; Pages 125, 128, 244, 359, 380, 395, and 461 courtesy of Jorge Valdez; Pages 143 and 144 courtesy of Tequila Corralejo; Page 150 courtesy of Familia Camarena Tequila; Pages 157, 216, 218–219 courtesy of Anna Bruce; Page 159 courtesy of Convite Mezcal; Page 183 courtesy of José de Jesus Garcia Natera; Page 190 courtesy of Jon Anders Fjeldsrud; Pages 197, 201, 204, and 205 courtesy of Derechito Tequila; Page 209 courtesy of Derrumbes; Page 224 courtesy of Excellia; Pages 226–227 by Lufang Cao on Unsplash; Page 231 courtesy of Emmy Photography; Page 242 courtesy of Ilegal; Page 252 courtesy of Mezcalero; Page 272 courtesy of El Tesoro; Page 277 courtesy of Pexels; Page 313 courtesy of Andrew Cebulka; Pages 319 and 320 courtesy of Los Siete Misterios; Page 331 courtesy of Roberto H.; Page 339 courtesy of Madre Mezcal; Page 343 courtesy of Mezcal de Leyendas; Pages 378 and 379 courtesy of Quiquiriqui; Pages 410 and 412 courtesy of Tequila Partida; Pages 426 and 434–435 courtesy of The Lost Explorer; Page 449 courtesy of Tiempo Tequila; Page 462 courtesy of Villa Lobos; Page 504 by Michael Kucharski on Unsplash; Page 532 courtesy of Tasting Kitchen; Pages 610–611 by Roger Ce on Unsplash; All other photos used under official license from Shutterstock.com.

ACKNOWLEDGMENTS

During the writing of *Big Tequila*, I met new people and received so much help and support from several brands. I will do my best to thank all of you. In case I forget you, please forgive me, and I appreciated any help from all of you.

Let's start with the distilleries that hosted me during my trip to Mexico, starting with Carmen and the Casa San Matías team. They were absolutely amazing.

Thank you to: the Siete Leguas team, who made me feel part of the family; Gabriela and Tapatío and Evelyn and Casa Maestri, for all your knowledge and kindness; Derechito and Alberto for finding the time to meet me and show me their products; Alex and the Banhez family, it was such an amazing adventure meeting all of you; Erik, Ignancio, and Los Amantes team for such a beautiful day; and Tiffany and The Lost Explorer team, you were absolutely brilliant.

A big thank you for answering my questions to Casa Amras, Tears of Llorona, Familia Camarena, Casa Don Ramón, Monita Tequila, Corralejo, and August Sebastiani II and the 3 Badge Beverage Corporation. And thank you to Ben and Pensador Mezcal, James and El Tiempo Tequila, Michael and Storywood Tequila, Jesse Estes and Tequila Ocho, Melanie and Quiquiriqui, Anne-Sophie from Bruxo, and Eduardo, Julio, and the Los Siete Misterios team.

Thank you to David Wood and Hal Stockley, Sophia Forino and Madre Mezcal, and the Calle 23 team for providing me with their great products.

Thank you to Agua Mágica, Corte Vetusto, Casa Cortés, Eduardo and Mezcal de Leyendas, Mal Bien, Marca Negra, Gracias a Dios, Alexandra from Speciality Brands, and Ansley and the Mezcalero team for providing me with some beautiful lifestyle pictures.

A special thank you to Phil, Jon, Emilio, and Jay for taking the time to have a chat with me and answering my numerous questions.

A big thank you to Urban Bar for providing me with such beautiful and elegant glassware.

I won't be able to say thank you enough to Tom Stockley from Collective Spirits for his patience, his time, and the wonderful gifts he sent me.

Thank you to James Wheeler for giving me the chance to take some pictures at the bar.

Thank you to Jorge and Diego for helping with the translations in Oaxaca. We spent an amazing day together.

Thank you to José for being such a great host; your love and passion for tequila are incredible.

Thank you to Heather and Oscar for sharing our adventure in Mexico. It was very special.

Thank you to Barnabas for always being there for me; thank you for your support and your help.

A special thanks to my dear friend Leo. You will never be forgotten.

Thank you to Selene for your massive support. As always, without you, all of this wouldn't have been possible. Big love, as always.

A big thank you and a lot of love to all my readers. I appreciate your support and love. Please, enjoy the cocktails and the read! Feel free to reach out with any feedback. You can find me on @cocktailswithlele.

ABOUT CIDER MILL PRESS
BOOK PUBLISHERS

Good ideas ripen with time. From seed to harvest, Cider Mill Press
brings fine reading, information, and entertainment together between
the covers of its creatively crafted books. Our Cider Mill bears fruit
twice a year, publishing a new crop of titles each spring and fall.

"Where Good Books Are Ready for Press"

501 Nelson Place
Nashville, Tennessee 37214

cidermillpress.com